Praise for *How to Make Money in Coins Right Now*

"A no-holds-barred examination of insider secrets that can be used for startling, quick profits. This stands alone as the most penetrating guide of its kind ever published."
—Maurice Rosen
Rosen Numismatic Advisory

"A revolutionary book. Scott Travers presents all the intricacies of buying and selling rare coins, including legal aspects found in no other market guide. A must-read for the sophisticated investor."
—Armen R. Vartian, legal counsel
Professional Numismatists Guild

"Collectors and investors alike will profit handsomely from Scott Travers' insider's advice on how to buy and sell coins professionally. Read *How to Make Money in Coins Right Now* and help yourself level a tough playing field."
—Don Alpert, former numismatics columnist
The Los Angeles Times

"If you're going to try and make money in rare coins or want to find out why you haven't, this is the book for you. It's an expert's guide written in lay language that can help you make real money right now!"
—David L. Ganz, past president
American Numismatic Association

ALSO BY SCOTT A. TRAVERS

The Coin Collector's Survival Manual
The Insider's Guide to U.S. Coin Values
The Investor's Guide to Coin Trading
One-Minute Coin Expert
Scott Travers' Top 88 Coins Over $100
Travers' Rare Coin Investment Strategy

How to Make Money in Coins Right Now

Second Edition

SCOTT A. TRAVERS

HOUSE OF COLLECTIBLES

THE CROWN PUBLISHING GROUP • NEW YORK

To my parents

Contents

Acknowledgments

The author extends credit to the following individuals who lent expertise, knowledge, and ability in the preparation of the text: John Albanese, David T. Alexander, Charles Anastasio, Richard A. Bagg, Jon Bahner, Rudy Bahr, Dennis Baker, Steve Blum, Steve Bobbitt, Q. David Bowers, James Brandt, Helen L. Carmody, Eric Li Cheung, William L. Corsa, Sr., Beth Deisher, Thomas K. DeLorey, Silvano DiGenova, Bill Fivaz, Harry Forman, Leo Frese, Michael R. Fuljenz, David L. Ganz, Larry Gentile, Sr., Sal Germano, William T. Gibbs, Richard Giedroyc, Brent Gutekunst, Cathy Hadd, David Hall, James L. Halperin, David C. Harper, Dorothy Harris, George D. Hatie, John Highfill, Steve Ivy, Robert W. Julian, Timothy J. Kochuba, Randy Ladenheim-Gil, Ronald E. Lasky, Julian M. Leidman, Robert J. Leuver, Jesse Lipka, Kevin J. Lipton, Dwight Manley, Steve Mayer, John McDonough, Raymond N. Merena, Bob Merrill, James L. Miller, Lee S. Minshull, Bern Nagengast, Donn Pearlman, Ed Reiter, Maurice Rosen, Will Rossman, Michael Keith Ruben, Mark Salzberg, Florence M. Schook, Harvey G. Stack, J. T. Stanton, David Sundman, Anthony J. Swiatek, James Taylor, Harvey C. Travers, Julius Turoff, Armen Vartian, and Keith M. Zaner.

Credit is also due the following companies and institutions: American Numismatic Association; Amos Press, Inc.; ANACS; Auctions by Bowers and Merena, Inc.; *Coin Dealer Newsletter;* Heritage Numismatic Auctions, Inc.; Krause Publications; Miller Magazines, Inc.; Numismatic Guaranty Corporation of America, Inc.; and Professional Coin Grading Service.

PREFACE

According to statistics released by the U.S. Mint in 2000, more than 100 million Americans are collecting coins. The 50 States quarters program has reenergized numismatics—the study of coins, paper money, and medallic art. In 1999, the Mint began releasing into circulation five different quarter dollars per year, each bearing a reverse commemorating a different state of the Union. The program will last until the end of 2008, when all fifty states will have been honored on distinctive 25-cent pieces—all of them part of Americans' everyday pocket change.

In 2000, the Mint also began producing a circulating golden-colored dollar coin, and that intensified interest in coins even more. A CNN/Gallup poll conducted in July 2000 revealed that 81 percent of Americans who received the new dollar coin were keeping or "collecting" it.

The lackluster performance of modern U.S. proof sets and commemorative coins up until just a few years ago seems like a distant bad dream. Today, all it takes are darts and a dartboard to pick modern proof sets and modern commemorative coins, battered by years of malaise, that will increase in value by 100 percent, 200 percent, 300 percent or more within a year or so. A number of modern Mint products have increased in value from $25 to $250—and done it so quickly that many dealers are not even aware that the almost overnight surge has taken place.

And modern Mint products produced in the millions are not the only coins appreciating smartly. Early Washington quarters—coins bearing dates from the 1930s—have seen a resurgence of interest. Some early Gem examples have doubled in value as a result of the rekindled interest in this once-dormant series, sparked by the interest in America's state quarters.

In the meantime, many truly *rare* "trophy" coins are selling nicely. For example, on August 30, 1999, an 1804 Class I Draped Bust silver dollar was sold at auction for $4,140,000—more than double what any other U.S. coin ever had sold for at public auction before that. The New York City sale was conducted under the auspices of Auctions by Bowers and Merena, Inc. This world-record price had special meaning to me, for I was one of the underbidders—and my bid of over $2 million shattered the old record.

The excitement of collecting state quarters is expected to build, but these coins with mintages in the millions are probably not the best long-term investment. Investors in coins want more. The quarter program represents an introduction for thousands of serious new coin buyers seeking fun and profit in the panorama of American numismatics.

After accumulating statehood quarters and being "bitten" by the collecting bug, droves of new coin collectors are flocking to dealer showrooms—spending thousands of dollars on individual coins in on-line auctions and making mail-order purchases for coins independently "certified" by grading services.

This book touches upon state quarters and the impact they are having on the coin-collecting hobby. But the overwhelming message of this book is about "real" coins—scarce and rare coins costing hundreds or thousands of dollars—and how to profit from them.

While no profit can ever be truly guaranteed, there are strategies available to maximize the chances that you will make money—even *big* money—buying and selling rare coins. That's the message of this book. And the mission of this book is to arm you with the knowledge you will need to put those strategies to work.

The climate in the *rare* coin marketplace is vastly different today from the almost festive atmosphere we saw throughout much of the 1980s. Nearly a decade of downward drift drove many investors away from coins and sapped the market itself of the underlying confidence that had buoyed it during setbacks in the past. But those difficult years also purged the market of unrealistic expectations and forced buyers and sellers to abandon old ideas that simply won't work in a time of new realities.

One of those old ideas is the notion that rare coins need to be bought and held for ten or twenty years in order to earn the best possible profit for their owners. This approach worked well for people who bought coins prudently a generation ago; for years, an annual survey by the Salomon Brothers investment house consistently rated coins at or near the top of the list of best-performing long-term investments. But times—and the marketplace—have changed. The coin market fell apart, beginning in 1989—and as this book is written, in August 2000, it still hasn't completely righted itself, despite all of the new state quarters and the collectors they have brought with them. As a consequence, some of those "guaranteed" profits haven't materialized. The buy-and-hold philosophy simply doesn't ring true in the current market environment. And Salomon Brothers doesn't even list rare coins in its surveys anymore.

Today's coin buyers don't want to wait ten or twenty years—or even five years—for their profits. They realize now that those profits may never come at all, so they want to see results in a much more immediate way. They want to make money *right now*. It's no longer enough to buy a coin for $50, put it into a drawer and spend the next five years reading price guides and watching it climb step by step toward $100. Today, people are looking to buy a coin for $90, alter its appearance in some way, resubmit it to a grading service for an upgrade—and then make a killing for thousands of dollars. They're looking to outguess and outsmart the grading services. In short, they're out to beat the system. And some of them are doing it quite successfully!

There are risks, to be sure—but, as this book shows, those risks can be minimized. *How to Make Money in Coins Right Now, Second Edition,* provides simple, straightforward strategies— low-risk, high-reward action strategies—for making handsome profits from coins in good times and in bad. The text is written in language easily understandable even by a layperson with little or no background in rare coins, and accompanied by exceptional illustrations. *How to Make Money in Coins Right Now,*

Second Edition, gives you all the information you'll need to get started making money in coins the new way—*right away*!

—Scott A. Travers
Scott Travers Rare Coin Galleries, Inc.
P.O. Box 1711, F.D.R. Station
New York, NY 10150-1711

212/535-9135
E-mail: travers@inch.com
Internet: http://www.inch.com/~travers/travers3.htm
http://www.pocketchangelottery.com

January 2001

How to Make Money in Coins Right Now

INTRODUCTION

Rare coins have captured mankind's imagination for many centuries. However, the notion of making money from coins—turning a profit from buying, holding, and selling them—is of recent origin, at least as a primary objective of those who covet and collect them.

Coins came of age as a vehicle for investment during the 1960s. Up to then, the coin field had been dominated by traditional-style collectors who pursued rare coins primarily for pleasure, rather than profit. The emphasis changed dramatically in the early 1960s when uncirculated rolls of modern U.S. coins—coins that were still brand-new—became the objects of widespread speculation nationwide.

It was during that decade that coin collecting—and investing—experienced the single biggest boom in the hobby's history. Coin prices soared to unprecedented heights; an uncirculated roll of Jefferson nickels struck at the Denver Mint in 1950, for example, was selling for as much as $1,200—an average of $30 for each of the 40 nickels in the roll. U.S. government proof sets of newly minted coins were snapped up by the public in staggering numbers each year, hitting an all-time high of more than 4 million sets in 1964, when the Kennedy half dollar made its first appearance on the scene. Major new coin periodicals sprouted up, and hobby publications reached circulation and advertising levels never approached since. In short, it was a time of tremendous excitement and growth.

THE END OF SILVER COINS

The roll boom sputtered in the mid-1960s, and late-date coin rolls have never regained the prominence they enjoyed prior to that. In part, this reflected the growing realization that coins which could be obtained in roll or bag quantities weren't likely to be scarce and desirable. Thereafter, the emphasis shifted to individual coins that possessed low mintage, high quality, or both. The market's decline involved more than rolls, however; interest and prices diminished across the board. A major reason for this was the U.S. government's action in eliminating, or greatly reducing, the silver content of circulating coinage.

In 1965, silver was removed entirely from the quarter dollar and dime, giving way to a "sandwich-type" base-metal composition consisting of an outer layer of copper-nickel bonded to a core of pure copper. The half dollar's silver content was reduced from 90 percent to 40 percent from 1965 through 1970, and then, in 1971, it joined the quarter and dime as a silverless coin. When these newfangled "clad" coins first appeared, President Lyndon B. Johnson asserted that silver dimes, quarters, and halves would never bring a premium simply because of their precious-metal content and that they would circulate side-by-side with the new coins for many years to come. He proved to be a prophet without honor: Almost overnight, silver coins vanished from circulation, for they were correctly perceived as stores of value. This greatly reduced the chances of finding worthwhile coins in pocket change, and that, in turn, dampened Americans' interest in coin collecting, for circulation finds had been a major factor in the hobby's rapid growth.

It took the introduction of the 50 States quarters program in 1999 to breathe new life into the coin market. Almost overnight, millions of Americans started searching their pocket change. Through good times and bad, the notion of using coins as a way to turn a profit—of making big money from collectible small change—has remained an important factor in many people's involvement with the hobby and the marketplace. And the hope of quick profit—of making money *right now*—has proven to be a particularly powerful lure.

A New Golden Era

After the roll boom faded, the coin market drifted aimlessly for the next decade or so before getting a boost in 1974 when

Uncle Sam restored the right to private gold ownership. That awakened millions of Americans to the investment possibilities of precious metals, and rare coins went along for the ride. Around the same time, astute coin dealers began promoting coins' investment potential through aggressive and sophisticated marketing campaigns, attracting a new breed of buyer—typically, a well-heeled professional man or woman with limited knowledge of coins but substantial financial resources. A company called First Coinvestors of Albertson, New York, and its founder, the late Stanley Apfelbaum, played pivotal roles in this process, and although they came under fire for the relatively high markups they charged, they deserve recognition for increasing public awareness that coins might indeed be a good investment.

Fueled by rampant inflation, gold and silver soared in price in 1979 and 1980, and again, rare coins boomed right along with them. Price guides could hardly keep up with the non-stop increases in value: Seemingly overnight, desirable coins were doubling and tripling in price. Within weeks, coins that had been worth $500 were trading for $5,000. In the inefficient marketplace of 1979 and 1980, a keen-witted young numismatist could go to a coin show and make a profit of $25,000 just by trading coins over a weekend. Many young collectors who got their start at that time went on to become professional numismatists—full-time coin dealers—and virtually all of them look back on the experience with wistful recognition that those were truly the good old days.

At the start of the 1980s, coin investing was really a shot in the dark. Prices were rising dramatically, to be sure, and some investors did fare very well—notably those who caught the wave on the rise and jumped off before it hit the shoals. But many ill-informed coin buyers lost their shirts, often because unscrupulous coin dealers took unfair advantage of their lack of expertise. It wasn't at all unusual for a well-heeled noncollector to visit a local coin shop in 1979, put $10,000 on the counter (and often much more), and tell the dealer, "Buy me something pretty." Big Brother wasn't watching the coin market then, wasn't looking over the shoulder of the coin merchant and saying,

"You need to disclose this and you need to disclose that." The buyer was on his or her own, and "caveat emptor" was an understatement. Many of the people who purchased coins in 1979 and 1980 received much less than what they paid for: They got coins that were grossly overgraded—described as being in a much higher level of preservation than they really were—and just as grossly overpriced.

THE GRADING REVOLUTION

As word of such abuses reached Washington, D.C., the Federal Trade Commission entered the picture in the mid-1980s and started bringing suit against some of the bigger offenders, charging them with engaging in false, deceptive, and misleading practices in commerce. In 1986, the industry itself launched a major counterattack with the founding of the Professional Coin Grading Service (PCGS), a company that offered independent certification of rare coins' authenticity and grade by seasoned coin dealers, plus encapsulation—or "slabbing"—of each coin in a sonically sealed, hard plastic holder. The Grading Revolution had begun!

PCGS experts provided an arm's-length opinion regarding the grade of each coin submitted for its review, using a 1-to-70 scale in which 1 represents a coin barely identifiable as to its type—a coin so worn it could hardly be identified—and 70 represents a perfect coin, a coin with no nicks, no scratches, no flaws, and no imperfections. PCGS was soon joined by the Numismatic Guaranty Corporation of America (NGC), another highly skilled coin-grading service which—like PCGS—encapsulated coins in sonically sealed, tamper-resistant holders. Together, these two companies instilled a sense of confidence in coin buyers—and especially in investors with limited knowledge (or no knowledge at all) about coins. Ripoffs were far less likely with certified coins, for the grades of those coins had been independently verified by experts.

Before long, the coin market's faith in PCGS and NGC was so great that many certified coins were trading "sight-unseen." Buyers and sellers accepted the accuracy of the companies' grades without even seeing and examining the coins. This caught the attention of Wall Street financiers, who reasoned that certified coins could readily be traded in much the same way that investors trade stocks and bonds. Several large brokerage houses began to test the waters by setting up multimillion-dollar funds based upon investments in rare coins. As the decade neared a close, Merrill Lynch and Kidder, Peabody both had established such funds, and coin prices were soaring in expectation that this was just the beginning.

THE BUBBLE BURSTS

Unfortunately, the end of the 1980s also marked the end of Wall Street's brief flirtation with rare coins. The coin market proved to be just too small—just too thin a market—to sustain the types of price gains that were taking place in 1989. As a result, rare coins plummeted in value just as quickly as they had gone up. Merrill Lynch and Kidder, Peabody both beat a hasty retreat, and the rest of the Wall Street crowd went out the exit with them. This had the effect of exacerbating the downturn in the market, driving prices even lower—and the slump even deeper—than would have been the case under normal circumstances.

The coin market has witnessed few rallies that rivaled that last major peak in May of 1989. And as this revised edition is written in 2000, many people—this author included—are gun-shy about recommending coins for people to buy and hold as a safe, long-term investment. Conventional wisdom simply doesn't seem all that wise anymore. In the old days, investment advisers had a tried-and-true formula: "Buy this coin today for $2,500, or buy this coin investment portfolio today for $25,000, and hold on to it for ten years and you'll be able to cash out at 20 percent a year." That kind of advice is now a fallacy; what's more, it has become politically incorrect. In fact, it has become so politically incorrect that even Salomon Brothers, the respected Wall Street brokerage house, has discontinued its once-ballyhooed survey of investment vehicles, which perennially ranked rare coins as the number one investment from the standpoint of long-term performance. In 2000, rare coins are simply not viewed as a long-term investment.

A NEW BALL GAME

It's a different kind of marketplace today. The advent of on-line auctions and the introduction of the states quarters and Sacagawea dollar have changed the look and feel of the rare coin marketplace. That doesn't mean you can't make money in coins; it means that you have to be smarter than smart, you have to exercise more caution, you have to be more careful with your funds, and you have to act more quickly than in the past.

To make money in the coin market today, you have to think and act like a dealer and you have to seek—and heed—advice from *extremely smart* dealers, who are also honest. *How to Make Money in Coins Right Now, Second Edition,* will show you how to do this.

Among other things, it will explain the three basic risks that confront coin buyers and sellers and give you the knowledge you need to minimize—and even totally neutralize—these worrisome hazards. The first of these pitfalls is the *acquisition risk*—the risk that you may pay too much to obtain a coin—and in this age of on-line auctions, the risk that you may receive *no* coin. Chapter 2 provides detailed information on how to determine the fair market value of a coin, including a thorough listing of the market's leading price guides and tips on how to gauge their accuracy, as well as the reliability of a dealer. Armed with these tools, you should be able to ascertain how much any given coin is really worth. Chapter 14 fortifies your defenses in transacting business through on-line Web sites such as eBay so that you won't be ensnared by a dealer spinning a web of deceit. Next comes the *market risk*—the risk that a coin may depreciate in value because of market conditions during the time you own it. This book will furnish price-performance data and insights on how to understand—and apply—the lessons of marketplace cycles. Finally, there is a *sale risk*—the risk that you may sell a coin for less than it's really worth. I'll give you expert guidance on how to get the maximum, rather than the minimum, when you sell.

PROFIT-MAKING TIPS

One of the best ways to *make* money in coins is to sell off investments that are *losing* money, then put the proceeds into something productive. This is a common practice among successful coin dealers. You need to cash out your nonperformers and free up your funds for coins that are winners. *How to Make Money in Coins Right Now, Second Edition,* will tell you how to do this and thereby obtain capital for profit-making purchases.

You also must avoid purchasing coins that are losers—and despite all the hoopla surrounding America's states quarters, a number of government Mint products rank high on that list. This book will explain why. It also will explain how to maximize your return by targeting your purchases at coins that will make you money *right now.*

Making money quickly in a lean marketplace requires recognition of opportunities. This book goes into great detail on how to recognize—and capitalize upon—these situations.

- It tells you, for example, how to make money from short-term increases in the price of gold—how to buy generic gold coins today and sell them tomorrow for possibly a quick 20 or 30 percent profit.
- It identifies the few coins that are winners, such as roll coins that have good potential to go up in value 20 or 30 percent.
- It talks about some of the sleepers that may increase in value dramatically in the months and years ahead.
- Most importantly, it examines grading arbitrage—the technique of enhancing a certified coin's value by resubmitting it to a major certification service and getting it regraded at a higher level.

You'll feel as if you are an inside trader—and an inside grader—as you read very special interviews with some of the most talented coin traders and graders in the world, including John Albanese, David Hall, and Jim Halperin. And a bombshell "tell-all" interview with veteran dealer Jesse Lipka might forever change the way you thought the coin market operates. The grading arbitrage strategies and other insights described by these experts will all be explored and explained in simple terms, so that you can play this game yourself and increase the chances of actually turning a profit.

How to Make Money in Coins Right Now, Second Edition, is a book that tells you how successful coin dealers play the game. It takes you behind the scenes and puts you in the experts' shoes, and shows you how you, too, can make the same kinds of profits. But don't think this is an area you can explore without risks; on the contrary, *the coin market is a high-risk area.* If you're merely curious about collectibles, you'll still find this book highly informative. But it's really aimed at somebody who is willing to take some big chances—somebody who lives by the motto, "No guts, no glory!"

If you feel inclined to *speculate* in coins—and coins at this point are a very speculative area—then this is the book for you. By reading it thoroughly and following the strategies I outline, the potential exists to come out better than even and maybe make some money—starting *right now*!

CHAPTER ◆ 1

HOW TO THINK LIKE— AND *BE*— A COIN COLLECTOR

What is a collector? Are collectors born or made? Why do collectors have an inherent advantage over others who acquire rare coins?

These are basic questions that need to be considered by anyone who's thinking of spending time and money on valuable coins. Whether a person's ultimate goal is financial profit, psychic income, or both, he or she needs to approach this pursuit with the proper frame of mind in order to achieve the best results—and the biggest returns.

THE NATURE OF A COLLECTOR

In a broad sense, anyone who assembles related items of interest as a hobby is a collector, whether those items are coins, stamps, matchbook covers, beer cans, or just about any other objects you might name. Over the years, however, the term *collector* has come to have a more specific meaning in the coin hobby—it designates someone who acquires and arranges coins in a systematic way (unlike a mere accumulator, who gets and keeps coins haphazardly, with little or no regard to their organization). It also denotes someone who is motivated primarily by intangible rewards such as the enjoyment of art, beauty, and history (unlike an investor, who tends to be preoccupied, even obsessed, with financial gain).

Time and again, experience has shown that dedicated collectors derive the most from coin collecting, including the biggest monetary rewards. Their discriminating taste and attention to detail result in the acquisition of coins with unusual appeal, and those kinds of coins tend to have greater value when they are sold, even though profit may not have been a motive when they were purchased in the first place. Clearly, then, the most fundamental way to make money in coins—right now or whenever you choose to sell them—is to view them and pursue them with the mindset of a dyed-in-the-wool collector.

THE LURE OF COINS

All collectibles hold a special fascination for those who pursue and peruse them. But coins' positive features are particularly appealing:

- They are small and portable, easily stored in large numbers, and easily hidden in times of emergency.
- They are durable, sometimes surviving for centuries—or even millennia—in much the same condition as when they were made.
- They record the panorama of human history—and human hopes and dreams—as few other collectibles ever have. A silver denarius of Julius Caesar . . . a shekel of the Jewish revolts against Rome . . . a denier of the Crusaders . . . silver shillings of Britain's King Charles I and his enemy Oliver Cromwell— to possess one of these is to hold a piece of history in your hand.
- They are hand-held works of art, sometimes bearing portraiture as breathtaking in its way as a masterpiece by Rembrandt or da Vinci.
- They can represent significant stores of value just from the standpoint of the metal they contain (in cases where that

metal is precious and rare), as with coins made of gold or platinum.

- On top of everything else, coins have historically offered the bonus advantage of rising in value substantially over time, provided that their owners choose items that are genuinely scarce and preserve them carefully.

THE COLLECTOR MENTALITY

In a very real sense, collectors are builders. They first lay a solid foundation for their collections, much as a contractor does in erecting a large building. Then, as they go forward, they follow a definite plan, much like an architect's blueprint, and implement this carefully over months and years and sometimes decades. In some instances, where an entire family is involved in assembling and maintaining a collection, the process may continue for generations–possibly as long as a century or more.

Collectors have very specific goals. Some of these may be short-term in nature–perhaps the acquisition of one example of every U.S. gold type coin with a portrait of Miss Liberty on the obverse, or front of the coin. Other goals may be long-range and more complex, such as the completion of a set of Bust dimes from every single year, or a set that includes every recognized variety of a particular coin. In each case, however, people who are collectors–truly solid collectors–have a mindset that entails completing a project. And when a collector does complete a set, the whole can be worth much more than the sum of the parts, for it then has heightened appeal–and tangible value–to other collectors.

THE EARLY DAYS OF COLLECTING

Coin collecting first became an avocation of consequence during the Renaissance. For centuries, however, it was limited almost exclusively to bluebloods and other men of wealth, leading people to dub it "the hobby of kings." Not until modern times did it take root with the masses and come to be known instead as "the king of hobbies." U.S. coinage first appeared in

1793, but collecting of that coinage didn't begin in earnest until the mid-1800s.

One of the first serious numismatists in the United States, Joseph J. Mickley of Philadelphia, became attracted to coins when a casual whim launched him on a virtual treasure hunt. As he neared the age of 20 in 1819, Mickley decided to look for a copper cent from his birth year, not realizing that 1799 cents were rare and elusive even then, a time when the large, heavy cents of the nation's early years were being encountered routinely in circulation. Mickley's search for this birth-year coin escalated into a wider quest: He sought to obtain copper cents from every date the U.S. Mint had made them. Soon, he expanded his interest to other U.S. coin series as well, blazing a trail for future collectors of series such as early silver dollars, quarters, and half cents.

Mickley, a maker of musical instruments, had an ideal location in which to pursue his new hobby: He lived within walking distance of the Philadelphia Mint and went there frequently to purchase new coins at face value. On one such visit, in 1827, he bought four newly struck quarters bearing that date—an acquisition that cost him just a dollar. The coins proved to be extremely rare, and after passing through several great collections, one of them changed hands at a 1980 auction for $190,000.

Mickley also owned an 1804 silver dollar, one of just 15 examples known to exist today of this famous rarity. He got the coin, he said, for little more than face value from a teller at the Bank of Philadelphia. When Mickley's coins were sold in 1867, this dollar fetched $750—a record price at the time for any U.S. coin. By 1993, the coin belonged to prominent Texas numismatist Reed Hawn, and when he chose to sell it in October of that year at an auction sale conducted by Stack's of New York, the winning bid was an eye-popping $475,000.

MAJOR AMERICAN COLLECTORS

Joseph Mickley blazed a trail that millions of others have followed. Most have been people of modest means, but the hobby has also attracted men and women of wealth—and some of these

Figures 1-1 & 1-2. *1913 Liberty Head nickel* (obverse and reverse). One of five known, this nickel sold for $1,485,000 in May 1996. This specimen was from the collection of Louis E. Eliasberg, Sr., and sold at public auction by Bowers and Merena (Box 1224, Wolfeboro, NH 03894). *Photos courtesy Auctions by Bowers and Merena, Inc.*

have assembled collections of almost legendary stature. Here are a few examples:

- In the late 1800s, Baltimore & Ohio Railroad executive T. Harrison Garrett formed an important collection of U.S. coins. His sons, Robert and John Work Garrett, expanded the collection. When it came up for sale at a four-part series of Bowers and Ruddy auctions from 1979 through 1981, it realized a total of more than $25 million, a record that stood for nearly two decades.

- Before his death in 1926, Chicago beer baron Virgil M. Brand amassed a collection containing more than 350,000 pieces, including large numbers of stunning rarities. Many of the coins were later dispersed piecemeal, but when a small segment belonging to Brand's niece came up for sale at a series of public auctions in the early and mid-1980s, they still brought a total of close to $10 million.

- Baltimore banker Louis Eliasberg startled the numismatic community in the early 1950s by announcing that he had formed a complete collection of all U.S. coins, including major varieties, by date and mint mark. The gold coins from the collection brought more than $11 million when sold at public auction by Bowers and Ruddy Galleries in 1982. The remaining coins were sold at auction in 1996 and 1997 and realized an additional $32.4 million, bringing the overall total to more than $44 million, a record that still stands. (See Figures 1-1 and 1-2.)

COLLECTING REACHES THE MASSES

Coin collecting remained a somewhat exclusive pastime for more than a hundred years after Joseph Mickley's entrance on the scene. Ironically, it took hold with Americans at large in the depths of the Great Depression, primarily due to a simple yet ingenious new invention. In the early 1930s, an enterprising Wisconsin man named J.K. Post devised a series of inexpensive boards to house and display U.S. coins by date and mint mark. These boards had die-cut holes where people could place each coin as they found it in their everyday pocket change. The Whitman Publishing Company of Racine, Wisconsin, acquired the rights to make and market these boards, and soon they were turning up in 5-and-10-cent stores across the country.

Low-cost forms of amusement and entertainment enjoyed great popularity during the Depression years. Movies, miniature golf, jigsaw puzzles—all of these flourished as Americans looked for ways to inexpensively escape from their worries. "Penny boards" fit this pattern perfectly: Filling a board with Lincoln cents plucked from circulation was well within the budgets of most Americans, even in those brutally hard times, and searching for those coins provided long hours of pleasure. As a bonus, completed boards could be sold for well over face value; many dealers advertised their interest in purchasing these from the public.

Yet another stimulus to coin collecting's growth was the enterprising ad campaign of Fort Worth, Texas, coin dealer B. Max Mehl. During the 1930s and 1940s, the flamboyant Mehl placed ads in newspaper Sunday supplements almost non-stop offering to pay $50 apiece for any 1913 Liberty Head nickel—and also offering, not just incidentally, to send his company's price list and other coin literature to those who would remit a small fee. Mehl was well aware that only five examples of the rare 1913 nickel were known to exist, but the offer got people's attention, and the literature he sent helped cultivate untold thousands of new collectors.

Those 1913 nickels are a story in themselves. Official Mint records make no mention of Liberty nickels of that date; all the five-cent pieces struck in that year are supposed to have been of the then-new Indian/bison design (commonly referred to as the Buffalo nickel type). Evidently, someone at the Philadelphia Mint surreptitiously made a few Liberty nickels with the 1913 date, using dies that the Mint had prepared as a contingency. At one point, all five of these nickels belonged to the eccentric Edward H.R. Green, son of reclusive financial genius Hetty Green, who was known as "the witch of Wall Street." The coins were dispersed following Edward Green's death in 1936, and over the years they rose in value astoundingly. In 1993, one of these nickels changed hands at a public auction conducted by Stack's of New York for $962,500—then the highest price ever paid at auction for a single U.S. coin. The seller, Texas numismatist Reed Hawn, had bought the coin in 1985 for $385,000. Then, in 1996, the Eliasberg specimen brought $1,485,000, becoming the first coin to realize more than $1 million at a public sale.

A DEALER'S-EYE VIEW OF COLLECTORS

I sat down recently with Julian M. Leidman of Silver Spring, Maryland, one of the nation's most prominent and respected coin dealers. Leidman represents many important collectors at public auction sales, helping them decide which coins they should pursue and executing bids on their behalf. Based on his perspective as a longtime dealer who has been an active participant in hundreds of major auctions, Leidman is convinced that collectors almost always derive the greatest rewards—both financial and emotional—from buying and selling rare coins, even though the monetary aspect of these transactions may be of limited concern to them.

During our conversation, Leidman spoke of one particular client who had been collecting coins for more than 50 years be-

Figures 1-3 & 1-4. *1873-CC, Without Arrows, Liberty Seated dime* (obverse and reverse). This, the only known specimen, is from the collection of Louis E. Eliasberg, Sr. It was sold at public auction by Bowers and Merena in May 1996 for $550,000.   *Photos courtesy Auctions by Bowers and Merena, Inc.*

fore he sold his collection—at a very handsome profit—at an auction sale conducted by Bowers and Merena of Wolfeboro, New Hampshire. This client, he said, was one of the most enthusiastic collectors he ever dealt with and, throughout his half-century of pursuing rare coins, he maintained a simple mindset: He was working on a project that he wanted to complete. Money was never the driving force behind this man's project; in buying coins, his first priority wasn't dollars and cents, but whether a given coin would enhance his collection. He didn't want to pay ludicrously high prices, to be sure—but, on the other hand, if something he needed and wanted was worth $1,000 in the marketplace, and he was presented with an opportunity to buy it for $1,200 or $1,300, he would seriously consider doing so and almost always gave Leidman carte blanche to buy on his behalf in such situations. He enjoyed coins' intangible qualities and never failed to project the pride of ownership. Furthermore, when he reaped a windfall upon his collection's sale, that was merely frosting on the cake.

COLLECTORS VERSUS INVESTORS

It's really the pride of ownership—of knowing they possess something scarce and desirable—that inspires many collectors to continue acquiring coins as time goes by. Collectors understand that the sets they are assembling have lasting—and per-

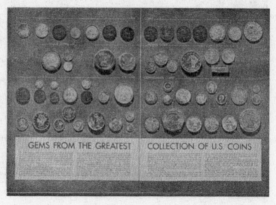

Figures 1-5 & 1-6. LIFE *magazine, April 27, 1953.* Q. David Bowers reports that this article about Eliasberg's sensational coin collection generated thousands of letters from readers. *Photos courtesy Auctions by Bowers and Merena, Inc.*

haps significant—value, but they simply aren't obsessed with making a profit. They view their collections as long-term projects and pay little heed to the day-to-day peaks and valleys in the marketplace. Investors, by contrast, get jittery whenever prices fall and look to unload their holdings at the first sign of clouds on the economic horizon; they feel no long-term commitment to the hobby or attachment to the coins they have acquired. (See Figures 1-3 and 1-4.)

The contrast between collectors and investors is evident in the way both groups regard "slabs"—the hard plastic holders in which coins are encapsulated after being graded by a third-party certification service. (A detailed discussion of grading and certification will appear in Chapter 3.) Investors look upon slabs, and the guarantee that accompanies them, as a vital security blanket to protect them against overgrading. Collectors, on the other hand, often remove slabbed coins from their holders because they want to be able to hold, feel, and touch them and examine every detail without obstruction.

Dealers have special incentive to treat collectors fairly, for unlike investors, who tend to come and go, collectors stick around for the long haul and develop a sense of loyalty to sellers with whom they establish a good relationship. Similarly, collectors are well advised to patronize dealers who are likely to be around for many years to come—dealers with proven track records.

These dealers will take pains to give good value and select nice coins if they feel those coins are going to clients who will buy from them again. They also will want to ingratiate themselves with hobbyists who are forming important collections in hopes that those clients will bring the coins back to them when they are ready to sell. I can vouch from my own experience that this is a powerful incentive. Some of the greatest collectors of our time have commissioned my firm to acquire rare coins on their behalf. Some of these same people have also subsequently engaged me to help them disperse their holdings, either through a lightning sale (a special kind of quick-turnaround auction my firm conducts), or by assisting them in selling their coins at public auction.

RECORD-KEEPING AND TAX OBLIGATIONS

The following section was prepared by prominent numismatic lawyer Armen R. Vartian of Manhattan Beach, California.

Tax Consequences of Coin Transactions

There is very little we do in the United States today that is not somehow affected by tax laws. Buying and selling coins is no exception. An understanding of basic principles of state and local sales tax, income tax, and estate tax will not only assure compliance with the law, but may save you money as well. Of course, although I have tried to accurately present this complicated subject, be warned that tax laws change quite often and differences in geography, income, and overall portfolio may change considerably the effect of taxes. You should always consult a competent attorney or tax advisor to update yourself and to tailor any tax strategies to your particular situation.

SALES TAX

Most states, and some county and city governments, impose a sales tax on all retail dealers for the privilege of retailing tangible personal property within their geographic limits. The tax is usually a percentage of the gross sale price of the goods and is remitted by the dealer along with a sales tax return. While the dealer is actually liable for sales tax, a nearly universal practice is to pass the cost of sales taxes on to the retail buyer. In a typical over-the-counter sale of coins, the dealer will add the appropriate sales tax to the invoice price of the coins.

The taxable event for sales tax is an in-state retail sale. This leads to two common exemptions to sales tax. First, sales tax is not due on wholesale (dealer-to-dealer) sales. Generally, a state will recognize this exemption only where the buyer holds a valid resale permit or certificate from that state or another state. Second, sales by out-of-state retailers are exempt from sales tax if (1) the customer orders goods directly from the retailer, and (2) the goods are shipped from outside the state and no in-state branch, office, outlet, or other place of business of the seller participates in the sale.

In certain states, some sales of coins are specifically exempted from sales tax for various reasons. States which do not apply sales tax to the sale of money exempt sales of "coins of the realm," defined as coins which remain legal tender of the United States or a foreign government. Others do not tax investment purchases and assume that purchases of over $1,000 are for investment. However, in most states, unless the sale falls into one of the common exemptions, sales tax will apply.

USE TAX

Recently, the numismatic marketplace has seen states become much more aggressive in enforcing their right to collect use tax on certain coin sales. While sales tax is triggered by a dealer's exercise of the privilege of doing retail business in a state, use tax is based entirely on the purchase of property for use in the taxing state. The taxable event is the purchase, not the sale, and the tax is due from the buyer, not the dealer. Use tax is far more difficult to predict than is sales tax. For one thing, the sale need not take place in the taxing state, provided that the buyer resides there. This means that mail-order purchases which are clearly exempt from sales tax nevertheless are subject to use tax. States are quite candid in saying that use tax levels the playing field between local dealers who have to pay sales tax and their out-of-state competitors who don't. Generally, states hold dealers responsible for collecting and remitting use tax on behalf of their customers, and for all practical purposes states will not attempt to collect back taxes from individual customers if the dealer is solvent. However, the liability is there, and it can continue indefinitely if the unwary buyer does not file a use tax return.

The states with the largest collectibles markets, such as New York and California, are leading the way on use tax. They stipulate that dealers with an in-state office, agent, warehouse, or other permanent physical presence have a close enough "nexus" with their states to require collecting use tax on all sales to their residents. But these states have also aggressively audited dealers with no permanent physical presence there, even dealers who just attend local coin shows. For example, in July 1995, California's Board of Equalization announced that attending a single retail coin show in California might create nexus, causing the American Numismatic Association to move its 1996 early spring fair from Santa Clara, California, to Tucson, Arizona. In June 1995, New York's highest court ruled that Orvis, a Vermont mail-order seller of outdoor equipment, acquired "nexus" with New York after Orvis' personnel made 12 trips to New York City over a three-year period to monitor product displays at independent stores which carry Orvis' products. Orvis' personnel did not attend shows or even make a single sale in New York. Nexus guidelines prepared by the Multistate Tax Commission, an organization created by state taxing authorities, hint that even a short appearance at a coin show will trigger nexus. This area of law is likely to change in the future as states realize the dangers of discouraging out-of-state dealers from doing business there.

INCOME TAX

Net income from the sale of coins is taxable. Beyond that simple fact, the income tax aspects of coin purchases and sales depend largely upon whether you are a collector, an investor, or a dealer for tax purposes. Sounds simple enough, but many people spend a lot of time and effort arguing with the IRS and state taxing authorities over this characterization, because the tax consequences of each can be quite different.

Collectors, who buy and sell coins primarily for personal pleasure, are the most tax-*disadvantaged* class. They must pay tax on income they earn from their coins, but cannot deduct net losses they might have from coin sales. They cannot deduct any expenses relating to their collection, such as insurance, security, membership dues for coin clubs, and subscriptions to numismatic periodicals, but can offset these expenses against any net income they declare from the sale of coins. Unfortunately, even this benefit is substantially limited because it comprises a "miscellaneous" itemized deduction on Schedule A subject to the 2 percent adjusted gross income floor. In other words, unless the collector's total miscellaneous expenses exceed 2 percent of adjusted gross income, there is no benefit. Collectors are entitled to treat their coins as capital assets after a one-year holding period, but the difference between tax rates for capital gains and ordinary income is not as great today as it has been in the past.

Those who purchase coins primarily for investment fare slightly better than collectors, being permitted to deduct expenses relating to their coins, but not net losses from coin sales. However, the IRS makes it more and more difficult to qualify as a coin investor, clearly preferring to characterize everyone interested in coins as a collector. The key is whether the taxpayer is engaged in the activity for profit or for enjoyment. Taxpayers who show a profit from their coin activities for three of the past five years are presumed to be engaged in those activities for profit, although the IRS has the right to rebut that presumption. Relevant factors are the amount of time the taxpayer spent on the activity, whether the taxpayer relied on advice of experts, and whether losses could be expected in a particular year (such as when the market drops in particular types of coins).

Finally, taxpayers who can establish that they buy and sell coins as part of a trade or business may acquire dealer status, enabling them to deduct expenses as well as net losses against their other income. As one might expect, the IRS is loath to treat a numismatist with other sources of income as a coin "dealer." However, over the years the regulations in this area have been expanded so that it is not impossible for a serious coin enthusiast to qualify. The "for profit" determination is similar to that described above for investors. Dealers pay tax at ordinary income rates, and may use losses to offset other ordinary income.

ESTATE TAX

This is an extremely complicated area of law, and because of estate tax thresholds tax-saving strategies are really only needed by persons whose estates are likely to exceed $600,000. For those in that category, however, it is important to work with competent professionals to develop an appropriate estate plan. Coin collections are sometimes difficult to administer, because their values are somewhat subjective as well as susceptible to "blockage." That is to say, different experts can differ over the value of a collection, and in addition the collection loses a certain amount of its value if it must be sold as a unit. In any event, a professional numismatist should be consulted about valuing coins held in an estate.

RECORD-KEEPING REQUIREMENTS

For various reasons, anyone purchasing a sizable amount of coins should keep detailed records regarding such purchases. The prices paid for each coin should be detailed as well as the date of purchase, so that if the coins are sold the gain (or loss) can be calculated and characterized, i.e., as capital gain or ordinary income. In addition, if the taxpayer intends to deduct any expenses relating to coins, those expenses should be paid by check and an invoice or receipt obtained. A note should state the purpose of the expense, so that if necessary it can be proven to be within the expenses allowable by law.

Buyers of coins should realize that dealers also have documentation requirements. Most dealers record every sale, no matter how small, and issue an invoice to the buyer. For cash transactions over $10,000, dealers must file a report to the IRS on Form 8300 and send a copy to the buyer.

When selling coins, all relevant records should be kept for at least 10 years after the sale. This enables the taxpayer to fulfill all record-keeping requirements for collectors, investors, and dealers. If possible, commissions, state and local sales tax, and other selling expenses should be itemized and in writing.

CHAPTER 2

RISK—A CANDID ANALYSIS

Speculating in coins is a game of chance. There are risks when you buy . . . risks when you sell . . . risks when you trade . . . and risks when you hold.

Like any good decision-maker, you need to approach these risks in a businesslike way. You have to take risks on occasion, but in doing so you need to make sure that the odds are clearly in your favor. "No guts, no glory" is an excellent guiding philosophy, but temper it with "Look before you leap." And keep in mind that coins are not for the faint of heart.

TRANSACTIONAL RISKS

Transactional risks are those you incur when buying, selling, or trading coins. Each of these activities involves a distinct risk, or combination of risks, and therefore all three need to be addressed individually.

Acquisition Risk

If you purchase a coin for $1,000 but its actual market value at the time of the transaction is only $100, you're obviously losing a lot of money. This is an acquisition risk—or "buy" risk—you confront each and every time you shell out your hard-earned money to purchase a coin.

Here are some of the forms an acquisition risk can take:

- After paying $1,000 for a coin—or any amount, for that matter—you could take it home and find that you've purchased an empty box, or your coin has been switched for another of lower value.
- If you're buying a coin that hasn't been authenticated and graded by an independent certification service, there's a risk that the seller could be misrepresenting it—overstating its grade, perhaps, or falsely representing it as a rare and valuable variety.
- Even if the coin you're buying is totally problem-free—a nice coin, properly certified, and honestly and accurately graded—there's still a risk that you could be overcharged and end up paying substantially more than the coin is really worth.

The way to minimize acquisition risk and avoid overpaying for coins is to learn all you can about the market and make sure you're getting *fair market value* for your money, or, in the case of a dealer-to-dealer transaction, make sure you're paying a *fair market wholesale* price.

Fair market value is the price at which a knowledgeable buyer and an equally knowledgeable seller would allow a coin to be sold when both are under no compulsion or compunction to consummate a transaction. *Fair market wholesale* is the price that would be agreed upon under similar circumstances by two professional numismatists, or other individuals acting as dealers, when both are fully informed about the coin or coins being sold.

Acquisition risk is substantial, but you can overcome it by arming yourself with knowledge. In particular, you need to become familiar with the *grading* of coins, and later chapters in this book will explain just how to do that. You also can reduce your acquisition risk by asking the seller to disclose how much he or she paid for the coin in the first place and asking to see a copy of the purchase invoice for that transaction before you agree to buy it. Knowledge is power, and you need to deal from strength when buying coins.

Sale Risk

Equally as dangerous as acquisition risk is the *sale risk* you face when selling a coin. If you purchase a coin for $100 and it subsequently increases in value to $1,000, you certainly shouldn't sell it for $50, or even $500. Yet many unscrupulous dealers will make lowball offers when you're ready to sell your coins, and unless you're prepared to cope with this, there's an all too real risk that you'll suffer an unnecessary loss or give up part of the profit that's rightfully yours.

Naturally, you want the highest possible price when you sell a coin. At the very least, however, you want to get fair market value. Here again, knowledge is the single most powerful weapon in your arsenal; knowing a coin's true value is the best possible protection against the con men waiting to fleece the unwary. It also can give you an edge in transactions with reputable dealers. For example, you may own a certified coin that very nearly qualifies for the next-higher grade. Knowing this, you can bargain for a premium beyond the going price for an average or low-end coin of this kind and grade. Conversely, if you know that your coin barely qualifies for the grade it has been assigned, you should try to sell it sight-unseen to a dealer who purchases certified coins on that basis.

Another way to overcome sale risk is to sell your coins at a public auction; that way, they'll be seen by many different potential buyers, rather than just one dealer. You shouldn't consign them, however, to just *any* auction; you need to choose a *good* auction, where your coins will benefit from broad exposure and spirited competition. I'll offer detailed advice about this in a later chapter. And in Chapter 14, I offer detailed advice about the acquisition risks associated with Internet auctions.

Trade Risk

When you trade one coin for another, you confront *both* buy and sale risk, because you're essentially buying one coin and selling another in the same transaction.

Trade risk can be insidious, because there is a tendency to let down your guard—lower your defenses—when engaging in a trade, rather than an outright purchase or sale. It's a clean and easy transaction; there isn't any money changing hands, and you don't see your bankroll getting smaller or the balance getting lower in your checking account, the way you do when purchasing a coin.

With this in mind, you need to be doubly vigilant when you engage in a trade. Otherwise, you could find yourself getting hit by a double whammy: You could undervalue the coin you're giving up and overvalue the one that you're receiving in return.

HOLD RISKS

In addition to the risks you face at the start and the conclusion of your ownership, you also must contend with risks during the time you own a coin. These are called *hold risks,* and they encompass all of the factors that bear upon the value of that coin while it is yours.

Hold risks fall into two principal categories: market risk and storage risk. These two risks require careful consideration.

Market Risk

If you purchase a coin for $1,000 and it subsequently goes down in value to $100, you've lost a lot of money—and potential loss of value is a very real risk when you own a coin. When the marketplace environment is hostile, coins will not rise in value unless there is strong economic justification. You need to seek conditions that provide such justification—inflation and rising bullion prices, for instance—and capitalize on them when they occur. Conversely, you need to be wary of conditions that heighten market risk.

These are some of the factors that tend to make coins go down in value:

- *Deflation.* When there is contraction of the nation's money supply, interest rates tend to fall and people feel less need for a hedge against inflation—the kind of hedge provided by tangible assets, including precious metals and rare coins.
- *Decreasing net worth.* When people suffer a setback in the overall value of their assets—when real estate values are falling, for example—they become more conservative in their

spending and curtail or eliminate expenditures on non-essential items such as coins. This reduction in demand translates into lower market prices.

- *A weak bullion market.* Many coin dealers also are regular traders of precious metals, and when the market for gold and silver bullion is healthy and active, they generate extra income, much of which they spend buying coins. If the bullion market is sluggish, these dealers don't do as well, and that hurts the coin market as a whole.
- *Recession or depression.* Hard times are bad times for coins and other collectibles. People become preoccupied with meeting their basic needs, such as food, clothing, and shelter, and everything else recedes in importance until the storm has passed.

Besides being cognizant of these general economic considerations, you also should be watchful for conditions that may pose problems within the coin marketplace itself. One of the most common—and potentially most troublesome—is the kind of market mania that develops on occasion because of ephemeral promotions or other hype. If prices have risen sharply because of such a promotion, you'll almost certainly see a downward correction shortly, and if you make the mistake of buying when those prices are at the top, your bank balance will plummet along with the value of the coins.

We saw this kind of mania from 1971 to 1974, and again from 1978 to 1980. Most recently, we saw it in the late 1980s when Wall Street–type investors poured tens of millions of dollars into rare coins. The involvement of traditional investors—and, more significantly, several major Wall Street brokerage houses—served as a tremendous catalyst for the coin market, driving prices exponentially higher for many of the coins that enjoyed special favor with these buyers. Unfortunately, most of the coins they favored weren't really rare enough to justify such high prices. Applying a stock-market mentality to the coin market, they preferred to buy and sell coins as if they were commodities or shares of common stock, and truly rare coins don't lend themselves to this approach, being too scarce and distinctive. The Wall Street crowd concentrated instead on "generic" coins— coins that exist in high enough quantities to be readily inter- changeable. These included Morgan silver dollars and Walking Liberty half dollars certified by one or more of the coin-grading services as being in high levels of preservation. While attractive and desirable, these coins are far from rare and certainly didn't merit the prices they were bringing at the height of the Wall Street coin boom in May 1989.

Predictably, the overpriced generic coins plunged in value, chasing Wall Street money out of the coin market. That, in turn, depressed the prices of coins across the board—including those of genuine rarities, which had benefitted along with everything else when the market was hot.

The lesson is clear: You need to be extra-careful when the coin market's riding high. Far from being a time to relax your vigilance, that may very well be when the risk is at its highest point as well. Even in the hottest market, coins don't go up in value indefinitely, and once they do go up, it's just a matter of time before they go down.

Storage Risk

If you buy a coin for $1,000 and drop it on the way home, its value might very well drop to $100 if it's damaged in the process. That's just the first in a series of risks you face in keep- ing the coin safe and free from harm while it is yours. These are known collectively as the *storage risk.*

The ultimate storage risk is the chance that a coin might be stolen. But you can be robbed of much of its value even if the coin remains in your possession; adverse storage conditions will steal your investment away just as surely as a bandit with a gun. Coins need to be stored in a dry, stable environment that's free from airborne particulate matter. Moisture and foreign matter are cancerous to a coin; they set in motion chemical reactions that often cause irreparable damage.

Before placing a coin in long-term storage, you should neu- tralize its surface with a non-reactive solvent or degreasing agent to protect it against reaction with chemicals in the environment. For many years, I recommended trichlorotrifluoroethane; this is a safe, effective substance that evaporates without leaving any residue. Unfortunately, the U.S. government has banned its sale because it is believed to contribute to the depletion of the atmosphere's ozone layer. A good, inexpensive—and unproscribed—alternative is denatured alcohol. This will remove airborne particulate matter from a coin's surface and help ward off chemical damage.

Obviously, your coins should be stored in a place where they're safeguarded against the regular kind of theft as well—the kind that's carried out with guns or burglary tools. For most people, that means a safety deposit box in a nearby bank. You should be aware, however, that a bank may not be liable for losses that you suffer in the admittedly unlikely event that your safety deposit box is burglarized. For that reason, you need to obtain insurance on your coins covering their value as collectibles (not just their face value, as is often the case with standard homeowner's policies, for example). Coverage for theft is relatively inexpensive if the coins are stored routinely in a bank box.

This may sound strange, but I recommend that you rent a *cheap* safety deposit box. There's a logical reason for this seemingly illogical advice: Elaborate (and costlier) safety deposit areas are designed to help preserve documents, and that means keeping moisture levels high. This is great for documents; it inhibits them from turning yellow. It's terrible for coins, however, since moisture is a catalyst for chemical reactions that can leave them with permanent scars. Choose a bank with cheaper boxes—and drier, safer air.

A new product, Intercept Shield, has been developed by John Albanese in conjunction with Lucent Technologies. This coin-storage product is supposed to prevent a coin from deteriorating. It is expected to be available as envelopes, boxes, and holder inserts. Watch for announcements.

REGULATORY RISKS

Government regulation can have enormous impact on the value of your coins, and there's a real risk that its impact could be detrimental. In fact, this could be the single biggest risk category some coin owners face in years to come.

Uncle Sam's interest in the rare coin market grew by leaps and bounds during the 1980s as the market itself expanded to include growing numbers of Wall Street–type investors who viewed coins not as collectibles but rather as alternatives to stocks, bonds, and other investment vehicles. The federal government has been sensitive to abuses in the stock and bond markets ever since the Wall Street crash of 1929 and has sought to keep a tight rein on those markets; it evidently saw government oversight of the coin market as a logical extension of this activist approach, once that market became an important haven for investors.

Loss of a Major Tax Break

One of the earliest instances of adverse federal involvement in the coin market—and one of the most damaging—was passage by Congress of the Economic Recovery Tax Act of 1981. Prior to enactment of this legislation, rare coins and other collectibles were eligible for inclusion in self-directed retirement plans, including Keogh plans. This was a significant inducement to purchase coins, for it sheltered them from federal income tax during the time they were held in a retirement plan, and many coin dealers actively solicited business on the basis of this selling point. In fact, some dealerships based most of their business on sales involving retirement-plan portfolios.

The Economic Recovery Tax Act eliminated this preferred tax treatment; from that time on, collectibles no longer could be sheltered in many self-directed retirement plans. Thus, in a single stroke, Congress wiped out a benefit that had become one of the most attractive reasons for buying rare coins. This had an immediate depressant effect on coin values, sending the marketplace into a tailspin—and it drove some dealers out of the business altogether.

Recently, there have been efforts to make collectibles eligible again for many self-directed retirement plans. Clearly, this would be extremely beneficial for the coin market, just as the loss of this eligibility was extremely damaging. The entire scenario involving this tax break demonstrates dramatically, however, that government regulation is a risk—a potentially far-ranging risk—for those who buy and sell coins.

Big Brother and the Computer Age

The Computer Revolution has been a boon to the coin market. Computerized trading has greatly facilitated many coin transactions, particularly those involving fungible coins—those that exist in large enough numbers to be readily interchangeable on a "sight-unseen" basis. Computers enable dealers and collectors to keep closer tabs on their coins and follow—and act upon—changes in price performance. Computers may even play a major role soon in grading coins. However, computerization is a double-edged sword: In the hands of government agencies, it provides a powerful weapon for regulating the coin business, and this can have a chilling effect on marketplace activity. In short, it can be a serious risk.

We first came to know the character Big Brother in the George Orwell novel *1984*. In real life, 1984 is quite a few years behind us, but Big Brother is alive—and all too well—in the form of the government's stealth squad of regulators and enforcers. Computers have given a powerful new weapon to the Internal Revenue Service and other government agencies, enabling them to peek over our shoulders and, through magnetic media reporting, look right into our bank books and receipts from our transactions. This can make coin transactions a risky business indeed for those who aren't careful—and even for some who are.

Buying or selling coins may be subject to one of several IRS reporting requirements. One of these regulations pertains to cash transactions. Here's the way the regulation reads:

> Each person engaged in a trade or business who, in the course of such trade or business, receives more than $10,000 in cash in one transaction (or two or more related transactions) must file Form 8300. For example, multiple receipts of cash from any person which in any one day total more than $10,000 should be treated as a single receipt (and therefore reportable).

A separate IRS regulation requires bullion dealers to file a report (Form 1099-B) on each transaction covered by contracts of the Commodity Futures Trading Commission (CFTC). This rule has its legal basis in Section 6045 of the Tax Equity and Fiscal Responsibility Act. Although it was intended primarily to regulate transactions involving precious metals in bullion form, the IRS has interpreted it to cover sales of bullion-type coins as well, and this has made many potential buyers more cautious about proceeding. That, in turn, acts as a brake on marketplace activity and values, and since there is a symbiotic relationship between the coin and bullion markets, the repercussions are felt in both.

The FTC and the Coin Market

Although the IRS has taken an ever-greater interest in the coin market, Big Brother's involvement has been even more apparent in the regulatory activities of the Federal Trade Commission. Since the late 1980s, the FTC has been a formidable presence in the coin arena—monitoring the marketplace closely, cracking down on abuses as it sees them, and promulgating (or proposing) regulations with far-reaching implications.

Much of this involvement has been healthy and helpful; ridding the market of unscrupulous dealers is certainly for the good. Some of it, however, has been less beneficial and even of questionable merit. In 1995, for example, the FTC proposed a series of regulations governing the activities of telemarketers—companies that conduct all or part of their business by telephone. There is ample documentation of abuses by certain telemarketers, including some companies that sell supposedly rare coins by phone, often at greatly inflated prices. These abuses have triggered numerous complaints to government agencies, and those were undoubtedly the catalysts for the FTC's proposals. But the telemarketing rules, as originally proposed by the commission, would have had a devastating effect on *every* firm that uses the telephone to do business, including not only the disreputable ones, but also the untold thousands of legitimate entrepreneurs for whom the phone is a vital lifeline to customers.

Fortunately, the FTC was persuaded to modify the regulations before they went into effect. It did so after hearing testimony from representatives of major business groups that would have been affected by the rules, including the Industry Council for Tangible Assets (ICTA), an advocacy group for dealers in coins and precious metals. But it's frightening to ponder how close the commission came to implementing these ill-advised rules, and how ruinous they would have been for the coin market as a whole—as well as for collectors and investors, whose holdings would have plummeted in value as a consequence.

Here's a brief summation of the rules as *originally proposed,* and also as adopted and implemented effective December 31, 1995:

- A *proposed* rule would have required sellers to mail written disclosures to all customers regarding the terms of their sales, then get these signed and returned before they could even ask for payment. This would have been required for every order. The adopted rule requires only oral disclosure.
- A *proposed* rule would have required sellers of tangible assets to disclose in writing the markup they were charging over their cost, and also tell clients how much they would receive upon immediate resale of the merchandise—a clearly untenable provision in a business where prices change constantly and sometimes dramatically. This provision was eliminated.
- A *proposed* rule would have prohibited a seller from contacting a customer with a new solicitation until *all terms and conditions* of any previous trade, including shipping and receipt, had been completed. This provision also was dropped.
- A *proposed* rule would have barred a seller from contacting a customer by phone more often than once every three months—a truly astounding notion that would have sounded the death knell for many coin dealers. Thankfully this, too, was eliminated in the adopted rules.
- A *proposed* rule would have prohibited a seller from providing or directing a courier service, such as Federal Express, to pick up a payment from a customer—a practice that is routine in the coin business, especially in transactions involving

bullion coins and other items whose prices can be highly volatile. Under the final rule, a seller may provide a courier for this purpose, or direct the customer to use one, as long as the required oral disclosures have been made.

- A *proposed* rule would have made business-to-business transactions subject to the same disclosure procedures as those proposed for retail clients: written notification and a signed receipt. The adopted rule applies this requirement only to sales of non-durable office and cleaning supplies, making it irrelevant to the coin business.

Coin dealers and their customers narrowly averted a body blow in this instance. Far from protecting coin consumers, the original regulations would have stripped away the marketplace infrastructure that supports the value of their holdings.

Perhaps the FTC and other government agencies have come away from this episode with a greater understanding of the coin market's workings and heightened sensitivity to the havoc they can wreak with wrong-headed overregulation. There's certainly a lesson for those who buy and sell coins: Regulatory risk could prove to be the greatest risk of all!

CHAPTER ✦ 3

STATE-OF-THE-ART GRADING

I now consider the basic premise of numerical grading to be seriously flawed—and the blanket application of the Sheldon 1-to-70 scale to all series to be a gross blunder on the part of the ANA.
—"Grading by the Number," Tom DeLorey
COINage magazine, September 1993

Numbers. Numbers. Numbers. When it comes to grading coins, there are numbers everywhere—and they're not always what they seem to be. Understanding these numbers is vital, however, to grasping the concept of how to grade coins. And understanding grading is crucial to making money from coins *right now*.

To a mathematician or scientist, numbers are absolute: 65 is always 65, because numbers don't lie. In the coin industry, nothing could be further from the truth. Numbers may not lie, but they don't always represent *exactly* what you think they represent.

Coins are graded, or rated, on a 1-to-70 scale. At the low end, the number 1 represents a coin which is so well worn it can barely be identified as to its type. At the high end, 70 represents a coin which is perfect—a coin with no nicks, no flaws, no

Figure 3-1. *Low-end Mint State-65 Morgan dollar.* The cheek, a grade-sensitive area, possesses various nicks and marks. If this coin were resubmitted for certification, a grade of MS-64 might be assigned. *Photo courtesy Professional Coin Grading Service.*

Figure 3-2. *High-end or "premium-quality" Mint State-65 Morgan dollar.* Notice the freedom from flaws on the cheek, as well as the satinlike luster. This coin is so close to the MS-66 grade that if it were resubmitted for certification, a grade of MS-66 might be assigned. *Photo courtesy Professional Coin Grading Service.*

scratches, and no imperfections of any kind. The 11 numbers from 60 to 70 constitute the Mint State grades—the numbers applied to coins which have not passed from hand to hand and exhibit no friction on their very highest points.

A coin that grades or rates 65 on this 1-to-70 scale could be worth thousands of dollars more than a coin of the same type grading 64. As a consumer, you might think that all 65s are alike and that all 64s are alike. Point-blank, you're wrong! Figures 3-1 and 3-2 make that obvious.

The coin shown in Figure 3-1, an 1887-P Morgan silver dollar, grades or rates Mint State-65. It was given this impartial, arm's-length-distance rating by the largest independent coin grading service in the world, the Professional Coin Grading Service (PCGS). PCGS rates coins using a consensus approach, then encapsulates the coins in sonically sealed, tamper-resistant holders. The coin shown in Figure 3-2, an 1879-S Morgan dollar, also was graded Mint State-65 by PCGS. It's obvious, however, that these two coins have significant differences. The coin in

Figure 3-1 has a number of nicks and scratches on the cheek of Miss Liberty, and the cheek is an important, grade-sensitive area. By contrast, the coin in Figure 3-2 has beautiful, satinlike luster on the cheek. Numbers don't lie, you say? Well, in the coin field, they may not lie—but they *can* mislead.

ORIGIN OF THE 1-TO-70 SCALE

The 1-to-70 scale used in grading coins seems puzzling to many newcomers when they first encounter the system. But then, even people deeply involved with rare coins—and thoroughly familiar with the grading scale—often find serious fault with it. Tom DeLorey, a former grader-authenticator at the American Numismatic Association Certification Service (ANACS), spoke for many dealers and collectors when he characterized the system in his thoughtful *COINage* article as "a gross blunder on the part of the ANA."

The ANA adopted the scale in 1977 while formulating a grading system for its book *Official A.N.A. Grading Standards for United States Coins.* However, it wasn't really an ANA creation. Rather, it was a modified version of a grading system first promulgated in 1948 by the late Dr. William H. Sheldon, an authority on early U.S. cents, as a way to reflect the values of common-variety large cents dated 1794, which have long been very popular with collectors. At that time, a badly worn 1794 large cent, barely identifiable as to its variety, was worth about $1 in the marketplace, so Sheldon designated that as Basal State-1. Specimens graded good were worth $4 to $6, so Sheldon assigned those the grades of G-4 through G-6. Cents in better grades got progressively higher numbers, always corresponding to their retail dollar value, up to the number 70 for a flawless uncirculated piece (at a time when $70 was deemed an astounding price).

In adopting the Sheldon system as the basis for its own, the ANA presumably was influenced by the fact that it was already familiar to many hobbyists. But while it appears to have been a useful form of shorthand for reflecting the grades and values of early cents, it has proven to be confusing and in many ways inadequate when applied to the broad range of U.S. coinage.

What's more, the numbers suggest a level of exactness that really doesn't exist. The system would be just as accurate—or inaccurate—if adjectives were used to describe the various grades, assuming that enough satisfactory adjectives could be found. DeLorey reports that the ANA originally considered a 1-to-100 scale, with Mint State coins occupying the range from 70 to 100. Given the widespread acceptance and usage of the decimal system, including its use in U.S. coinage, this would seem to have been a far more promising approach.

Initially, the ANA set aside just three grades for Mint State coins: 60, 65, and 70. It soon added 63 and 67 for intermediate-grade coins, and marketplace demand resulted in the addition of 64 and 66, as well, in the early 1980s. Soon after that, when independent third-party grading services appeared on the scene, it became common practice to recognize and use all 11 numbers from 60 to 70.

Today, the recognized standard definitions for the 1-to-70 scale can be found in *The Official Guide to Coin Grading and Counterfeit Detection,* by PCGS (edited by Scott A. Travers; text by John W. Dannreuther and Richard S. Montgomery). This gargantuan Random House book contains hundreds of black-and-white photographs, as well as spectacular digitized images and definitive standards for all the grades.

THE COIN GRADING SPECTRUM

Coin grading is performed on a spectrum, or a continuum. Not all coins graded 65, or graded 64—or graded *any* number on the 1-to-70 scale—are necessarily equal. Coins are like snowflakes; each one is different from every other. Some coins grading 65 might be high-end 65s—almost 66s. An example of this is the 1879-S Morgan dollar shown on the right in the previous set of photos. Some coins grading 65 might be low-end 65s—barely better than 64s—like the 1887-P Morgan dollar on the left.

For people who earn a living as traders of coins—who buy and sell coins on a regular basis to make money—much of the money-making activity centers around the seemingly small detail of whether a coin is high-end or low-end for its grade. If you were to take a rare-date coin grading 65—but *high*-end 65—and send it back to the grading service and get it recertified as a 66, you might make thousands of dollars. On the other hand, you would have downside risk, rather than upside potential, if you were to purchase a coin such as the one shown on the left, with scratches all over the cheek—an attractive, Mint State-65 coin, yes, but not high-end for its grade. If you were to take that coin, crack it out of its holder, and resubmit it to a leading grading service such as PCGS, it might end up being regraded as a 64.

High-End and Low-End Coins

I worked for a time as a grader for the Numismatic Guaranty Corporation of America (NGC), another of the nation's preeminent grading services. During that time, we were cognizant of the differences among coins with the same numerical grade in the spectrum. For internal purposes only, we graded coins using the letter suffixes A, B, and C, with A signifying a coin that was at the high end of the spectrum for its grade, C denoting a coin at the low end, and B representing a coin right in the middle. As a high-end Mint State-65 coin, the 1879-S Morgan dollar pictured would have been graded 65-A. As a low-end coin, the 1887-P Morgan dollar would have been graded 65-C.

Coin grading is a process of subjective evaluation. However, it becomes somewhat objective when groups of experts examine coins and achieve a consensus of subjectivity. It is common practice at the leading grading services for three expert graders to examine each coin. In most cases, they concur in their assessments. On borderline coins, however, they sometimes split—and this is where shrewd submitters sometimes make big money.

Let's say three graders examined the 1879-S dollar previously shown and two of them concluded it was Mint State-65-A, while the third grader decided it was Mint State-66-C. In that event, the coin would probably be graded Mint State-65. (The grading services don't indicate A, B, or C on their holders.) Now let's suppose that the coin were resubmitted and a different team of graders were to look at it —and instead of two graders rating it 65-A and one rating it 66-C, two were to grade it 66-C and one 65-A. In that case, the coin would probably be regraded as a 66. Thus, for the submitter, wealth would be created—perhaps many thousands of dollars. Small differences in grade can have big implications for the price of a coin, and recognizing—and capitalizing upon—these subtle but critical differences is one of the central themes of this book.

HOW GRADERS AT THE BEST SERVICES EVALUATE COINS

When a coin is submitted to a grading service, the experts base their rating on certain key characteristics. You need to consider these factors yourself in deciding whether a coin is a strong or weak candidate for resubmission and possible upgrading.

Eye Appeal: This is probably the most important element. Is the coin pretty or is it ugly? Does it look as if Godzilla might have used it as a teething ring, or is it dripping with luster and free from any obvious imperfections? Does it have attractive concentric-circle color or toning about the periphery, or is it totally black—so black that you can identify imperfections on it only with great difficulty?

Strike: Was the coin well struck or weakly struck?

One of the most intense debates in the entire history of U.S. coin grading centers on the issue of weak strike. Since grading is such an important element in pricing, strike has become a vital concern. The problem in understanding the role of strike is that many of today's collectors tend to look at early U.S. coins through 20th-century eyes. Such issues as Colonial coins and early U.S. Mint issues are generally weak compared with products of modern high-speed presses.

To some, striking weakness and wear are indistinguishable, but strike and loss of metal to circulation are wholly different things. Slow striking on antique presses that lacked the power to force silver into every cranny of the dies can be detected on nearly all early U.S. dollars and half dollars, though smaller coins generally did better. Being relatively soft and malleable, gold allowed successful, needle-sharp strikes as a matter of routine. Early copper coins were struck with far less care, resulting in the tremendous array of collectible die states so beloved by early copper specialists.

As a commercial factor, weak strike first became the source of debate on Morgan dollars from the New Orleans Mint. O-mint coins were simply not struck with the same precision and force as their Philadelphia counterparts, resulting in blurry feathers or a flat lock over Miss Liberty's ear. Since the Morgan dollar fueled the 1980s investment market, under-standing the realities of New Orleans minting procedures really was vital to understanding that uncirculated "O" dol-lars did not exhibit wear—they exhibited weak strike. Even today, this distinction is not fully understood by all collec-tors or dealers.

The lightest wear results in an interruption of the microns-thin layer of mint luster that enhances the beauty of a truly uncirculated coin. This break in the luster can be seen clearly under a glass as a coin is slowly rotated and tilted back and forth under a pinpoint light source, as I have illus-trated in my best-selling book, *The Coin Collector's Survival Manual* (4th edition, Bonus Books, 2000). By contrast, a weakly struck coin shows full luster covering the entire surface—even on the highest areas, such as Liberty's locks and the eagle's feathers on Morgan dollars; the headband on Indian cents; or the cheek on a Boone commemorative half dollar.

Pricing may well rest on whether a coin has the subtle eye appeal sought by a collector. At one time, numerically graded coins that were weakly struck but otherwise exactly as they came from the dies could be called MS-65 or MS-67 examples. But this drew fire from some rather strident dissenters, especially in the silver dollar world, who denied that any weakly struck dollar could ever be considered a high-grade Mint State specimen.

Luster: Does the coin have natural, original luster? Does it reflect light the same way an ocean does? When you look at an ocean, it always reflects light. When you tilt and rotate a truly Mint State coin under a pinpoint light source, that coin also reflects light in a circular pattern. A coin that is not quite Mint State—one that grades About Uncirculated—reflects light in the same kind of pattern, but the pattern is disturbed in some way. Coins are struck with flow lines, which can be likened to the ridges on an ocean. When a coin is cleaned or dipped in a mildly acidic solution, microscopic portions of that coin's metal are removed. As a result, the flow lines—those tiny ridges that give the coin its vibrant luster, its ability to reflect light—are flattened, and the coin can appear to be overdipped. Grading services view this as an important factor in assigning a grade to a coin.

The surfaces of the coin: Has the coin been cleaned? <u>Important Tip</u>: Always examine coins under a halogen light source. Halogen clearly reveals any imperfections a coin may have—in particular, any evidence that the coin has been cleaned. If a coin has been cleaned abrasively, PCGS and NGC will not certify and encapsulate that coin. It will be placed in what is called a "body bag" and returned to the submitter without a grade. Figure 3-3 shows a "whizzed"

Figure 3-3. *Whizzed 1795 13 Leaves Capped Bust eagle.* The harsh, abrasive cleaning is evident from the parallel striations which crisscross the coin. *Photo courtesy Heritage Numismatic Auctions, Inc.*

1795 Capped Bust eagle. Whizzing refers to the simulation of Mint luster by the use of a wire brush to remove the top layer of the coin's metal. This form of abrasive cleaning is evident from the parallel striations which crisscross the coin. These can be readily detected by tilting and rotating the coin under a halogen light. <u>Caution</u>: *Be careful of extended exposure to halogen; halogen lamps emit relatively high levels of electromagnetic radiation. Unlike computer screens, halogen lamps are not rated according to their levels of low-level magnetic field emission. There are no regulations governing halogen lamp usage in the workplace, either in the United States or abroad.*

Toning: Does the coin have beautiful, original color or has it been toned artificially? In many cases, you can look beneath the toning and see imperfections. If you're not sure whether a coin has been toned artificially, examine the coin carefully under a halogen light source. If you see big scratches, gouges, or signs that the coin has been altered in any way, it might have been subjected to artificial toning. "Coin doctors" engage in very sophisticated methods of coin alteration and restoration, and many times these have fooled grading services. The Albany commemorative half dollar pictured in

Figures 3-4 & 3-5. *Returned as a "no grade" because of questionable toning.* Coins returned ungraded by NGC and PCGS are sent back in a "body bag." These two services charge the same fee to "no-grade" a coin as they would to certify and encapsulate it. *Photos courtesy Professional Coin Grading Service.*

Figures 3-4 and 3-5 was returned to its submitter because of questionable toning.

Environmental damage: Grading services don't like to encapsulate coins that pose a significant risk of deteriorating in their holders. For the most part, it's a good idea to neutralize or degrease your coins before long-term storage, using denatured alcohol. You should be aware, however, that if you have a coin with polyvinyl chloride—a chemical found in certain kinds of plastic—on its surface, a grading service is very unlikely to certify and encapsulate the coin, because the chances are good that it would deteriorate while it was housed in the company's holder, thus imposing financial liability on the service.

These are the factors that experts look for at the best grading services, and the factors that you should check for yourself as you embark upon the challenging but potentially rewarding process of grading Mint State coins—and, for that matter, grading *all* coins, including even circulated coins.

The Development of Coin Grading

Precise coin grading is a relatively new phenomenon. Up until the mid-20th century, coin dealers and collectors got by with just a handful of grade designations, and Mint State coins were all lumped together as *uncirculated.* Gradually, descriptive adjectives came into use to call attention to coins of exceptional quality; these would be designated as *brilliant, gem,* or *choice,* for example. At that point, there was no urgency for more specific language, since prices were relatively modest and didn't increase dramatically, in most instances, from one broad grade level to the next.

The need for precision grading began to become apparent during the 1970s, as large numbers of well-to-do outsiders started buying coins as an investment. These investors placed heavy emphasis on quality, limiting their purchases almost exclusively to Mint State coins—and this, in turn, drove up the prices of these coins, breaking the long-standing pattern whereby values had increased in a steady and consistent manner from one grade level to the next. Suddenly, Mint State coins were commanding far higher premiums than their circulated counterparts.

In the absence of industry-wide standards, abuses developed, or rather, existing abuses became greatly magnified, because so much more money was at stake. Unscrupulous dealers could and did use very creative language in describing the grades of their coins, and proving them wrong was difficult at best. Demand arose for action to remedy the problem, specifically for the establishment of official grading standards that could be applied in a uniform way nationwide.

THE ANA CERTIFICATION SERVICE

The logical choice to oversee this project was the national coin club, the American Numismatic Association. The ANA was deeply involved already in authenticating coins—certifying them to be genuine. In response to earlier concerns regarding the sale of fake and altered coins, it had set up the ANA Certification Service (ANACS) in 1972, and this agency had taken major strides toward exorcising that demon. Now, responsible dealers and collectors turned to the ANA again, and it responded by drawing up official grading standards and expanding the role of ANACS to encompass not only coin authentication but grading as well.

ANACS started grading coins in March 1979, at just about the peak of the coin market's greatest boom. In contrast to the unalloyed success the service had enjoyed with authentication, though, its assumption of this new role turned out to be a mixed blessing. ANACS grading was wildly successful from a commercial standpoint, attracting many thousands of submissions and generating enormous revenue for the ANA. But many in the marketplace came to be dissatisfied with it, and while it was predictable that unscrupulous coin sellers would oppose it, the critics also included highly legitimate merchants.

Almost at once, ANACS grading certificates became important marketing tools for many dealers and a huge bone of contention for many others. Critics complained that ANA grading was often inconsistent and even downright inaccurate. But ANA certification was helping to feed the frenzy in the marketplace, so dealers continued to deluge the service with coins to be graded. At one point, these coins were arriving at ANA headquarters in Colorado Springs at the rate of 12,000 per month.

A Dilemma for ANACS

As prices fell and many dealers' grading tastes grew more finicky, ANACS faced a dilemma: If it adhered to the liberal standards set in its early months of operation, its grading would be out of step with the new reality; but if it tightened its standards, the earlier ANACS certificates would be cheapened and the service would suffer a loss of credibility. In the end, it seemed to straddle the two approaches and, in the process, really satisfied no one.

By February 1982, ANA President Adna G. Wilde, Jr., felt compelled to appoint a committee to review the many complaints and formulate guidelines for improving the situation. The committee's chairman, scholar-researcher-dealer Q. David Bowers, reported a few months later that the panel had uncovered a number of inconsistencies in ANACS grading and that these were "embarrassing to the ANA." He said there was ample evidence "that a coin graded one way on Tuesday may be graded another way Friday, or that a coin graded at 10 a.m. may be different at 4 p.m." ANACS remained the dominant grading service for several years thereafter, but its reign was an uneasy one.

Perceptive dealer and market analyst Maurice Rosen of Plainview, New York, pinpointed ANACS's problem—and accurately predicted its subsequent decline—in a 1982 interview published in *COINage* magazine.

"I strongly approve of the concept of an independent grading service," Rosen told *COINage*'s Ed Reiter, "but only if it is competent. In the case of ANACS, the level of competence and experience simply isn't great enough now. I believe it can be improved to the point where it will gain broad acceptance—but in order for that to happen, the ANA will have to spend some money and get the right people to run it. In other words, the grading service itself must be upgraded." Unless that happened, Rosen said, ANACS might wither and die, and a new grading service beyond the ANA's control might take its place.

PCGS AND THE GRADING REVOLUTION

Those who were dissatisfied with ANACS organized a number of competing grading services during the early and middle 1980s. Most had one thing in common: They were formed by coin dealers. And this was no coincidence. Influential dealers were among the most vociferous critics of ANACS, primarily because they didn't believe it was giving proper weight to commercial considerations in its grading. Essentially, they viewed ANACS as too academic and out of touch with reality as reflected in the marketplace.

The search for an alternative ended successfully in 1986 when David Hall of Newport Beach, California, one of the nation's most talented coin traders, announced the formation of the Professional Coin Grading Service (PCGS). It was clearly an idea whose time had come—and come in a big, big way. PCGS scored the equivalent of a first-round knockout, quickly dethroning ANACS as king of the coin-grading hill. In a very real sense, 1986 meant as much to the grading "revolution" as 1789 did to the French Revolution and 1917 to the Russian Revolution. That was the year certified coins came into their own, the year the coin market witnessed and accepted a new order in grading.

The PCGS Formula

Several key ingredients made up the revolutionary PCGS formula. First, the new company engaged leading dealers—including Hall himself—to do the grading. And they graded by consensus: Three different experts would view a given coin and assign it a grade, then the grade would be examined by a "finalizer," who would weigh the consensus and assign it a final grade. (See Figure 3-6.)

Second, PCGS introduced the use of a sonically sealed, hard plastic holder to encase both the coin and a PCGS tab stating the

Figure 3-6. *PCGS-certified and graded.* *Photo courtesy Professional Coin Grading Service.*

coin's date, denomination, variety, and grade. This holder (soon dubbed the "slab") made it possible to buy and sell coins sight-unseen, almost like commodities. And that process was further eased by a third major feature of PCGS's program: its guarantee to purchasers. PCGS dealer members agreed that they would accept the grade assigned to any coin by the service and buy it, sight-unseen, at their current bid price for that grade.

ANOTHER MAJOR GRADING SERVICE EMERGES

PCGS soon overtook ANACS as the coin market's No. 1 grading service. But the new leader's dominance didn't go unchallenged for long. Soon after PCGS began operations in Newport Beach in February 1986, one of its organizers, highly respected coin dealer John Albanese, withdrew and began drafting plans for a new grading service of his own. Albanese felt that PCGS had an Achilles' heel: the possible conflict posed by the fact that its principals were dealing in coins. He set out to form a service that would offer the best of both worlds—the professionalism of PCGS and the independence of ANACS. In the process, he stopped buying and selling coins himself.

Albanese's grading service opened for business in August

Figure 3-7. *NGC-certified and graded.* Shown is the back of an NGC holder which displays the American Numismatic Association's logo. NGC is ANA's official grading service. *Photo courtesy Numismatic Guaranty Corporation of America, Inc.*

1987 as the Numismatic Guaranty Corporation of America—or NGC, for short. It is based in Parsippany, New Jersey, some 35 miles west of New York City.

Like PCGS, NGC encases each coin in a hard plastic holder along with an ID label. (See Figure 3-7.) A flexible white plastic insert grips the coin securely, preventing it from rattling around and possibly being damaged. By contrast, PCGS uses a clear plastic holder. To enhance the security of their holders, NGC and PCGS both incorporate holograms into their packaging. These make it much more difficult to produce effective counterfeit holders. Both services' holders have raised edges, making them easy to stack.

NGC appears to have relaxed its original policy barring its principals and full-time employees from dealing in coins; Albanese acknowledged that he himself bought and sold coins. However, this shift does not seem to have caused a loss of consumer confidence in the service. In 1999, Albanese sold his interest in NGC. He remains active as a dealer, as well as a manufacturer of Intercept Shield, a coin preservation product. (See Chapter 2.)

A Different ANACS

In 1989, the ANA sold its coin-grading operation to Amos Press, Inc., of Sidney, Ohio, publisher of *Coin World,* the hobby's largest-circulation weekly newspaper. The new owner retained the acronym ANACS as the name of the service, although the letters no longer stood for the original words and the ANA now has no connection with the business. (See Figure 3-8.) The operation was moved to Columbus, Ohio, where it remains, and over the years it has carved out an important niche in the marketplace. The ANA retained the authentication portion of its formerly two-pronged service.

Independent Coin Grading Company

The Independent Coin Grading Company (ICG) is a relative newcomer to the ranks of the nation's coin-grading services, having been founded in 1998. That is only two years ago as this is written in August 2000, but the company has already carved out an important niche for itself and is competing aggressively with the established leaders in the field. In fact, its volume of business compares favorably with the Big Three that existed when ICG entered the field. In large part, that's because

Figure 3-9. *Coin certified by ICG.*
Photo courtesy Independent Coin Grading Company.

1928 $20
ICG - MS63
1234567890

ICG handles large numbers of high-grade modern U.S. coins—considerably more, percentagewise, than the other leading services. In fact, its encouragement of these submissions has been a significant factor in the rapid growth that sector of the marketplace has enjoyed.

Unlike PCGS and NGC, ICG does not have a network of authorized dealers. Rather, it accepts submissions from all dealers and provides an incentive by giving dealers a 20 percent discount on all submissions. To receive this, they must use a Dealer Submitter Number (DSN), which they can obtain without charge simply by requesting one from ICG. At the time this number is assigned to a dealer, he or she is furnished with ICG submission forms.

"Independent" is ICG's first name, and not just by coincidence. The company has proclaimed its determination to avoid even the appearance of conflict of interest, notably by ensuring that its graders do not know the identity of clients who submit coins for review. Toward this end, it requires that submissions not go to ICG directly, but rather to an affiliated third-party company called Corporate Security Solutions, also located in Englewood, Colorado. Corporate Security removes all shipping and identification labels and assigns a computerized random tracking number to each incoming coin—and then, once coins are certified, graded, and encapsulated, it packages and ships them to the submitters.

Standard service at ICG has a normal turnaround time of fifteen days, but coins are shipped sooner if they are ready for return. One-day service is available, with coins received by noon being ready the next day by 5 P.M. The company charges no grading fee for "no-grade" coins—those it declines to certify. However, a $5 processing fee is charged to the submitter's account in such instances. The full submission fee is assessed for no-grade coins which the company deems to be counterfeit or altered.

ICG is off to a fast start and has a good chance to remain a major part of the coin-grading industry for many years to come. It remains well behind the other leading services, though, in the volume of coins it handles from the pre-modern era. Those are considerably rarer and more valuable as a group, and grading decisions have greater financial implications for them than for modern U.S. coins. ICG's long-term stability and growth will hinge in large part on how successful it is in penetrating this part of the market and expanding its role there.

GRADING FEES

Grading fees are comparable at all of the major coin certification services. Typically, it costs about $30 to have a coin graded and encapsulated in the standard manner, which involves a turnaround time of about a month. Faster processing is available for a higher fee; it costs approximately $150 for "walk-through" service, in which a coin can be certified literally while the submitter waits. Current fee schedules can be obtained by contacting the individual services.

These services will accept submissions from the public or through authorized dealers. Write first. Lists of dealer members can be obtained by writing to the services in question.

The addresses of these services are as follows:

Professional Coin Grading Service
P.O. Box 9458
Newport Beach, CA 92658

Numismatic Guaranty Corporation of America, Inc.
P.O. Box 1776
Parsippany, NJ 07054

ANACS
P.O. Box 182141
Columbus, OH 43218-2141

Independent Coin Grading Company
7901 East Belleview Ave., Suite 50
Englewood, CO 80111

POPULATION REPORTS

All of the major grading services issue periodic "population" or "census" reports showing how many coins of each date in each U.S. series they have certified in each of the 11 proof or Mint State grades. These have become valuable tools for coin buyers, sellers, and researchers for they offer a good picture of relative rarity within each series. However, they cannot be viewed as totally accurate reflections of rarity and availability, since the same coin may be counted more than once—many times, in fact—if it is resubmitted in quest of a higher grade.

GRADING GUARANTEES

From the beginning, PCGS and NGC have furnished guarantees to protect their customers against loss of value caused by overgrading or deterioration of coins while housed in the services' holders. These guarantees provide for regrading of coins where such loss has occurred or is suspected. If the grade assigned during this second procedure is lower than the one originally assigned, the services will pay the difference in value between the two grades. NGC does not cover copper coins under its guarantee; PCGS does, giving buyers a special incentive to limit their purchases of certified copper coins to those in PCGS holders.

DETECTING COUNTERFEIT HOLDERS

In the late 1980s, the integrity and acceptance of certified coins suffered a scare when overgraded coins began turning up in counterfeit PCGS holders. Fortunately, the holders had fundamental flaws which permitted knowledgeable dealers and collectors—as well as the service itself—to identify them. As shown in Figure 3-10, there were small but significant differences in the lettering on the tab that is inserted in each holder. The fake holders differed, too, in having a more pronounced raised area along the side of the plastic.

Since that time, PCGS and other grading services have adopted more sophisticated techniques—including the use of holograms—to safeguard their holders and render them more difficult to counterfeit. There have been no major security problems since then, and the perpetrators of the original fraud have been brought to justice.

CHANGES IN GRADING STANDARDS

Consistency was a goal of all the major grading services when they began operations; all of them recognized that faithful adherence to constant grading standards would be a crucial factor in winning and keeping consumers' confidence. For the most part, they have done a highly commendable job of meeting this goal. However, there have been perceptible deviations over the years—sometimes in the direction of stricter grading, other times toward looser interpretation or enforcement of the established guidelines. For this reason, coins graded during one time period may differ by as much as a point—or even more—from virtually identical coins that passed through the same grading service at a different time. These differences can be disconcerting. At the same time, however, they can work to the advantage of those who can identify holders from the various periods.

Dealer-author Q. David Bowers has monitored this situation closely over the years, obviously retaining the same keen interest he had when he headed the panel that reviewed ANACS grading in the early 1980s. "It is my opinion that grading standards, or at least interpretations of standards, are changing once

IDENTIFYING
ILLICIT PCGS COIN HOLDERS

Step #1 From the insert

Determine if the insert is genuine.

 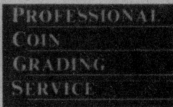

GOOD INSERT   **BAD INSERT**

The serifs on the good insert slant from the letters at a 45° angle. Note the S and the E in SERVICE. The serif on the G is longer.

The serifs on the bad inserts are vertical. They cut off squarely and do not angle out. Also there is no serif on the G.

Step #2 From The Plastic Cases

It is important to check the plastic holder even if the insert is o.k.

 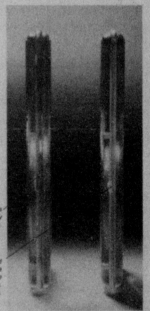

Area to examine on case

Bad case has a more obvious raised area which is approximately 3/16" long.

Good case has small raised area along the edge where the holder was cut from the injection molded sprue. About 1/16" long.

Figure 3-10. *Tipsheet for identifying fake PCGS certification (old holders).* PCGS has since modified and improved its holder and built in anti-tampering mechanisms such as a hologram.   *Photo courtesy Heritage Capital Corporation.*

again," Bowers wrote in his *Coin World* column, "The Joy of Collecting," in late 1995. "In many instances, what the grading services used to call Mint State-65 is now MS-66. In order to buy the same quality that was sold as MS-65 a few years ago, it is often necessary to buy MS-66 today." Since writing that column, Bowers has purchased an interest in PCGS, putting himself in position to gain even greater insight—from an insider's perspective—on the workings of the certification business, including the grading standards used.

But his ownership interest in a grading service hasn't affected his outspokenness about grading service standards. In 1999, in his same "Joy of Collecting" column in *Coin World,* Bowers authored a series of articles under the "grade inflation" banner. In one of them, he wrote, in part:

> ... I spied a certified holder containing a Mint State 1839-O quarter eagle. This is quite an exciting coin to contemplate, and in more than forty-five years of professional numismatics I've seen only a handful.... However, upon inspection I found it, in my opinion, to be an acid-etched Extremely Fine 45 coin at best, a real "dog." ... I would not have bought it even at a price for a Very Fine coin! It was a dog, indeed! Presumably, some bargain-seeking investor, who buys "numbers" instead of coins, owns it now.

In a later *Coin World* column he opined: "There is a peculiar aspect to certification numbers. Populations never contract. They keep getting larger!" In his column, he explained these ever-increasing population numbers as follows:

> Part of the higher numbers is due, in my opinion, to grading inflation, but the practice of resubmission is also important. I recall that one of the leading West Coast dealers once told me that he had a very nice 1916-D dime, for which there was a big jump in market price between MS-63 or MS-64 and the grade he desired, MS-65. He sent the coin in twenty-four times—yes, twenty-four

times—until, *finally,* it was certified MS-65! The data show two dozen Mint State 1916-D dimes sent to a particular service when, in fact, only a single coin was involved.

Bowers' remarks are particularly fascinating when you consider that his coin companies were acquired by Collectors Universe (parent company of grading service PCGS) in early 2000.

Michael Keith Ruben, a prominent South Carolina dealer, has submitted tens of thousands of coins to the certification services—notably NGC—over the years. In his opinion, the grading standards were "unquestionably softer" at NGC and PCGS in the mid-1990s than they had been a few years earlier. He believes, however, that in at least one instance, the marketplace forced a *tightening* of standards: "Prior to 1988, a deeply toned original coin had its grade increased, but today NGC and PCGS lower the grade for toned specimens." Ruben offers this capsule comparison of these two grading services: "For the most part, PCGS is more conservative than NGC; but NGC is more consistent than PCGS."

John Albanese has a unique perspective on the birth pains of the two biggest services: He was one of the original owners and graders at PCGS, then went on to found NGC a short time later. "I can speak both for NGC and PCGS concerning their first six months of operations," Albanese says. "The grading standards of both services were too tight." Today, he says, the companies provide grading of comparable quality: "NGC is marginally looser in grading a certain group of coins, but overall is on par with PCGS standards." He made those statements in 1996, and he sold his interest in NGC in 1999.

David Hall, founder and president of PCGS, has acknowledged that some of the coins graded by his company in its first few years—and especially its first six months—might receive higher grades if resubmitted today because the standards were overly strict at that time. During an appearance on a radio program I hosted, he agreed that it might be advisable to seek regrading of such coins—particularly very high-grade, high-end pieces—before selling them.

Coins that were graded by PCGS and NGC during their earliest years can generally be identified by the absence of a hologram on the holder—a security feature both firms adopted only later. However, this is not a foolproof way to distinguish these potentially profitable coins from all the rest, since some of the coins graded in the early months were subsequently reholdered without being regraded.

How to Grade Rare Coins

From your perspective as a buyer or seller, the most important part of the grading spectrum is the grading of Mint-State coins—coins that have not passed from hand to hand, have not circulated, and have no wear on their very highest points. The difference in price in these "upper-end" coins is tremendous; you literally *can't afford not to know how to grade these coins.*

Grading services furnish invaluable assistance to buyers and sellers of coins, particularly to those who lack in-depth knowledge of grading. But to maximize your potential for making money from coins, you need to become familiar with how to grade coins yourself—particularly how to grade coins in the 11 Mint State levels.

PCGS Coin-Grading Standards

In 1997, PCGS shared its grading secrets with the public through the publication of a major new book, *The Official Guide to Coin Grading and Counterfeit Detection.* I served as editor of the book, which was published by House of Collectibles, an imprint of Random House. The book won three major literary awards in the coin field.

The following is an excerpt from that book, incorporating the basic PCGS coin-grading standards.

Mint State Standards
MS-70: Perfect Uncirculated

Marks: An MS-70 coin has no defects of any kind visible with a 5X (5-power) glass. **Note: Minor die polish, light die breaks, and so on are *not* considered defects on business-strike coins.**

Strike: The strike is razor-sharp and will show 99+ percent of the detail intended.

Luster: The luster is vibrant and undisturbed in any way. Any toning will be attractive. Only the slightest mellowing of color is acceptable for red copper.

Eye Appeal: The eye appeal is spectacular—the ultimate grade!

MS-69: Superb Gem Uncirculated

Marks: A virtually perfect coin. It usually takes an intense study of the surfaces to ascertain why the coin will not grade MS-70. Only the slightest contact marks, nearly invisible hairlines, the tiniest planchet flaws, and so on are allowable for this grade. **Note: Slight die polish, medium die breaks, or slight incomplete striking are *not* defects.**

Strike: The strike is extremely sharp and will show 99+ percent of the detail intended.

Luster: The luster will be full and unbroken. Any toning must be attractive. Only the slightest mellowing of color is acceptable for red copper, and only the slightest unevenness of color for red-brown and brown copper.

Eye Appeal: Superb!

MS-68: Superb Gem Uncirculated

Marks: A nearly perfect coin, with only slight imperfections visible to the unaided eye. The imperfections (tiny contact marks, minuscule hairlines, a small lint mark, etc.) will almost always be out of the range of the coin's focal points.

Strike: The strike will be exceptionally sharp.

Luster: The luster will be full (or virtually so) and "glowing." Any luster breaks will be extremely minor and usually restricted to the high points. Slight unevenness in toning is acceptable, as long as it is still attractive. Red copper may show some mellowing, and there may be some unevenness of color for red-brown and brown copper.

Eye Appeal: Exceptional, with no major detractions.

MS-67: SUPERB GEM UNCIRCULATED

Marks: Any abrasions on the coin are extremely light and/or well hidden in the design and do not detract from the coin's beauty in any way. As with MS-68 coins, the fields on smaller coins are usually nearly flawless, especially on the obverse. On large silver coins with smooth devices (Morgan dollars, for instance), the flaws will usually be found in the fields; on large gold coins (such as Liberty Head $20s), the fields will usually be superb in this grade, with only minor flaws in the devices.

Strike: The strike will be very sharp and almost always full.

Luster: The luster will be outstanding. Any toning (even if slightly uneven) must be attractive and not impede the luster in any way. Red copper can have mellowing of color, and there can be unevenness of color for red-brown and brown copper. Minute spotting, if present, should be virtually unnoticeable.

Eye Appeal: In almost all cases, the eye appeal will be superb. Any negativity will be compensated for by another area that is spectacular.

MS-66: GEM UNCIRCULATED

Marks: There may be several noticeable, but very minor, defects. If marks or hairlines are in an important focal area, they must be minimal and compensated for by the rest of the coin's superbness.

Strike: The coin will be well-struck.

Luster: The luster will be above average (usually far above average), and any toning should be attractive and should only minimally impede the luster. Red copper can have mellowing of color, and there can be unevenness of color for red-brown and brown copper. Very minor spotting may be present, although it should be noticed only upon close examination. A dipped coin must be "fresh" in appearance and never give the impression of having been cleaned.

Eye Appeal: The eye appeal will almost always be above average for a gem-quality coin, and many MS-66 coins will be superb in this category. Any negative factors must be compensated for in another area.

MS-65: GEM UNCIRCULATED

Marks: There may be scattered marks, hairlines, or other minor defects. If the flaws are in a main focal area, they must be minor and few. Hidden marks and hairlines can be larger. On dime-type and smaller, they almost always must be in the devices or must be very minor if they are in the fields. On larger coins, there can be marks/hairlines in the fields and in the devices, but no major ones.

Strike: The coin will be well-struck.

Luster: The luster will be at least average (almost always above average), and any toning can only slightly impede the luster. Copper coins can have mellowing of color for red and unevenness of color for red-brown or brown coins: **Note: There can be a little minor spotting for copper coins.**

Eye Appeal: The eye appeal will be average or above. This is a very nice coin. However, there are many ways a coin can grade MS-65. This grade (or MS/Proof-64) may have the largest range of eye appeal. A coin may grade MS-65 with scattered light marks, but with great luster and strike—or a coin with virtually no marks but a slightly impeded luster also could be MS-65. The overall eye appeal still must be positive or the coin does not merit MS-65.

MS-64: CHOICE UNCIRCULATED

Marks: There may be numerous minor marks/hairlines, several significant marks/hairlines, or other defects. There may be a few minor or one or two significant marks/hairlines in the main focal areas. On minor coinage (dime coinage and lesser), there may be several marks/hairlines in the fields or main focal areas, but none should be too severe. On larger coins, these marks/hairlines may be more severe in the fields or main focal areas. However, a severe mark/hairline would have to be of a size that would preclude grading the coin MS-65, though not so severe as to reduce the coin to MS-63. If there are several fairly heavy marks/hairlines in obvious areas, the coin would grade MS-63.

Strike: The strike will range from average to full.

Luster: The luster can be slightly below average to full, and toning can impede the luster. On brilliant coins, there may be breaks in the luster caused by marks or hairlines. Red copper can be considerably mellowed. There may be noticeable spotting for this grade, although heavy or large spotting would reduce the grade to MS-63 or below.

Eye Appeal: The eye appeal can range from slightly negative to very positive. This is a nice coin, so anything too negative would preclude the MS-64 grade. Balance is a key. A coin with marks/hairlines in obvious focal areas would have to have great luster or some other positive factor to attain MS-64. A coin with less severe marks/hairlines hidden in devices could have impaired luster or some other problem and still be graded MS-64. Coins with deficiencies and no redeeming characteristics are graded MS-63 or lower.

MS-63: CHOICE UNCIRCULATED

Marks: There may be numerous marks/hairlines, including several major marks/hairlines in main focal areas. If there are distracting marks/hairlines on the major devices, the fields should be relatively clean. If there are distracting marks/hairlines in the fields, the devices should have less disturbance.

Strike: The strike will range from slightly below average to full.

Luster: The luster can be below average to full. The toning can seriously impede the luster. On brilliant coins, there can be significant breaks in the luster. Red copper can be considerably mellowed. There can be noticeable spotting, including several large spots or a group of small ones. **Note: If the luster is poor, then the coin would *not* be graded MS-63, even if the strike were full and the marks/hairlines were acceptable for the grade.**

Eye Appeal: The eye can be slightly negative to very positive. The "average" MS-63 will have neutral eye appeal (noticeable marks/hairlines, average to above-average strike, and average luster). However, quite a few coins are graded MS-63 because of their negative appearance. If either the luster, strike, or marks/hairlines are below the standards set forth here, then one of the other criteria must be exceptional for the coin to attain MS-63.

MS-62: UNCIRCULATED

Marks: The marks/hairlines may cover most of the coin. If the marks/hairlines are light, they may be scattered across the entire coin. If there are several severe marks/hairlines, the rest of the coin should be relatively clean.

Strike: The strike can range from very weak (some New Orleans Mint Morgan dollars, for example) to full.

Luster: The luster can range from poor to vibrant.

Eye Appeal: The eye appeal will be negative to slightly positive. The negativity in this grade usually involves excessive marks/hairlines and/or the strike and/or lack of luster and/or unattractive toning. There can be one to three of the major criteria that contribute to negative eye appeal. Even coins with overall positive eye appeal usually have one or two areas that are negative. Thus, a coin with numerous marks/hairlines but with average strike and luster may grade MS-62, while a coin with just a few marks (probably in the wrong places) and weak strike and luster also may grade MS-62.

MS-61: UNCIRCULATED

Marks: There may be marks/hairlines across the entire coin. There may be several severe contact marks/hairlines. If there are numerous large marks/hairlines in the main focal areas, the fields should be cleaner, although they still could have contact marks/hairlines. On larger coins (half dollars and larger), there may be areas with almost no marks/hairlines.

Strike: The strike can range from very weak to full.

Luster: The luster may be poor, average, or full.

Eye Appeal: The eye appeal will be very negative to very slightly positive.

MS-60: UNCIRCULATED

Marks: Numerous. The marks/hairlines will probably cover all of the coin's surface. On larger coins (half dollars and higher), there may be some areas that have few or no marks/hairlines. The marks/hairlines can be large and in prime focal areas. **Note: Sometimes the mark is *not* from "normal" contact with other coins or from circulation, thus would be considered damage and the coin might not be graded.**

Strike: The strike can range from very weak to full.

Luster: The luster may be poor, average, or full.

Eye Appeal: The eye appeal can be very negative to neutral.

Circulated Standards
AU-58: CHOICE ABOUT UNCIRCULATED

Wear: There will be slight wear on the highest points of the coin. In some cases, 5X magnification is needed to notice this wear, and sometimes it can be noticed by slowly tilting the coin in the light source. This method often may show the slight friction as discoloration. Very often, the obverse will have slight friction and the reverse will be full Mint State (often MS-63 or higher).

Marks: There are usually very few marks for this grade. Instead of marks, the principal detractions on the typical AU-58 coin are rub or hairlines. The few marks should not be major or in prime focal areas. A coin that would grade AU-58 from a wear standpoint, but has numerous marks, would be graded AU-55 or lower.

Strike: The strike can range from below average to full. **Note: A very weak strike would be downgraded to AU-55 or lower.**

Luster: The luster can range from poor to full. There will be noticeable breaks in the luster on the high points. These areas will be visible to the unaided eye, but should be less than 10 percent of the surface area.

Eye Appeal: The eye appeal is usually very good. Since marks are usually very minor, the eye appeal will be determined mainly by strike, luster, and originality. Many AU-58 coins are lightly cleaned or dipped uncirculated coins that are no longer considered uncirculated because of the light cleaning or rubbing that is now present. These coins can be just as attractive as coins that are graded AU-58 because of slight circulation—and sometimes even more so. Often these coins will have fewer marks than low-grade uncirculated coins.

AU-55: CHOICE ABOUT UNCIRCULATED

Wear: There will be slight wear on the high points and some friction in the fields. The reverse will now usually show wear similar to that on the obverse. In a few instances (coins stored face up that have acquired friction), the reverse will still be uncirculated.

Marks: There usually will be several minor marks/hairlines and a couple of major ones. These should be scattered between the devices and fields, with nothing too severe on the prime focal areas.

Strike: The strike will range from slightly weak to full.

Luster: The luster can range from poor to full, although the areas of wear will not show full luster. There will be breaks in the luster covering 10 to 25 percent of the surface.

Eye Appeal: The eye appeal is usually good. The main criteria will be surface preservation, lack of and placement of marks/hairlines, the luster remaining, and originality.

Proof Standards
PROOF-70: PERFECT PROOF

Marks: There can be no defects visible with a 5X glass. A Proof-70 coin is 100 percent free of hairlines, planchet flaws, lint marks, and any other mint-caused or post-striking defects.

Strike: The strike is full, showing all of the intended detail.

Luster: The surfaces are fully reflective (if applicable) and undisturbed in any way. Any toning must be attractive. Red copper must have no breaks in the color, and only the slightest mellowing is acceptable.

Eye Appeal: Nothing short of spectacular.

PROOF-69: SUPERB GEM PROOF

Marks: This coin will appear perfect to the unaided eye. Upon magnification, one or two minute imperfections (extremely minor hairlines, a previously hidden lint mark, a flake from the planchet, etc.) will be evident. **Note: Slight die polish, very minor die breaks, or incomplete striking will *not* preclude a coin from attaining this grade.**

Strike: The strike will be full, showing all of the detail intended.

Luster: The surfaces must be fully reflective (if applicable) and not negatively affected by toning or patina. Any toning must be attractive. Slight mellowing of color is allowed for red copper and only the slightest unevenness of color for red-brown and brown copper.

Eye Appeal: Superb! **Note: Darkly toned proof coins will *not* grade Proof-69.**

PROOF-68: SUPERB GEM PROOF

Marks: A Proof-68 coin will have minor defects barely visible to the unaided eye—defects that usually go unnoticed at first look. These will usually include one of the following: virtually undetectable hairlines, a small planchet flaw, or an unobtrusive lint mark. Such defects, no matter how minor, should not be in a conspicuous place such as Liberty's cheek or the obverse field.

Strike: The strike will be full, showing virtually all of the detail intended.

Luster: The coin must be fully reflective (if applicable) or virtually so. Any toning must be attractive, but slight unevenness is allowable. Some mellowing of color is allowed for red copper and some unevenness of color for red-brown and brown copper.

Eye Appeal: The eye appeal will be exceptional. Any hint of negativity will be compensated for in another area.

PROOF-67: SUPERB GEM PROOF

Marks: Any defects visible to the unaided eye will be minor. These could include unobtrusive hairlines, one or more very minor contact marks, a stray lint mark or two, a well-hidden planchet flaw, and so on. If the eye is immediately drawn to a defect, that will almost always preclude the coin from grading Proof-67.

Strike: The strike will be full or exceptionally sharp.

Luster: The reflectivity must be nearly full (if applicable). Toning may be dark or uneven, but not both. Red copper can have mellowing of color, and there can be unevenness of color for red-brown and brown copper. Minute spotting, if present, should be virtually unnoticeable.

Eye Appeal: Superb, or nearly so. Any negativity must be compensated for in another area. Darkly toned coins are almost always penalized at least one grade point at this level—for example, a Proof-67 coin that is dark would grade at least Proof-68 if the toning were attractive or nonexistent.

PROOF-66: GEM PROOF

Marks: A Proof-66 coin can have a few light contact lines/hairlines, but nothing detracting or concentrated in one area. It may have small lint marks or planchet flaws, but any defects must be minor. If the eye is drawn to a flaw, the rest of the coin must be superb to compensate for it.

Strike: The strike must be sharp and will almost always be exceptionally sharp.

Luster: The reflectivity will usually be excellent (if applicable). Any toning must be positive, and reflectivity must be good (if applicable). A Proof-66 coin may have some extremely positive attributes that offset slightly too much negativity in another area. For instance, Coin X has two or three too many hairlines to qualify as Proof-66, but the toning is fantastic, the devices are heavily frosted, and the eye appeal is outstanding, so the coin is graded Proof-66 anyway. Red copper can have mellowing of color, and there can be unevenness of color of red-brown and brown copper. Very minor spotting may be present.

Eye Appeal: Overall eye appeal for this grade is great, since this coin just misses Proof-67. Any deficiency in toning (too dark for Proof-67 because of impeded reflectivity, "splotchy" almost to the point of being negative, etc.) will be slight. If the coin is brilliant, the deficiency usually will be minuscule—contact/hairline/slide marks that preclude a higher grade.

PROOF-65: GEM PROOF

Marks: There may be several minor problems. These may include light contact, hairlines, lint marks, planchet flaws, or other minor defects. Since there may be several minor problems, there are many ways to attain the grade of Proof-65. For example, a coin with virtually no hairlines may have slight contact/slide marks on the high points and still grade Proof-65. In another case, a coin with no contact/slide marks might still grade no higher than Proof-65 because of minor but noticeable hairlines. Any other minor defects, such as lint marks or planchet flaws, should be unobtrusive.

Strike: The coin will be well-struck and, in most cases, very sharp.

Luster: The reflectivity will be average or above. Any toning present can impede the reflectivity only slightly. On untoned coins, the reflectivity can be moderately subdued, but coins with "washed-out" surfaces cannot be graded Proof-65. Red copper can have mellowing of color; color coins can have minor spotting.

Eye Appeal: The eye appeal will be average or above. This is a coin almost everyone finds attractive. The comments for eye appeal under MS-65 are just as relevant for Proof-65. There is a wide range in the appearance of Proof-65 coins. Any slightly negative factors must be compensated for in another area.

PROOF-64: CHOICE PROOF

Marks: There may be numerous minor problems. These may include contact marks, many small hairlines, or several large hairlines. Other defects—such as lint marks or planchet flaws in focal areas—may be allowed.

Strike: There can be some weakness in strike. **Note: This is the highest Proof grade where some distracting weakness of strike in the major devices is allowable. Weakness in stars and other minor devices is not usually enough to reduce the grade.**

Luster: The reflectivity can be impeded. If the coin is toned, the reflectivity can be noticeably subdued. On untoned coins, there can be dullness or a "washed-out" appearance, but these coins should have fewer contact lines/hairlines than a coin with more of the mirror surface intact. Red copper can be considerably mellowed. There may be noticeable spotting for this grade, although large or numerous spots would reduce the grade to Proof-63 or lower.

Eye Appeal: The eye appeal can range from slightly negative to very positive. This is an attractive coin. However, there can be some negativity in toning (too dark, hazy, splotchy, etc.)—or, with untoned coins, there can be dullness in the mirrored surface. The amount of hairlines acceptable for this grade is directly proportional to the eye appeal. If a coin has great contrast (frosted devices), the hairlines or other defects can be quite noticeable. On a coin that has less contrast and is either darkly toned or dull brilliant, the hairlines must be minor.

PROOF-63: CHOICE PROOF

Marks: There may be immediately noticeable defects. There may be quite a few contact marks/hairlines or a group of concentrated hairlines, lint marks in prime focal areas, medium-to-large planchet flaws, or a combination of these or other defects. Obvious "slide marks," which usually result from an album's plastic sliding across the devices, will almost always result in a grade of no higher than Proof-63.

Strike: The strike can range from average to full. This is the highest Proof grade where considerable weakness of strike is allowed. If the coin is poorly struck, a grade of Proof-62 or below would be appropriate.

Luster: The reflectivity can be below average to full. On untoned coins, the surfaces are often dull—and on toned coins, there can be dark or uneven toning that will seriously impede the amount of reflectivity. Red copper can be considerably mellowed. There can be noticeable spotting, with several large spots or numerous small ones. **Note: If the mirrored surface is almost totally obscured, the grade of Proof-63 will *not* be attained and a grade of Proof-62 or lower is warranted.**

Eye Appeal: The eye appeal can be slightly negative to very positive. The "average" Proof-63 coin will have neutral eye appeal (noticeable hairlines, well-struck, slightly dulled surfaces). Some coins can still grade Proof-63, even if one or more of the major criteria are negative, but that must be compensated for by strength in another area.

PROOF 62: PROOF

Marks: There may be some light contact marks, numerous light hairlines, medium-to-heavy hairlines, or a combination of the above covering most of the coin's surface. There also may be concentrated patches of hairlines, with some areas remaining relatively free of contact marks/ hairlines.

Strike: The strike can range from extremely weak to full.

Luster: The reflectivity can range from below average to nearly full. On toned coins, there may be very little of the mirrored surface left, and with brilliant coins the reflectivity may be almost completely impaired by hairlines.

Eye Appeal: The eye appeal will be negative to slightly positive.

PROOF-61: PROOF

Marks: The surfaces may have some contact marks and numerous light-to-heavy hairlines. There may be several small marks hidden in the devices. The entire surface may be covered with contact marks/hairlines, or there may be several areas with concentrated hairlines and some others relatively free of them.

Strike: The strike can range from very weak to full.

Luster: The reflectivity will range from poor to slightly impaired.

Eye Appeal: The eye appeal will be very negative to very slightly positive.

PROOF 60: PROOF

Marks: The surface may have quite a few contact lines or myriad medium-to-heavy hairlines and may have several marks. There should be no large marks for this grade. If there are large marks, the grade would be Proof-58 or lower.

Strike: The strike can range from very weak to full.

Luster: The reflectivity may range from poor to slightly impaired.

Eye Appeal: The eye appeal can be very negative to neutral.

PROOF 58: CIRCULATED PROOF

Wear: There usually is very little wear on the high points. With Proof coins, wear usually takes the form of slight friction in the fields. Since the mirrored surfaces of Proof coins are so delicate, any minor circulation or mishandling will cause marks and hairlines to become immediately apparent. In some cases, the reverse may have no impairment and will grade Proof-60 or higher. **Note: It is much easier to discern wear on a Proof than on a business strike. Proofs and prooflike business strikes reveal marks/hairlines much more easily because of the mirrored surface.**

Marks: There could be a few major marks. There can be scattered contact marks, with a few allowed on the devices and in the fields. If there are more than a few marks, a Proof coin would be graded Proof-55 or lower.

Strike: The strike can range from average to full. **Note: A weak strike would be downgraded to Proof-55 or lower.**

Luster: The reflectivity will be somewhat impaired. This is not always true with Proof-58 coins, since many coins in this grade will have full reflectivity, which is disturbed only by hairlines, marks, or minor wear.

Eye Appeal: The eye appeal is usually very good. There usually is nothing other than slight contact marks/ friction on Proof-58 coins. Appearance is usually *not* the problem with this coin.

PROOF-55: CIRCULATED PROOF

Wear: There will be slight wear on the high points and up to half of the fields will have friction. The reverse will now be impaired in most cases.

Marks: There may be several marks and quite a few contact marks/hairlines. These should be scattered about and should not be concentrated on prime focal areas.

Strike: The strike will range from slightly weak to full.

Luster: The reflectivity may be severely impaired. Up to 50 percent of the mirrored surface is now slightly to fairly severely impaired. There can be a few areas that have lost complete reflectivity.

Eye Appeal: The eye appeal is usually good. The main criteria will be surface preservation, lack of and placement of marks/hairlines, reflectivity remaining, and originality.

PROOF 53: CIRCULATED PROOF

Wear: There will be obvious wear to high points. Friction will cover 50 to 75 percent of the fields.

Marks: There may be several minor and major marks/ hairlines. There can be scattered marks/hairlines in all areas of the coin, including prime focal areas, but a severe disturbance in those prime areas will result in a lower grade. Some small areas may have heavy concentrations of hairlines.

Strike: The strike will range from below average to full.

Luster: The reflectivity may be severely impaired. The amount of "mirror" still visible will depend on the original depth of the mirrored surface.

Eye Appeal: The eye appeal now is a function of surface preservation, lack of and placement of marks/hairlines, reflectivity remaining, and originality.

PROOF-50: CIRCULATED PROOF

Wear: Wear is evident. There can be friction in the fields ranging from half to all of the unprotected areas. The high points will have wear that is very obvious to the unaided eye.

Marks: There may be many marks/hairlines. Many times, hairlines and small marks will now start to "blend" into the surfaces. These will appear as discolored areas.

Strike: The strike will range from below average to full.

Luster: The reflectivity may be completely impaired. There may be parts of the surface with no mirror at all. The Proof surface may be visible only around protected devices.

Eye Appeal: The eye appeal is now a function of surface preservation, lack of and placement of marks/hairlines, reflectivity remaining, and originality.

NOTE: COINS THAT GRADE PR-45 AND BELOW ARE GRADED ESSENTIALLY THE SAME AS REGULAR STRIKES. SINCE THE CRITERIA FOR DETERMINING THE OVERALL GRADE WILL MOSTLY BE THE SAME FOR BOTH MINT STATE AND PROOF COINS, THESE GRADES ARE LISTED ONLY UNDER THE MINT STATE STANDARDS MENTIONED EARLIER, WITH ANY EXCEPTIONS NOTED.

A Photographic Guide to Precision Grading

If your coin purchases are for trading, you should buy only coins graded by grading services listed in the *Certified Coin Dealer Newsletter.* THERE ARE NO EXCEPTIONS TO THIS RULE. EVEN THOUGH SOME OTHER COINS MIGHT BE GRADED CORRECTLY BY AN UNKNOWN SERVICE, USE ONLY THE SER-

VICES LISTED IN THE *CCDN*. OTHERWISE, YOUR INVEST-
MENT'S LIQUIDITY COULD BE JEOPARDIZED.

Morgan Dollars

Let's start by looking at Morgan dollars. The 1880-S illustrated
in Figure 3-11 trades as an MS-66. The single tiny mark on Miss
Liberty's cheek, between her nose and lips, keeps this coin from
being assigned the MS-67 grade.

Figure 3-12 shows another 1880-S Morgan dollar, this one
grading MS-65. Here a detraction appears in the same area as
in this coin's MS-66 counterpart. The photographic lighting
slightly exaggerates this imperfection, though. Notice the unin-
terrupted luster and freedom from flaws.

The 1880-S Morgan dollar illustrated in Figure 3-13 also displays stunning, satiny luster. However, various interruptions of
the frost remove it from the MS-65 category. This coin really is
a lovely MS-64, though; and the whitened high points are *not*
wear, merely breaks in the frost.

The 1881-S Morgan dollar grading MS-63 (Figure 3-14) possesses more scratches and abrasions than the coins that are assigned higher grades. But the 1881-S graded MS-62 (Figure 3-15)
has scattered imperfections, thus preventing even the MS-63
grade. However, by far the most hideous looking coin of the
group is the coin assigned MS-60 (Figure 3-16)—the minimum
Mint State grade.

Walking Liberty Half Dollars

Another popularly traded coin type is the Walking Liberty
half dollar. In Figure 3-17, a 1947 Walking Liberty half dollar
grading MS-65 is displayed. Notice the lovely lustrous surfaces and lack of any significant marks. The 1939 specimen
(Figure 3-18) is of nearly equal beauty except for a few minor detractions. The most obvious flaw is the hit on the leg. The 1946
example (Figure 3-19) grades MS-63 and has marks visible to the
unaided eye in the right obverse field.

Figure 3-11. *MS-66 1880-S Morgan dollar.*
Photo courtesy Museum of the American Numismatic Association.

Figure 3-12. *MS-65 1880-S Morgan dollar.* The lighting exaggerates the tiny facial nick. *Photo courtesy Museum of the American Numismatic Association.*

Figure 3-13. *MS-64 1880-S Morgan dollar.* This coin grades MS-64 under the standards of PCGS and NGC. *Photo courtesy Museum of the American Numismatic Association.*

Figure 3-14. *MS-63 1881-S Morgan dollar.* *Photo courtesy Museum of the American Numismatic Association.*

SAINT-GAUDENS DOUBLE EAGLES

The Saint-Gaudens double eagle enjoys great popularity, but many persons are confused about how to grade this series. The "Saint" grading MS-64 (Figure 3-20) displays attractive luster but possesses too many surface abrasions to qualify for the MS-65 grade. The MS-63 example (Figure 3-21) is not nearly as

Figure 3-15. *MS-62 1881-S Morgan dollar.* Photo courtesy Museum of the American Numismatic Association.

Figure 3-16. *MS-60 1897 Morgan dollar.* **This most unattractive piece earns the minimum grade of Mint State.** Photo courtesy Museum of the American Numismatic Association.

lustrous and displays marks more prominent and deeper than its MS-64 counterpart. The MS-62 Saint (Figure 3-22) is heavily abraded, but it's not a borderline problem coin like the MS-60 Morgan dollar displayed earlier (Fig. 3-16). The 1923 Saint (Figure 3-23) has light wear on its highest points and grades About Uncirculated-55.

LIBERTY HEAD DOUBLE EAGLES

The Liberty Head double eagle is another heavily traded coin type. But despite these coins' large size, many people have difficulty grading them. The temptation is great to grade many of these coins MS-64 or above, especially since gold retains its original luster. But a great number of them deserve only MS-63 or lower grades. In fact, NGC and PCGS have not assigned the MS-65 grade to very many Liberty Heads.

The 1900 $20 Liberty graded MS-63 (Figure 3-24) has great luster and eye appeal but is marred by abrasions on the neck. The 1904 $20 Liberty assigned the grade of MS-62 (Figure 3-25) has a prominent scratch on the cheek, a grade-sensitive area. The 1907 $20 Liberty (Figure 3-26) is not a borderline problem coin but is substantially abraded and just makes the MS-61 grade, although the MS-60 designation is tempting.

Figure 3-17. *MS-65 1947 Walking Liberty half dollar.* Lovely, satiny luster on peerless surfaces. *Photo courtesy Museum of the American Numismatic Association.*

Figure 3-18. *MS-64 1939 Walking Liberty half dollar.* PCGS and NGC would assign the MS-64 grade to this coin. *Photo courtesy Museum of the American Numismatic Association.*

Figure 3-19. *MS-63 1946 Walking Liberty half dollar.* *Photo courtesy Museum of the American Numismatic Association.*

Figure 3-20. *MS-64 1928 Saint-Gaudens double eagle.* Both PCGS and NGC would opt for the MS-64 grade, but NCI might assign it MS-65. *Photo courtesy Museum of the American Numismatic Association.*

How to Identify a Circulated Coin

Locating wear on a coin's high points requires a pinpoint light source and your ability to tilt and rotate the coin. The close-up of the Liberty Seated figure (Figure 3-27) reveals signs of this coin having passed from hand to hand. Examine the arm, knees, and breasts.

Figure 3-21. *MS-63 1924 Saint-Gaudens double eagle.* Photo courtesy Museum of the American Numismatic Association.

Figure 3-22. *MS-62 1923 Saint-Gaudens double eagle.* Photo courtesy Museum of the American Numismatic Association.

Figure 3-23. *AU-55 1923 Saint-Gaudens double eagle.* This coin has passed from hand to hand and has circulated. Photo courtesy Museum of the American Numismatic Association.

Figure 3-24. *MS-63 Liberty Head double eagle.* PCGS and NCG grade very few coins of this type MS-65, although MS-64s are available. Photo courtesy Museum of the American Numismatic Association.

The Most Difficult Coins to Grade

I authored the following article, which appeared in *NGC News,* NGC's in-house dealer-only newsletter.

THE "TOUGH 7"—THE COIN TYPES MOST DIFFICULT TO GRADE

At NGC, all coins submitted for grading are treated equally.

Figure 3-25. *MS-62 1904 Liberty Head double eagle.* Photo courtesy Museum of the American Numismatic Association.

Figure 3-26. *Low-end MS-61 Liberty Head double eagle.* NGC's internal grading would read "MS-61C." Photo courtesy Museum of the American Numismatic Association.

By their very nature, though, some coins are harder to grade than others.

Based on my experiences as an NGC grader, I've compiled a list of what might be called the "Tough 7"—the seven coin types that I have found most difficult to grade.

I'd like to extend special thanks to Maurice Rosen, a fellow NGC grader, and John Albanese, NGC's founder and president, both of whom lent a helpful ear while I was preparing this article.

(1) Line Coins

"Line coins" are coins that qualify to be graded, say, either MS-64A or MS-65C. Either grade would be fair—but with many such coins, traders have paid a price commensurate with the lower grade and are hoping to receive the higher grade from NGC.

On business strikes, it usually comes down to the quality of the surfaces; this is what determines whether a line coin gets the higher grade—although impaired luster can reduce the coin's chances for the next grade

Figure 3-27. *Lightly circulated Liberty Seated figure.* Photo courtesy Bill Fivaz

(2) Law-Breakers

If you were to assign a technical grade of MS-67/64 to a coin, any old-timer would tell you that the overall grade would have to be MS-64, for it used to be conventional wisdom that a coin couldn't be assigned an overall grade that was higher than the lowest grade of any one side.

Wrong! The overall grade might well be MS-65, since the obverse can "carry" a coin. But if it were the other way around—an MS-64/67—the final grade probably *would* be MS-64.

An MS-65/65 coin with some weakness of strike might be graded MS-64—or lower—at NGC to reflect marketplace standards. NGC grades in such a way that coins can be traded sight-unseen, and a weakly struck coin graded MS-65 could restrict the fluidity of the system.

(3) Incuse-Design Gold

Coins with incuse designs are difficult enough to grade. With gold coins, this problem is compounded. Gold retains its mint luster indefinitely, and gold coins with incuse designs—like the Indian $5 and $2½—have characteristics that make it hard to tell whether or not there is wear on the high points.

(4) Coins with Sensational Eye Appeal

If you have a magnificent Barber quarter—one with a cameo contrast between its watery fields and snow-white devices—but the coin has a tiny hit on the *obverse,* can you still grade it Proof-65? Probably. Personally, I don't like seeing the 65 grade assigned to such coins, but it's the consensus that rules. (See Figures 3-28 and 3-29.)

If you have a proof Seated Liberty half dollar with light hairlines that make it a technical 63-A, can phenomenal toning make it a 64? Yes, as long as the eye appeal isn't counted for more than ¼ of a point.

(5) Rare Dates

If you come across a shimmering proof 1936 Walking Liberty half dollar and it is identical *in every respect* to 50, 1942 Walking

Figures 3-28 and 3-29. *Technical Mint State-62 Indian three-dollar gold piece graded MS-64 by NGC* (obverse and reverse). I graded this coin Mint State-62, visible marks, before it was certified. The dramatic reflective surfaces apparently elevated the grade in the eyes of NGC. Heritage sent it to NGC before selling it for me at auction. *Photos courtesy Heritage Numismatic Auctions, Inc.*

Liberty halves which were just graded Proof-64, does the 64 grade apply to the 1936 as well? If the '36 is a technical 64-A, compensation for the date by ¼ of a point is acceptable. Thus, the Proof-65 designation is acceptable. (See Figure 3-30.)

Compensation for rarity is satisfactory, as long as you don't go overboard and upgrade a technical MS-62 coin to MS-65.

(6) Small Coins

Graders spend more time examining small coins than any other kind. We have to be extremely careful about looking for imperfections, and even have to exercise more care in holding these coins. This is not to say that larger coins don't get complete consideration; it's just that smaller coins require closer scrutiny.

A tiny mark on a silver three-cent piece is weighted differently from a mark of the same size on a Morgan dollar. The three-cent silver is tiny *itself,* and even a *tiny* mark can be a considerable detraction.

Figure 3-30. *Rare 1895 Morgan dollar graded PR-64 by NGC.* Notice the few faint hairline scratches. This high-end, *premium-quality* example might qualify for a PR-65 grade. *Photo courtesy Heritage Numismatic Auctions, Inc.*

(7) Problem Coins

Coins with PVC (polyvinyl chloride) on them, or coins with imperfections, or coins that are bent or tampered with—these are problem, or "no-grade," coins.

Sometimes, however, it becomes a problem to determine whether a coin is, in fact, a no-grade—or whether it simply should have its grade lowered to reflect the imperfection.

For example, a Morgan dollar which under normal circumstances would grade MS-64 might be assigned a grade of MS-62 or MS-63 because of a rather eye-catching ding on its rim. But a Walking Liberty half dollar which normally would grade MS-67 but has a deep gouge on the obverse—a gouge so deep that it nearly travels through to the other side—would be no-graded.

Some coins are, indeed, tougher to grade than others. But the grading process at NGC is designed to maximize the use of *independent,* arm's-length grading to assure equitable grading opinions for everyone.

IMPORTANT GRADING TIPS

Knowledge is more than power; in the case of rare coins, it also can mean enormous profit. With that in mind, here's my personal list of the top 10 coin-grading tips, which first appeared in *COINage* magazine:

> *Check the high points for wear.* Even if a grading service certifies a coin as Mint State-63, that doesn't mean it won't come back with a lower grade—possibly even About Uncirculated-58— if you resubmit it. A coin should stand on its own merits; you should buy it for itself and not for the plastic. Look at the very highest points of the coin. If they're different in color from the rest of the coin, or if you see friction, the coin may not be Mint State; it may be About Uncirculated. Telltale signs of wear are indicated by the color of the high points. On coins made of copper, the high points after friction are dark brown. On coins made of nickel, the high-point color after friction is dark gray. On coins made of silver, the color

is dull gray. And on coins made of gold, the high-point color after friction is dull, dark gold.

If it's ugly, don't buy it. Use your common sense. Blotchy toning, obvious scratches, and spots which penetrate the surface of a coin are unattractive. And if a coin appears unattractive to you, it probably will appear that way to other people, too. Therefore, you should stay away from it. Even coins with very high grades—coins which have been certified as 67, 68, or 69 by a major certification service—are subject to personal taste, and you should always rely on yours. Rare-coin grading is subjective, and so is the beauty of coins. Among the few characteristics which are universally attractive is concentric-circle toning. If you observe this on a coin, you should view it as a highly positive feature.

Examine grade-sensitive areas. Some flaws are more obvious than others. On Morgan silver dollars, for example, a scratch on Miss Liberty's cheek is immediately apparent because that part of the coin is so smooth and open. By contrast, a scratch in her hair wouldn't be noticed as readily because it would be camouflaged by the intricate details in that portion of the design. High, exposed areas such as Miss Liberty's cheek are said to be "grade-sensitive," and you should be more hesitant to purchase any coin with an imperfection there, even though that coin may carry a grade of Mint State-65 or Proof-65 or above from one of the major grading services (Figure 3-31). If you have a choice between one coin graded Mint State-66 with a scratch on the cheek and another coin in the same grade *without* that scratch on the cheek, always opt for the latter. Everything else being equal, it's always best to purchase coins whose flaws are in non-grade-sensitive areas. Grade-sensitive areas for all the major U.S. coin series are identified and illustrated, with color grading maps, in James L. Halperin's book *How to Grade U.S. Coins.*

Figure 3-31. *1890 Proof-64 Liberty Head double eagle.* Dramatic cameo contrast between the golden-pondlike reflective fields and heavily frosted devices *doesn't compensate* for the hit on Miss Liberty's cheek.
Photo courtesy Heritage Numismatic Auctions, Inc.

Look beneath the toning. This is probably the most important point of all. It's also the easiest way to determine whether a coin has artificial toning. Toning can cover up a multitude of imperfections—scratches, hairlines, tooling, thumbing, and chemical alteration, to cite just a few. Many times, coins with imperfections are artificially retoned to conceal these flaws (Figure 3-32). By examining these coins closely under a magnifying glass, you can detect not only the hidden imperfections but also the artificial toning.

Examine every coin under a halogen lamp or a high-intensity pinpoint light source. When looking beneath the toning of a coin or otherwise searching for imperfections, it's essential that you use the right kind of lighting. A halogen lamp is especially beneficial when looking at proof coins. It will help you spot hairline scratches, which can detract considerably from a proof coin's overall grade (Figure 3-33.) As a rule, a Tensor lamp is adequate for Mint State business-strike coins. Ordinary light sources such as floodlamps or bare-filament

Figure 3-32. *Rare 1896-S Barber quarter with questionable toning.* Suspicious gray toning, such as that shown here, can cover a multitude of imperfections. *Photo courtesy Heritage Numismatic Auctions, Inc.*

Figure 3-33. *Light hairline scratches as they would appear under a halogen lamp.* Look carefully: This flashy 1892 Liberty Head quarter eagle has hairlines that detract from its grade. *Photo courtesy Heritage Numismatic Auctions, Inc.*

lights—the kind commonly used in chandeliers—make coins appear more attractive than they actually are. For that reason, if you're looking at coins at an auction-lot viewing session, you should always make sure there is a halogen lamp or a Tensor light source nearby.

Resubmit upper-end coins—coins which are high-quality for the grade—and coins graded 67 by PCGS. You stand a reasonably good chance of getting a higher grade if you resubmit such coins, especially if you acquired them in 1986 and 1987 when the grading services were extremely tough in assigning grades. David Hall, the founder and president of PCGS, has admitted publicly that a number of PCGS coins graded 67 a few years ago might well come back today at a higher grade. The difference in price between a 67 and its 68 counterpart can be tens of thousands of dollars, so this could represent a $20,000 gift for you, just for taking the trouble to crack a coin out of its holder and resubmit it.

"Read" every coin. Looking at a coin is similar to proofreading a letter. And individuals who possess book knowledge combined with practical experience at buying, selling, and trading coins have learned how to look at a coin and size up its flaws rather quickly, just as expert editors have learned how to scan a manuscript for errors and typographical mistakes. Often, a coin's imperfections won't be noticeable at a glance, or even after somewhat closer perusal by an unskilled observer. This may happen, for example, when a coin has one feature so overwhelmingly attractive that it causes you to lose sight of everything else. Let's say you're shown a Saint-Gaudens double eagle with blazing golden luster; the luster may be so intense that it causes you to overlook a bump or a ding on the rim, which in turn might cause the coin to be downgraded. You should learn how to read all the key information on every coin you handle and properly identify all the imperfections. Don't be dazzled by any one feature of a coin, no matter how attractive it may be, to the point where you miss important details in the "fine print."

Look for hairlines. A proof coin with overwhelmingly beautiful toning can be powerfully appealing. And, to the naked eye, its surfaces may appear pristine and original. But even on gorgeous proofs such as this, and even on coins in very high grades, you may very well find hairline scratches, and the number of hairline scratches is a very important element in determining the grade of a proof coin (Figures 3-34 and 3-35). Spotting hairline scratches is easier on brilliant modern proofs—proof Mercury dimes, for example. It's somewhat more difficult on older coins with heavier toning—say, Liberty Seated half dollars from the 1880s with concentric-circle toning. On coins such as these, the toning may cover the scratches.

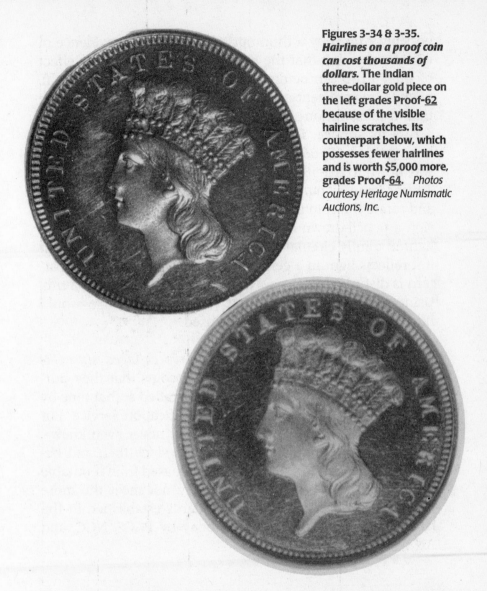

Figures 3-34 & 3-35. *Hairlines on a proof coin can cost thousands of dollars.* The Indian three-dollar gold piece on the left grades Proof-62 because of the visible hairline scratches. Its counterpart below, which possesses fewer hairlines and is worth $5,000 more, grades Proof-64. *Photos courtesy Heritage Numismatic Auctions, Inc.*

Beware of the rub. Checking for wear on the high points of a coin is relatively easy—and that's a good thing, since wear, after all, is the single most crucial factor in determining grade. Detecting rub on a coin is considerably more difficult, for rub is far more subtle. It's also far more hazardous to the health of that coin. As the term suggests, a "rub" is a small area on a coin—possibly no bigger than a thumbprint (and possibly *caused* by a thumbprint)—which bears evidence of friction, showing that the coin has been rubbed. The effect of such a rub can be devastating. Suppose you had a gem, pristine, magnificent coin, blazing with luster, and just one time a perspiration-soaked thumb rubbed ever so slightly across its surface. Even if the coin otherwise might have been graded 65, 66, or 67, that rub could knock it all the way down to AU-58. To identify rub, you need a good, solid Tensor lamp or pinpoint light source, and you have to tilt and rotate the coin under that lamp. You then need to envision a pencil-drawn circle fully formed. If the coin reflects light in a fully circular pattern, it's probably Mint State. But if it reflects light in a generally circular pattern but the pattern is disturbed in any way, then the coin may have a rub. Using the same analogy, that pencil-drawn circle would have just a couple of segments erased.

Remember that grading standards have changed since the early 1980s. A lot of people still own coins that they purchased in the early 1980s which were graded at that time by reputable dealers or by the ANA Certification Service. But many of these people tend to forget—or never even knew—that grading standards have tightened since then and become more consistent. Even coins purchased from reputable dealers in 1981, 1982, and 1983 may not meet the more rigorous, consistent, impartial standards established in the late 1980s and being observed today by PCGS, NGC, and ANACS.

CHAPTER 4

THE SECRETS OF COIN PRICING

WHAT'S IT WORTH?

That's the first question most people ask when someone shows them a rare and valuable coin. Coins are correctly perceived as stores of value—and quantifying that value is one of the marketplace's most important functions. It's a function we know as *pricing.*

Pricing—fair, honest, accurate pricing—is the cornerstone of consumer protection for those who purchase coins and the key to turning a profit on those coins. To get good value, you have to avoid overpaying. Those who overpay in the coin market lose their chance to reap financial gain, or at least postpone it needlessly.

DETERMINING VALUE

The value of a coin is determined on the basis of three main components: *grade, supply,* and *demand.* Under certain circumstances, one of these factors might outweigh either or both of the others.

Grade: As a general statement, a coin's value tends to rise arithmetically as its level of preservation—or *grade*—improves within the circulated range. Thus, a given coin might be worth 10 percent more in very fine condition than in fine, the next-lower grade, and an additional 10 percent more in extremely fine condition than in very fine. Often, however, the rate of increase becomes geometric as a coin moves up in the Mint-State range. Thus, it might be worth twice as much in Mint State-65 as in Mint State-64, and twice as much again in Mint State-66 as in Mint State-65.

Supply: The term *supply* refers to the number of examples of a given coin that are available in a given level of preservation. In recent years, buyers and sellers have gained an important new tool in determining just how many coins exist for a given type, denomination, date, and mint: The major grading services have issued population and census reports stipulating the number of specimens each service has certified for every different coin in each grade level. These reports provide crucial—and often surprising—insights into the relative rarity of each coin in each different grade. A word of caution, however: Dealers sometimes resubmit the same coin over and over in hopes that it might be assigned a higher grade, and these resubmissions can seriously distort the profile of a given coin. If the same coin were submitted 10 different times, for example, the population or census report probably would indicate that 10 different coins had been graded, masking the coin's true rarity by making it appear to be more common than it is.

Demand: The term *demand* refers to the number of people who want a particular coin at a given time. A coin with a mintage of only 500 is certainly rare in an absolute sense, but its value will be greatly diminished if there are just 200 people actively seeking to acquire it. Conversely, a coin with a mintage of 500,000 can command a handsome premium—far beyond the level this figure might suggest—if 2 million people are pursuing it.

How to Become an Astute Deal-Maker
To maximize your return when buying, selling, or trading rare coins, you need to become an astute deal-maker. And that,

in turn, means mastering the art of deal-making. I've prepared a list of tips (gleaned from my many years of hands-on experience dealing in millions of dollars' worth of coins) to guide you in putting together the best possible deal every time.

- *Know the value of every coin you hope to buy or sell.* Buying or selling a coin without knowing its current market value is like navigating a plane without a compass.
- *Master the use of your emotions.* With coins as with cards, a poker face will help you come out ahead by keeping the other person guessing about your intentions. No matter how badly you want to buy or sell a particular coin, try to appear composed and unemotional. Sometimes, however, judicious use of an emotional reaction at an appropriate time will clinch the deal for you.
- *Never bluff and never lie.* Bluffing and lying will only get you into trouble, damaging or destroying your credibility for future deals. They might even ruin your chance to make the deal that's at hand.
- *Let the other party make the first offer.* Deal-making is one situation where it often doesn't pay to go first. There's always a chance that the other person will offer you a coin for substantially less than you expected—or offer to buy a coin from you for substantially more than you would have offered it for. If you do have to go first, always start very low when making an offer to buy. You can always come up, but you can rarely go down.
- *Never make an offer you're uncertain about, and never withdraw an offer once you make it.* In buying or selling rare coins, your word is your bond, and you must be careful never to give it lightly. If you vacillate and dither after making an offer, you'll infuriate the person with whom you're making the deal and possibly kill any chance for future deals.
- *When making an offer, count out the money or write out a check on the spot.* Cash (or a check) on the barrel head can be very persuasive. Let's say a dealer is asking $2,000 for a coin and you've offered $1,600. Chances are, he might suggest

splitting the difference—but if you pull out your checkbook and write a check for $1,600, he may simply say, "OK, I'll take it," saving you $200.

- *Always assume the position of power.* Simply stated, this means giving yourself every psychological edge. If you're sitting down with someone to negotiate a deal, always try to get the most dominating seat. If you're trying to appear businesslike, always wear a suit and tie. Above all, never let yourself seem vulnerable; always strive to be in command.

- *Be flexible and be ready to change the conditions of a deal, if you must.* Sometimes a deal may seem hopelessly deadlocked; rather than lose it entirely, be prepared to improvise and modify the structure in order to save it. Suppose you're unwilling to pay more than $400 for a coin, but a dealer insists on getting $500. Look through his inventory for something else on which you can make up the difference—possibly a $600 generic gold coin that you can sell elsewhere for $700. By adding that to the deal, you can still come out just the way you wanted.

- *Make the other person feel that it's in his or her best interest to do the deal.* Convince the other party that you—and only you—are the right person for this particular deal. Stress the advantages of selling the coin to you, rather than any other prospective customer.

- *Don't take things personally.* If a dealer rejects your offer or counter-offer, don't go away mad; after all, this is only a game—even though the money involved is real. Maintain a positive, enthusiastic outlook and leave the door open. He or she may even reconsider and make the deal with you after all.

PRICING PROBLEMS

The 1990s witnessed a new kind of assault on the coin market's integrity and the pocketbooks of those who purchase coins: blatant, bare-faced overpricing. Instead of defrauding customers by selling them counterfeit or altered coins—or cheating them by overgrading coins, and thereby inflating the cost of those coins indirectly—at least one unscrupulous dealer brazenly overcharged them simply by pricing very rare coins at a multiple of established market levels. And while the dealer in question has been dealt with firmly by the legal system, I have reason to believe that others are engaging in similar practices on a less outrageous—but still highly profitable—level.

The success of such ripoffs is especially disconcerting in view of the fact that their victims could have avoided them so easily. All they needed to do was check the coins' value *before buying them* in one of the numerous price guides that are readily available today. The price listings vary from guide to guide, it's true, but on the whole, the values are reasonably accurate and would raise a caution flag in cases where the asking prices far exceeded these figures.

PRICE GUIDES

Price guides come in a number of different forms, and some will appeal to a given coin buyer more than others. The important thing is not *which guide* a person uses, but rather that he or she uses *some kind of guide* before shelling out his or her hard-earned money to buy a coin.

Following are some of the best-known and most popular annual price guides devoted to U.S. coins:

- *A Guide Book of United States Coins,* by R.S. Yeoman, edited by Kenneth Bressett. This book, available in both hardcover and softcover versions, has been a hobby bestseller for half a century. It is commonly referred to as the "Red Book" because of the color of its cover. (Whitman Coin Products, St. Martin's Press)
- *Coin World Guide to U.S. Coins, Prices and Value Trends.* This softcover guide is prepared by the editors of *Coin World,* a respected weekly journal of the numismatic field. (Dutton Signet, division of Penguin Books USA, Inc.)
- *The Insider's Guide to U.S. Coin Values 2001,* by Scott A. Travers. This paperback guide book, which I have authored since 1993, contains pricing data on all relevant coins in both circulated and Mint State condition. Unlike some other guides, it includes prices for very high grades and very rare

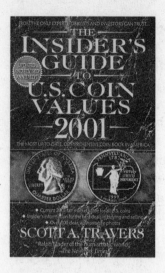

Figure 4-1. Front cover of *The Insider's Guide to U. S. Coin Values 2001*, by Scott A. Travers. *Courtesy Scott A. Travers and Dell Publishing/ Random House.*

coins. (Dell Publishing, division of Random House, 1540 Broadway, New York, NY 10036)

• *The Official Blackbook Price Guide of United States Coins,* by Mark Hudgeons. This handy, pocket-size paperback provides values not only for U.S. coins but also for tokens, medals, and other related collectibles. In addition, it contains detailed tips on buying coins and a special section on grading. (House of Collectibles, division of Random House)

For obvious reasons, yearly price guides can't be completely up-to-date; fast-changing market conditions often overtake them even before they are released. However, they do provide extremely useful facts and figures regarding relative rarity and value, and their listings serve as base-line points of reference that can be of great assistance in calculating long-term price performance. What's more, while market values may be somewhat higher or lower at any given point during the year, the listings in these books are close enough to the market to sound a clear alarm when grossly overpriced items are checked out.

Monthly price guides appear in two leading hobby magazines:

• *COINage* publishes a section called "The *COINage* Price Guide," which provides current values for selected U.S. coins in up to 14 levels of preservation. It also furnishes "*COINage* Price Averages," which track the market's overall performance in two important grade levels—very fine and Mint State-65. (Miller Magazines, 4880 Market St., Ventura, CA 93003)

- *Coins Magazine* features a "Coin Value Guide" which charts the price performance of both regular U.S. coins and commemoratives in up to nine levels of preservation. (Krause Publications, 700 E. State St., Iola, WI 54990)

Of all the printed price guides, those that appear weekly come closest to reflecting actual market values at a particular point. Instead of being prepared months before publication like listings in annual guide books, these are compiled no more than a few weeks in advance—and sometimes just a few days. Thus, while they may lack the comprehensive coverage of the yearly guides, they can offer greater immediacy and better reflect rapid movements up or down.

Weekly guides to U.S. coin values can be found in both of the two leading newspapers serving the hobby:

- *Coin World* publishes a "Trends" section listing current values. This comprehensive listing covers the gamut of U.S. coinage in three-week stages. (Amos Press, P.O. Box 150, Sidney, OH 45365-0150)
- *Numismatic News Weekly* contains a "Coin Market" section covering all of the popular coin series and providing accurate data on current values. In most editions, the listings encompass only certain series; every four weeks, however, Coin Market furnishes comprehensive listings for all the coins embraced by this report. (Krause Publications, 700 E. State St., Iola, WI 54990)

Among professional numismatists, two of the most closely monitored price guides are *The Coin Dealer Newsletter* and the *Certified Coin Dealer Newsletter.* These twin weekly publications— referred to as the *Greysheet* and the *Bluesheet,* respectively, because of their distinctive colors—are essential tools not only for those who deal in coins but also for serious collectors and investors.

- *The Coin Dealer Newsletter* provides the most accurate, up-to-date information available in printed form on current U.S. coin values. It contains detailed listings for all of the most popularly traded series, along with analysis and commentary on important market developments and trends. It uses a "bid" and "ask" format, and thus is a wholesale, rather than retail, price guide. The values pertain to uncertified coins—those that have not been graded and encapsulated by a coin certification service.
- *The Certified Coin Dealer Newsletter* parallels its sister publication, but covers coins certified by PCGS, NGC, and ANACS. *Bluesheet* listings facilitate sight-unseen trading of these coins.

Both the *Greysheet* and the *Bluesheet* are published by The Coin Dealer Newsletter, Inc., a California company whose in-house experts, including former coin dealers, follow the marketplace closely and understand not only the ebb and flow of price trends, but also the psychology that underlies the industry. The company also publishes *The Monthly Summary and Complete Series Pricing Guide* as a supplement to its weekly price guides. Contrary to what its name might suggest, this is not a summary of developments in the marketplace during the preceding month. Rather, it is an overview of the coin market as a whole, including price listings for coins less frequently traded than those in the weekly newsletters. The *Summary* is distributed without charge to regular subscribers. (The Coin Dealer Newsletter, Inc., P.O. Box 11099, Torrance, CA 90510)

THE BLODGETT CASE

Earlier in this chapter, I referred to a case in which one unscrupulous dealer perpetrated a scam by overpricing coins far beyond legitimate market levels. I'm pleased to report that I played a personal role in helping to bring the dealer in question to justice. But while this is a source of great satisfaction to me, the case itself serves as an object lesson in the need for constant vigilance, for when there is a potential for enormous financial gain, the temptation will inevitably give rise to abuses.

The abuses were every bit as enormous as the potential benefits in the case of Dr. Michael W. Blodgett, the Minnesota dealer who stands at the center of this sordid episode. According to charges lodged against Blodgett by the federal government, his company—T.G. Morgan, Inc.—defrauded more than 200 customers out of a total of $30 million by grossly overpricing coins that it represented as good investments.

The coins that Blodgett sold were completely genuine, and he didn't exaggerate their level of preservation; indeed, he sold nothing but certified coins whose grade had been determined independently, honestly—and, by and large, quite accurately—by either PCGS or NGC. His crime was simple and shameless: He priced the coins at levels that were astronomically higher than the going market levels at the time—and then assured clients that they were good values.

Flagrant Fraud
The United States Attorney for the District of Minnesota, Francis X. Hermann, and Assistant U.S. Attorney, Andrew Luger, engaged me as a consultant when their office was preparing to prosecute Dr. Blodgett. I then continued to furnish expertise throughout the trial. The abuses that came to light appalled and enraged me.

Consider these examples:

In August 1990, Blodgett charged a client $203,150 for an 1890-CC Morgan dollar certified as Mint State-65. Its true market value at the time was just $11,000, according to NGC founder John Albanese, who served as an expert witness for the government. Four months later, in December 1990, Blodgett advised the client that the coin's value had risen to $289,310. On the contrary, Albanese testified, the coin had actually *lost* value, and was worth only $6,000.

In July 1989, Blodgett sold a different client a 1901-S Barber quarter certified as Mint State-67—a legitimately rare coin in exceptionally pristine condition. The coin was certainly worth a pretty penny: $200,000, according to Albanese. Blodgett's price, however, was more than five times that amount: a staggering $1.1 million. Seventeen months later, in December 1990, Blodgett told the client that the coin had soared in value to more than $2.6 million. In point of fact, Albanese said, it had lost one-fourth of its value and was worth only $150,000.

Some might say the victims of these frauds "don't deserve sympathy" because they entered into these transactions—deals involving huge amounts of money—without challenging Blodgett's outlandish prices, when they could have discovered the fraud simply by purchasing a guide book costing less than $10. But this kind of attitude misses the point: Gullibility and ignorance aren't crimes; fraud is.

Incredibly, Blodgett might have gotten away with his scheme if overpricing the coins had been his only transgression. The prosecution's fraud case against him rested primarily not on the outrageous prices, but rather on his claims that the coins were good investments at those prices. With the help of expert witnesses such as John Albanese and prominent coin dealer Dwight Manley, the government was able to demonstrate conclusively that these claims were grossly untrue.

Blodgett was convicted on 11 counts of mail fraud, four counts of interstate transportation of stolen property, and three counts of wire fraud. He was sentenced to a prison term of 76 months. The expert witnesses' testimony also was significant in establishing the point that major rarities—like all rare coins—have definable market values which can be arrived at through a process of consensus by leading authorities. Far from being isolated and arbitrary, Albanese's estimates were corroborated and reinforced by Manley and other witnesses, undercutting the argument that these were just one man's opinions.

Following the trial in 1993, Assistant U.S. Attorney Andrew Luger, writing for U.S. Attorney Hermann, sent me a letter expressing satisfaction with the outcome and thanking me for my efforts in helping to achieve it.

> *It is a testament to your love for numismatics that you dedicated so much time and energy to our efforts without once requesting compensation. It was a pleasure working with you in common cause to punish this astonishingly successful con man. . . .*
>
> *Someday, perhaps, there will be no need for the prosecution of coin dealers in the United States. When that day comes, you will be among those who can say that you helped rid the industry of unsavory characters.*

The discussions in this book about Blodgett and his coin company are based on testimony and other evidence offered at the trial of *United States of America v. Michael W. Blodgett.* After his release from prison, Blodgett continues to proclaim his innocence.

CHAPTER 5

REALIZING A PROFIT RIGHT NOW!

I'm against the holders. I'm against the guys that run the business of the holders. I'm against the people who buy the stuff in the holders. I'm against the dealers who deal in the stuff in the holders. I'm against Bullet Auctions and all the other [baloney]. I'm against the morons who buy the stuff to get rich quick. I'm against everything—the whole concept. The crack-out game is a form of low-level larceny. The convention circuit boys who deal in slabs aren't interested in collectors or numismatics; these guys are parasites.

Anybody who pays an extra $10,000 for a coin that grades one point higher is a nut. That one point might be smoke. You're paying ten grand extra for something that might be ephemeral.

—John J. Ford, Jr., former longtime dealer
and outspoken coin collectors' advocate

The people who play the rare-coin game may be hobbyists, but the stakes can be high and the payouts can be substantial—higher and more substantial than the stakes and payouts those same people would play for if they went to a casino. On the other hand, the risks can be equally high.

At a casino, these people might put down a couple of hundred

Figure 5-1. *Money-making activity for Heritage Capital Corporation at a coin-convention bourse table, as two professional numismatists examine coins.*

dollars and hope to double their money. In the coin market, by contrast, they might put down $50 in the slab/crack-out game and get back $350 . . . put down $300 and get back $1,400 . . . or put down $600 and get back close to $2,000.

It isn't pie in the sky to think you might put down a couple of hundred dollars here, when you play a rare-coin game, and get back a couple of thousand dollars there. All three examples I just gave, in fact, are real-world cases you will see illustrated with actual coins in this chapter.

I want to thank James L. Halperin, co-chairman of the board of Heritage Capital Corp. of Dallas, for sharing his secrets with me—and you—to help make this chapter so invaluable. Jim is one of the most successful coin traders in the business and one of the greatest experts on coin grading standards. He understands these standards—and uses them to his advantage—better than just about anyone else in the business. I'm proud to say that Jim and I have worked together on a number of projects and have maximized the returns that were realized by coins when we sold them at public auction or in the day-to-day marketplace. With Jim's assistance, many of my clients have profited tremendously through selling their coins at the optimal time and for the most money that could reasonably have been expected, given marketplace conditions.

THE CRACK-OUT GAME

The crack-out game is a relatively new phenomenon: It dates back to the late 1980s, when independent third-party coin grading services first appeared on the scene. Because of the strong demand for certified coins in pristine uncirculated condition, large price gaps often developed between the market values of coins in one Mint State grade level and those just a single grade higher, especially in levels of MS-65 and above. Thus, a certain type of coin might be worth $200 in MS-64 and five times that much—or more—in MS-65. Savvy traders soon began acquiring premium-quality (PQ) coins—those at the high end of their grade level—and "cracking" them out of their hard plastic holders in order to resubmit them to one of the grading services in hopes of receiving a higher grade and thereby reaping a windfall profit.

The coin crack-out game is just that—it's really a game. It's a high-stakes gamble, not unlike a poker game, where you can ante up a nominal sum of money and win a sizable pot. Jim Halperin has been playing this game for years, and winning more than his share of hefty pots. His success is apparent from the powerful position he holds as co-chairman of the board of Heritage Capital, a coin company generating $125 million in revenue a year. When experts such as Jim play the crack-out game, they don't put their trust in dumb luck or random chance. They approach the game scientifically, calculating the odds and playing their hands only when they believe that those odds are in their favor. They take risks, to be sure, but only when they are justified by the potential reward. This cautious, methodical approach works for them—and it can do the same for you!

JIM HALPERIN'S CRACK-OUT STRATEGY

When Jim Halperin calculates the risk-reward ratio for cracking out coins and resubmitting them, he draws up three columns on a piece of paper. The center column shows the value of each coin at its current certified grade. The left-hand column shows what it's worth in the next-lower grade; this represents the downside risk—the amount that Jim could expect to lose if the coin was downgraded the second time around. The right-hand column shows the current market value in the next-higher grade; this is the upside potential—the profit Jim would realize if the coin were upgraded instead.

Halperin follows a very simple philosophy in playing the crack-out game: "Stick with coins that have not too much risk and fantastic upside." Nobody's perfect—not even Jim Halperin. Everybody makes a mistake now and then in resubmitting a coin, no matter how good a grader he or she may be. Sometimes even premium-quality coins may be downgraded; perhaps a coin may have a hairline that you—the expert—missed. And even the experts have their weaknesses. Jim Halperin, for example, has never had a lot of success getting upgrades on MS-64 Indian quarter eagles; as he admits with a laugh, "there may be certain neurons missing" in his brain when it comes to grading these coins. But if you play the percentages, and develop and apply sharp grading skills, you'll greatly improve the odds in your favor. Learning to play the crack-out game is a matter of practice, practice, practice; the more experience you have, the better you get. And sometimes it's also a matter of being in the right place at the right time. As Halperin remarks: "I try to get there first, but I can't get there all the time. There are an awful lot of coins out there."

CHARTING POTENTIAL WINNERS

Let's consider one of the coins in the accompanying chart, which Jim prepared especially for this book: a 1944-S Walking Liberty half dollar graded Mint State-64 by the Professional Coin Grading Service (PCGS). With a certified grade of Mint State-64, this coin was worth $46 at the time the chart was prepared, in 2000. At that time, it would have been worth $35 in Mint State-63 and $290 in Mint State-65. A premium-quality Mint State-64 specimen—the best candidate for an upgrade—would have cost $4 to $14 extra, increasing the cost to $50 to $60. Let's say you bought a PQ MS-64 example of this coin and it cost you $50. The downside risk would have been negligible; even if the coin was regraded as MS-63, the loss in value would have been only $15. But the upside potential would have been enormous:

five times your cost (the purchase price of the coin plus the grading fee). If you buy a nice MS-64 coin under these circumstances, crack it out of its holder, and get it graded MS-65, it's salable for $290. If you lose out and the coin is downgraded to MS-63, it's still salable for $35. You have tremendous upside and very little downside—and that's the name of the game.

The following chart illustrates the high potential profits that exist in the crack-out game. It reflects the market values for a series of popular coins when certified and encapsulated by either PCGS or NGC in the grade levels of Mint State-63, 64, and 65. In addition to the 1944-S half dollar we've already examined, the coins in question are a 1914-S Buffalo nickel, an 1888-S Morgan silver dollar, a Type 3 gold dollar (any date), and two U.S. com-

Jim Halperin's Sample Crack-Out Winners

Coin	Service	Grade and 7-14-00 *Bluesheet* Bids		7-14-00
1914-S 5¢	PCGS	MS-63 $260	**MS-64 $330**	MS-65 $1,175
1944-S 50¢	PCGS	MS-63 $35	**MS-64 $46** (PQ add $4–$14)*	MS-65 $290
1888-S $1	NGC	MS-63 $182	**MS-64 $350†**	MS-65 $2,180
Indian $1 gold T-3 (1856–89)	PCGS	MS-63 $530	**MS-64 $710‡**	MS-65 $1,275
Isabella 25¢	PCGS	MS-63 $550	**MS-64 $725** (PQ add $60)	MS-65 $1,900
1905 Lewis & Clark commemorative $1 gold	NGC	MS-62 $800	**MS-63 $1,900**	MS-64 $4,080

*You have virtually no risk buying nice, premium-quality 64s, assuming you can buy them for $50 or $60. You have tremendous upside—*five* times your cost—and they are quite liquid.

†If it goes down in grade by a point, you're risking $168. If its grade increases by a point, you stand to make $1,830.

‡Gold type coins can be pretty wonderful because they are so liquid.

memorative coins: an 1893 Isabella quarter and a 1905 Lewis and Clark gold dollar. The prices are those that appeared in the *Certified Coin Dealer Newsletter,* also known as the *Bluesheet,* on July 14, 2000. In each case, the downside risk was minimal at that time and the upside potential was high. The coins in this chart are not necessarily the very best candidates for upgrades, by the way; they are simply good examples of how you can play the crack-out game and win. And as Jim Halperin notes, similar opportunities abound: "There are thousands of them around." The footnotes are Jim's.

WHEN *NOT* TO PLAY THE CRACK-OUT GAME

The crack-out game works best with premium-quality coins—coins that are at the high end of their grade level, such as the "A" coins described in Chapter 3. If there is a question as to whether a given coin is 64A or 65C and it's certified with a grade of 64, there's a reasonable chance that it might be regraded 65 if you resubmit it. A different set of graders, a fresh perspective from the same set of graders—these and other factors could produce a higher grade the second time around, since the call is a close one anyway.

There are certain times, however, when it would be inadvisable to play the crack-out game, even with PQ coins. *Coins with hairlines are unlikely to be upgraded,* for example. These fine lines may be hard for the naked eye to detect, but experienced graders can spot them, and they tend to preclude an upgrade.

Jim Halperin has an interesting suggestion on how to circumvent the grading problems posed by hairlines. It isn't a quick fix, by any means, and it's certainly not a way to make money *right now,* but it can pay big dividends in the long run. Let's say you have a flashy white coin that looks at a glance like an MS-65 but is certified as only 63 or 64 because it has hairlines. Halperin suggests cracking out that coin, placing it in an old Wayte Raymond holder, and storing it in your safe deposit box for several years—perhaps as long as six or seven years. Often, he says, the coin will develop beautiful, natural toning, which, in turn, will hide the hairlines completely. Then, when the coin is sub-mitted for grading again, it may very well come back as 65. There is a degree of risk: If the toning isn't attractive, the grade of the coin might be lowered instead of raised. But if the upside potential is great and the downside risk is minimal, this might be a chance well worth taking.

You also should *be wary of resubmitting coins where the down-side risk is substantial*. In all of the examples in Jim Halperin's chart, the price gap is modest between the grades of MS-63 and 64; thus, if a 64 coin happened to lose a point during the crack-out game, the loss would not be onerous. Take the 1888-S silver dollar, for example: The price at the time dropped from $350 to $182 between the grades of 64 and 63, so the downside risk was $168—not trivial, but not traumatic. On the other hand, the upside potential was handsome, for the price in 65 was a whopping $2,180. This kind of risk/reward ratio certainly would justify a crack-out. But suppose a different coin was worth $1,000 in MS-64, $3,000 in MS-65—and only $50 in MS-63. The potential reward—a $2,000 increase—would justify resubmission. But the downside risk—a possible loss of $950—most assuredly would not. In that kind of situation, discretion would definitely be the better part of valor.

THE BEST PLACE TO BUY CERTIFIED COINS

In looking for certified coins to use in the crack-out game, your best bet is to buy them at public auction. That is Jim Halperin's view, and I agree with him. For one thing, as Jim points out, you have a security blanket: The price you pay will be just one bid higher than what any dealers bidding at the sale would have paid. For another thing, the selection is likely to be extensive, and some of the coins in any given sale are almost sure to be overlooked and sell for less than they should. When Halperin goes to an auction, he studies each coin carefully and decides "the absolute most" that he would be willing to pay. He writes that number down next to the coin's listing in his catalog and never goes higher. "Never chicken out, either," he advises. "Trust your judgment, and learn from your mistakes."

Halperin has found that premium-quality coins can often be purchased at auctions for little or no more than the going market prices for regular-quality coins of the same type. And if you buy them at auctions, you won't be subjected to high-pressure tactics to pay a premium; sizing up the coins and deciding what to pay will be up to you alone. By contrast, Jim observes, if you find a PQ coin in a dealer's inventory, the dealer will try to convince you that the coin will get an upgrade and charge you a higher price on that basis. Halperin reports that the "bullet sales" conducted by his own auction company include many premium-quality coins. So do the "lightning sales" held by my company, Scott Travers Rare Coin Galleries. Buying coins at auction is "an ideal way to practice your skills," Halperin says: "These sales are the best vehicle for learning how to grade coins . . . the best place for a person willing to do his homework to buy coins."

A word of caution: The average consumer should not pay large premiums—say, 50 or 75 percent—for coins being sold at auction, or anywhere else for that matter, just because they look like good candidates for upgrades. Jim Halperin recommends paying no more than a 5 to 15 percent premium for a coin which appears to be PQ. He also recommends that before even bidding at an auction, would-be buyers first attend auctions at coin shows in their area and get a feel for which coins command extra premiums. "The biggest danger with an auction," he says, "is getting carried away with the mood and buying coins that you ordinarily would not buy. Never get carried away with the mood."

COMMENTS ON CRACK-OUTS

Jim Halperin estimates that 20 percent of all the coins now certified have been cracked out of their holders at least once. (See Figure 5-2.) There are good reasons for this. First, it isn't possible for any mere mortal to grade coins with absolute consistency, so until a foolproof system is devised, there will always be a temptation to seek an upgrade based upon the fallibility, and unpredictability, of human nature. Then, too, a certain

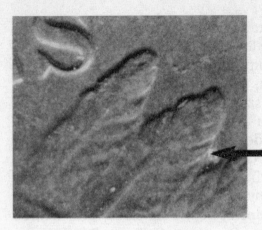

Figure 5-2. *A tiny piece of plastic is a telltale sign of a cracked-out coin.* Small plastic particles often adhere to a coin after it has been cracked out of a slab, unless the coin was airbrushed. *Photo courtesy Anthony Swiatek.*

number of coins will always be near the borderline between one grade and the next, and thus in a position to go either way. Also, some coins are confusing. If an otherwise gem coin has a tiny bit of rub, do you call it About Uncirculated-58 or Mint State-64? The very same coin can be graded—and has been graded—both ways at different times. And certain coins present special problems for graders. Indian Head half eagles and quarter eagles ($5 and $2½ gold pieces) are difficult to grade, for example, because their design elements are incused, or sunken below the surface. This makes them excellent candidates for crack-outs when they're graded on the low side.

Figure 5-3. *Indian quarter eagle graded MS-63 in an old PCGS holder without a hologram.* This coin would regrade as an MS-64 under today's standards. Consumers should carefully examine coins in these 1986-type holders for upgrades.

Halperin has found that if NGC grades a coin 65, then PCGS almost always will do likewise—eventually, if not immediately. He finds PCGS's grading to be "not quite as consistent" as NGC's. "I wouldn't say that the standards are significantly different," he adds. "NGC tends to give the coin the highest grade they will give it the first time, probably because they have fewer graders." Halperin's remarks were made for the first edition of this book in 1996.

Being active dealers, PCGS owners and their affiliates bid on PCGS coins. This, Halperin says, helps explain why some PCGS-graded coins have higher sight-unseen values than their NGC counterparts. NGC coins frequently are submitted to PCGS for crossovers, he adds, because PCGS coins sometimes sell for more—and then the process becomes a self-fulfilling prophecy. "PCGS will tend to put the better coins in their holders and reject the lower-grade coins—on average," Halperin says, "but that could reverse itself easily if there were more demand for NGC coins." *It would be an interesting play, he says, to buy coins that sell for considerably less in NGC holders and wait until the NGC coins become more popular than the PCGS coins.* Again, these opinions were expressed in 1996 and might not apply today.

DIPPING COINS

Silver coins often are dipped in a mildly acidic solution—thiourea—to remove toning or tarnish from their surfaces (Figure 5-4). This process, which is *cumulative,* can improve the appearance of a coin, making it brighter and enhancing its aesthetic appeal. Unfortunately, it also can expose underlying defects such as scratches and hairlines that were hidden by this layer before it was removed. What's more, it can leave the surfaces with a dull and washed-out look.

Coins which are original—that is to say, have never been subjected to artificial toning or other unnatural tinkering—tend to dip well. If you can't tell whether a coin is original or not, you shouldn't dip it. And if you want to test your skill, you should start with low-priced coins while you're still learning. Jim Halperin has an uncanny knack for spotting original coins, but to maximize his success rate, he has to look at coins out of their

Figure 5-4. *Jeweluster.* **This is a popular, mildly acidic dip.** *Photo courtesy Bill Fivaz.*

holders in order to determine if they will dip well. He can judge their potential, however, while they're still holdered. Jim has a word of advice for would-be dippers seeking to use this technique to improve their chances at upgrades: "Anyone who plays this game is going to have to pay for the education."

CRACKING OUT COMMEMORATIVE COINS

Anthony J. Swiatek, a nationally known coin dealer and author from Manhasset, New York, is widely regarded as the world's preeminent authority on U.S. commemorative coins—special coins issued periodically since 1892 to honor some significant person, organization, place, or event in our nation's history. Over the years, Swiatek has followed the crack-out game closely within this important segment of the rare coin marketplace, and he has concluded that certain "commems" stand a much better chance than others of being upgraded upon resubmission.

Swiatek has identified seven coins which are most likely to achieve an upgrade from MS-63 to 64, MS-64 to 65, or MS-65 to 66. All seven are half dollars issued by the U.S. Mint during the "traditional" period of the nation's commemorative coinage, which extended from 1892 through 1954. (The so-called "modern" period began in 1982, after a hiatus of nearly three decades.) Here are his six selections:

1. The 1936 Norfolk, Virginia, bicentennial half dollar (Figures 5-5 and 5-6)
2. The 1936 Wisconsin territorial centennial half dollar
3. The 1936 York County, Maine, tercentenary half dollar
4. The Texas centennial half dollar, including any of the coins struck from 1934 through 1938
5. The 1936-P Oregon Trail Memorial half dollar, a specific issue within a series that was issued sporadically from 1926 through 1939
6. The 1946 Iowa centennial half dollar

In general, Swiatek says that a commemorative coin has the best chance of gaining an upgrade if its mintage is relatively high and the price spread between grades is not significant. He adds:

"The coin must be eye-appealing, displaying an original white or very lightly toned lustrous surface or possessing an attractively colored toning—such as a rainbowlike play of colors—on one or both sides." And what if the coin is dull, dark, or unattractive, rather than flashy? In that case, Swiatek says that the person hoping for an upgrade should practice humming or singing "The Impossible Dream."

At the other extreme, Swiatek has identified seven coins with

Figures 5-5 & 5-6. *Superbly toned Norfolk commemorative graded MS-65 by PCGS which might qualify for an upgrade.* Anthony Swiatek recommends this coin type as a prime "crack-out" candidate. *Photos courtesy Heritage Numismatic Auctions, Inc.*

the *least* chance of winning an upgrade through resubmission. Their prospects are dimmed, he says, because all are scarce in Mint State grades and "practically nonexistent" in grades above MS-65. Here is his list of the six "worst bets" in the crack-out game:

1. The 1900 Lafayette dollar (Figures 5-7 and 5-8)
2. The 1893 Isabella quarter
3. The 1921 Missouri centennial half dollar
4. The 1915-S Panama-Pacific Exposition half dollar
5. The 1926 Sesquicentennial of American Independence half dollar
6. The 1923-S Monroe Doctrine centennial half dollar

Figures 5-7 & 5-8. *Lafayette dollar graded MS-65 by PCGS* (obverse and reverse). Anthony Swiatek says that the odds are against you to get this coin type upgraded to Mint State-66. *Photos courtesy Heritage Numismatic Auctions, Inc.*

Many of the gold coins from the traditional period of U.S. commemoratives also fall into this second category, Swiatek says.

PROFITING FROM GENERIC GOLD COINS

Grading arbitrage—the crack-out game—is a wonderful way to make money in coins *right now*. There are other ways to turn a hefty profit, as well, and one of the best is to purchase what are known as generic gold coins and then cash them in when gold bullion rises in value. The term "generic" is applied to gold coins which are numismatic in nature but whose mintages and available populations are relatively high—common-date Saint-Gaudens double eagles, for example. A significant rise in the price of gold will trigger an even sharper rise in the value of these coins, since they possess not only precious-metal content but also the cachet of being collectibles. And yet, because they are not really rare, they often can be purchased for only a modest premium over the current value of the metal they contain.

Generic gold coins occupy a market niche midway between bullion-type gold coins and gold rarities. Bullion coins—the American Eagle, Canadian Maple Leaf, and South African Krugerrand, for example—typically are sold for just a small premium over their metal value, with metal value serving as the overriding determinant in their price at a given time. Rare-date gold pieces, such as the 1907 high-relief Saint-Gaudens double eagle, frequently command premiums in the tens of thousands of dollars, and their value is based overwhelmingly on their low mintage, not their metal content. Generic gold coins exist in sufficient quantities to be traded as like-kind units—very much like commodities—and when the precious-metals markets are calm, their prices tend to hover not much above the value of gold bullion. But when the markets get hot, they benefit psychologically from their status as collectibles, and this drives up their value far beyond the rise in gold itself.

Precious-metal content is a key consideration in the value of generic gold coins, far more than it is for rare gold coins. This is especially true for coins in the highest circulated grades—AU-55 and AU-58—and those in the lowest Mint State grades. In these grades, generic gold coins are virtually bullion coins, very much like the American Eagle and the Maple Leaf: They rise and fall in value in lockstep with gold itself. The price differential widens, however, in grade levels of MS-63 and above. And coins in these grade levels tend to perform especially well when gold bullion gets "hot" and its price goes up dramatically within a short period of time.

GENERIC GOLD'S PRICE PERFORMANCE

High-grade generic gold coins were flying high in May 1989, when the coin market scaled its last major peak. They plunged in value thereafter, reflecting the sharp downturn in the coin market as a whole—even though gold itself never took a similar tumble in price. As of this writing, gold is selling for about $400 an ounce—a modest advance over its average price of $372 in May 1989. Yet high-grade generic gold coins are far below the levels they enjoyed at that time; most are worth less than half— even less than a third—of their 1989 highs. But if we were to witness meaningful upward movement in the price of gold bullion . . . say, $25 or $50 an ounce . . . these coins would almost certainly surge in value by hundreds of dollars apiece—far more, percentagewise, than the metal itself. And those who purchased the coins when the market was in a lull could reap a handsome dividend in the whirlwind.

Potential profits exist from trades in generic gold even during periods when the bullion market is flat. Gold itself has been remarkably steady—some would say stagnant—from 1989 through 2000, but during that time it has made modest moves on several different occasions, and high-grade generic gold coins have invariably flexed their muscles and made even stronger gains at such times. Traders who were shrewd (or fortunate) enough to ride these waves in the marketplace—buying at low ebb and selling at high tide—landed on the beach with big profits.

Consider these examples:

- On May 26, 1989, the *Bluesheet* assigned a value of $3,950 to common-date Saint-Gaudens double eagles graded Mint State-65 by PCGS. As this is written, in August 2000, those same coins are listed at $725—less than 19 percent of what they were worth at that peak. But they didn't fall to this point in a straight line. For an eleven-month period during 1992–1993, they actually rose in value more than 40 percent. And similar price swings have taken place several times since 1989.

- On May 26, 1989, the *Bluesheet* reflected a market price of $2,400 for Indian Head eagles ($10 gold pieces) graded Mint State-63 by PCGS. At this writing, those coins are down to

$450, or less than 19 percent of that amount. But again there have been significant upward spikes along the way. For instance, the price rebounded from $790 in July 1992 to $1,400 in June 1993—an increase of more than 77 percent.

- On May 26, 1989, the *Bluesheet* showed a value of $3,050 for Liberty eagles with motto (dates bearing the motto IN GOD WE TRUST) graded MS-63 by PCGS. Today, those coins are worth just $410—not even 14 percent of that lofty peak. But here, too, there have been some highly impressive ups along with the downs: The price bounced back, for example, from $875 in July 1992 to $1,240 in June 1993—a gain of more than 40 percent.

Not all generic gold coins have fallen as far as these—or fluctuated as greatly—since 1989. But many have experienced significant swings in value, creating opportunities for keen-witted traders to buy and sell advantageously, and each time they have risen, they have done so more dramatically than gold bullion.

RARE GOLD COINS' PERFORMANCE

In contrast to generic gold, rare gold coins have evidenced little price movement in recent years. Since plunging in value along with the rest of the coin market in 1989 and 1990, they have been depressed almost unremittingly. There's a simple reason for this: Rare gold coins don't exist in quantity, so they cannot be promoted by entrepreneurs. As a result, they don't enjoy the temporary price boosts created by such promotions. Rather, they lie dormant until the market regains more permanent underlying strength.

Truly rare gold coins are much better buys from the standpoint of long-term investment. They benefit more dramatically than generic gold coins when market conditions are bullish, for just as their malaise is more pronounced and persistent during slumps, their gains are more spectacular and sustained when the market is strong. They have the potential to soar far faster and higher in value when a turnaround occurs, for they are more elusive and desirable. But during bear markets, such as the one we've seen since 1989, generic gold coins offer much greater opportunities for action—and gains—in the short term.

A HIGH-RETURN GENERIC GOLD GAME

Many generic gold coins lost 50 percent of their value during the first year of the coin market's lengthy slump—the 12-month period from May 1989 to May 1990. They then regained roughly half the lost value before beginning to slide again. This ebb-and-flow pattern has been repeated several times since then. Let's say a certain generic gold coin was worth $10,000 in May of 1989 and you bought it a year later for $5,000. You probably could have sold this coin for $7,500 when the market rebounded temporarily, then bought it back for $5,000—or even less—the next time it hit bottom and sold it again when the market hit another upward spike. By repeating this process several times, you could have doubled or tripled the money you initially invested—right in the teeth of a raging bear market.

Rolling the dice repeatedly on gold's price performance is not for the faint of heart. It's very much a gambler's game—one that can be extremely risky. In a way, it's like playing musical chairs with your money, and I don't recommend it for ordinary consumers. Even expert dealers have difficulty doing it successfully. But there's far less risk involved in rolling the dice just once, assuming you make your purchases at a time when the markets in coins and precious metals are inactive.

You should buy generic gold coins at a time when both gold itself and the coins you are acquiring are relatively low in price, compared with near-past levels. You should sell them when you see prices trending upward without much apparent economic justification. Inflation, an expanded money supply, and increased federal spending all could be viewed as true economic justification for gold and gold coins to rise in value. In their absence, a sudden rise in generic gold coins' value could simply reflect a major market promotion, and that would be a signal to sell your coins. In any case, I urge you to limit your expenditures to totally discretionary funds—money that isn't essential to your economic health.

PROFITING FROM A TURNAROUND IN THE MARKET

The surest way for *everyone* to profit from rare coins would be for the lingering slump to end and give way to a genuine market boom. As of this writing, there's no apparent reason to break out the champagne and celebrate a turnaround; prices remain depressed in many major segments of the marketplace. But nothing lasts forever; bad things—like good things—must end. And now, while things are slow, is the time to position yourself to take full advantage of the boom that almost certainly will energize the market sooner or later.

In recent months, we have seen a recovery—even a resurgence—in rare coins, largely fueled by the 50-states quarter program. Gold and silver coins have not yet participated fully in this upward movement, but precious metals may well be on the verge of a recovery of their own. Despite record highs in the stock market and other positive indicators, many Americans seem to be feeling a sense of malaise regarding their economic well-being and security, a sense undoubtedly heightened by widespread job layoffs. That same kind of malaise—even the word "malaise," as uttered by then-President Jimmy Carter—helped give rise to the coin market's greatest boom in 1979 and 1980.

REASONS FOR BUYING NOW

Psychologically, most people feel uncomfortable buying coins when the market is weak; they're much more disposed toward making major purchases when the bulls are running, not the bears. Shrewd financial analysts have long since proven, though, that the optimum time to buy is when a market is weak, not when it's strong. Buying conditions today are particularly attractive in the coin market, for we're seeing not only relatively low prices—prices far below the levels they enjoyed in 1989—but also unusually thin supplies. Many desirable coins are scarcer than most people realize, and it would take only a small increase in demand to push their prices geometrically higher.

Many dealers' stock is low or depleted altogether, and they've had no incentive—and perhaps no capital, either—to replenish their supplies because of the prolonged market slump. It's my considered opinion that if we were to see $5 million or $10 million in new money enter our marketplace over a period of just a few weeks, and if that money was spent primarily on scarcer-date material, the type-coin market would rise in value anywhere from 20 to 40 percent.

There's another good reason for buying better coins at this time: Many dealers have sharply reduced their commissions, including the extra charge they tack onto the price of premium-quality coins. In May 1989, a PQ coin typically commanded 20 to 40 percent more than a regular-quality coin of the same type, date, and grade. Thus, if a regular-quality coin was selling for $1,000, a corresponding PQ coin probably would have cost $1,200 to $1,400. As this is written, in August 2000, the PQ differential for that same coin might be only $50. But if a market turnaround were to develop, it's possible—even probable—that the premium would return to its previous higher level. Indeed, I am convinced that when the market does turn around, premium-quality coins will be among the biggest winners of all.

COIN PROFIT SECRETS

Making money from coins—*right now* or any other time—depends to a great extent on establishing and following a set of prudent guidelines on when, what, and how to buy, on the one hand, and when, what, and how to sell on the other. The extent to which you do this will go a long way toward determining how much profit you make—or if you make any at all.

I've drawn up a list of pointers that you would do well to follow. Some may seem like simple common sense; others won't be so obvious to people outside the coin market's inner circle. All of them, however, are secrets to success for those who make money from coins—and they can help *you* achieve the same success.

Become a collector/investor. One of the most often-heard pieces of advice in coin books and periodicals is that people who invest in coins should first become collectors. I like to turn this around, though: People should look upon coins not only as collectibles but also as investments. Too often, collectors put so much emphasis on the historical, cultural, and aesthetic aspects of coins that they don't pay enough attention to the real—and important—financial implications of their purchases. Investors should indeed get a feel for the intangible aspects of coins—but by the same token, collectors should make it their business to learn all they can about the market value of coins they are considering for their sets. In years to come, the collector/investor will play an increasingly dominant role in the coin marketplace. To maximize your success, you need to possess both mentalities.

Know a coin's value at all times. Recently, I read an article suggesting that when a coin buyer negotiates with a seller, the buyer should always start by offering the seller a certain fixed percentage below the asking price. This is, pure and simple, one of the worst ideas I've ever heard. It totally ignores the clear and present danger that the asking price might be far above the coin's true market value. To use an extreme example, let's say a given coin is worth $1,000 and someone is offering it for sale for $10,000. It would be preposterous for you to offer to buy it for $5,000, simply because your strategy was to open negotiations at 50 percent of the asking price. Then again, if someone offered you that same $1,000 coin for just $50, there would be no point in trying to haggle the price down to $25. You would simply say, "OK, $50 is fine," buy the coin, and sell it for a very handsome profit. If you don't know the value of a coin, you shouldn't be negotiating to buy it. If you do know the value, you have a big advantage over other people who don't.

Buy low and sell high. This is one of those tips that seems self-evident. But following it successfully is easier said than done. If prices have fallen sharply within a short period of time, that might be an excellent time to buy. If prices are rising rapidly, that might be a very good time to sell. One way to avoid getting burned by fast-changing market values is to cost-average your purchases. If you plan to invest $10,000 in coins, don't spend it all at once, figuring you can outguess the marketplace—even experts have trouble doing that. Instead, spend a set amount—say, $1,000 a month—over an extended period of time. You'd make more money with a single lucky guess, but spreading out your purchases will give you far greater protection against unforeseen market changes.

Read books and stay informed. Knowledge is power in the coin market, and there's really no such thing as knowing too much. The more you know about coins, the likelier it is that you'll recognize a bargain when it appears—or seize an opportunity to sell a coin and pocket a hefty profit. Many excellent books are available today—more than ever before in the coin hobby's history. You also should monitor current market values by checking and analyzing the prices listed each week in the *Certified Coin Dealer Newsletter,* or *Bluesheet,* and its sister publication, *The Coin Dealer Newsletter,* or *Greysheet,* which covers market activity in coins that have not been certified. And I strongly recommend that you keep abreast of developments by reading all the excellent coin periodicals now being published.

Be decisive and take action. Quick action pays big dividends in the coin market—more so than in almost any other field. If you order a coin through the mail and it doesn't meet your standards when you get it, don't waste time: Return it to the seller right away. The same goes for coins that you purchase at a show. The longer you wait, the less chance you will have of getting your money back and the greater the chance will be that the dealer's return privilege will expire. Conversely, if you have a coin that rises in value quickly, it would be a good idea to sell it and take your profit. Go to the cash window, celebrate—and don't even think about looking back.

Make sure you have the coins. This may sound ridiculous, but I can assure you it isn't. Many people buy coins in very large quantities, much like commodities. For instance, they may order a thousand generic Morgan dollars—common-date pieces such as the 1881-S—and the coins may arrive in a box from a mail-order dealer. Months or years later, when they go to sell the coins, they may find to their chagrin that the box really contains only 600 silver dollars, not 1,000. Worse yet, the dealer from whom they bought the coins may be out of business by that time. It just stands to reason that you can't count your profits if you can't count your coins. And speaking of counting coins, always make sure that you don't get shortchanged when you purchase coins by the roll. And if you show a roll of your coins to a dealer, make sure that he doesn't palm one or two before handing it back.

Get rid of underperformers and junk. Everyone accumulates losers along with winners when buying coins. You need to weed your garden, to use a figure of speech, from time to time: Pull out your off-grade modern rolls, your common coins—and yes, your downright junk—and sell them all, even if you have to take a loss. Better coins offer far greater opportunities for profit. Keep this in mind: Coins which are scarce today can become rare in the future, and coins which are rare today can become rarer, but coins which are common today will almost surely remain common, at least for the foreseeable future. Incidentally, I would include virtually all of the modern commemorative coins issued by the U. S. Mint—those produced since 1982—under the heading of "common."

Limit yourself to coins which have been certified by PCGS, NGC, ANACS, or ICG. This is among my most important pointers, but I'm putting it near the end, rather than at the beginning, because I don't want you to use the grading services as a crutch. Certification is crucial in the current coin marketplace. Many buyers and sellers won't even handle coins unless they have been certified by one of the major services—and it's hard to find fault with their thinking. Third-party grading removes the nettlesome guesswork that used to plague buyers and sellers, and also much of the risk that used to exist. At the same time, however, you must never lose sight of the fact that when you buy certified coins, what you're really paying for is the coin and not the holder. True, the certification gives the coin greater liquidity, but when all is said and done, the coin should stand on its own merits.

Crack out any slabbed coins that appear to be undergraded. We covered this subject in great detail at the outset of this chapter. Getting a high-end coin recertified in the next-higher grade can pay you an instant dividend of hundreds—even thousands—of dollars. Surely this is a case where knowledge is not only power but also the passkey to profit.

Store your coins properly. This final recommendation is last but surely not least. Buying wisely is, of course, a major first step in making money from coins. But all the skill and know-how that go into getting bargains will end up being wasted if you store those coins improperly after you get them. You need to store your coins in a dry, stable environment. You also need to check to make sure that each coin's surfaces are free from airborne pollutants before you place the coins in long-term storage. And when you handle your coins, you need to exercise proper care and judgment at all times. Never place bare fingers on the front or back of a coin; always hold it tightly by its edges. All of us are simply custodians of the coins in our collections and portfolios. You owe it to future collectors to maintain your coins in the same level of preservation they were when you received them. Beyond that, you owe it to yourself—if you don't, you're likely to lose a lot of money.

CHAPTER 6

THE BIGGEST MISTAHES AND HOW NOT TO MAHE THEM

Mistakes are bound to happen in any field, and when they occur, a price must be paid. It's often said that doctors bury their mistakes, and coin dealers like to joke that they do likewise. Let's say a coin dealer makes a mistake by paying $1,000 too much for a certain coin. Often, he'll dig himself out of this hole by selling the coin to a non-knowledgeable investor for even more than he, the dealer, paid for it—burying the buyer with a bad investment, perhaps for years to come.

To avoid digging yourself a deep financial grave when buying and selling coins, you need to be aware of the pitfalls that await you in the marketplace. The best way to avoid them is to learn just where they are—and *what* they are. And the way to do that is to learn from the mistakes already made by others.

I've drawn up a list of commonly made mistakes, gleaned from many years of experience in the marketplace, including not only my own, but also that of other market analysts. By studying these mistakes carefully, you can gain some valuable—though not expensive—lessons in how to buy and sell coins advantageously.

Mistake No. 1: *Failing to think as an investor first and as a collector second.*

Many people who buy and sell coins look upon themselves as "pure collectors." They take a dim view of anyone who mentions the investment potential of coins or even—perish the thought—admits to buying coins with the notion of turning a profit. Coin collecting can certainly be enjoyable, and putting together a set of coins does have some of the aspects of a project or a game. It's no fun, however, to lose a lot of money because you've overpaid by many hundreds of dollars for a coin, or possibly held it too long in a falling market.

There are many reasons for buying coins, and pleasure is certainly one of them; in fact, it's a good idea to buy only coins that you like. But this doesn't mean that you shouldn't pay close attention to financial implications, as well, in every coin transaction to which you're a party. It's fine to consider aesthetic appeal and historical significance, if these are aspects that make a coin attractive to you. But don't lose sight of the bottom line: Even if investment is not your motivation, it makes no sense to throw your money away; that beautiful, historic coin will make you feel even better if you know you got good value when you bought it.

Awareness of value is especially important when buying and selling higher-priced coins. It's one thing to disregard a coin's investment potential when you're paying $100—or even $1,000. It's quite another matter, though, to shell out $10,000 or $100,000 and not review the financial aspects carefully. You wouldn't buy a car or a house without regard to potential resale value, and you shouldn't buy expensive coins that way, either.

Mistake No. 2: *Expecting to get full value.*

People who enter the coin market without first educating themselves about its idiosyncrasies have a tendency to look upon coins as a surefire investment—one that will always increase in value and one that possesses little risk. As I explained in Chapter 2, there is in fact significant risk in this marketplace.

What's more, the average markup paid by uninitiated buyers is substantially higher than most people realize. If you as an average consumer bought a coin from a typical dealer for $10,000, you'd probably expect to get close to that amount if you turned around and sold it right away. The reality is, you'd almost certainly get a whole lot less. To maximize your potential return when buying rare coins, you need a higher level of sophistication and insight into the marketplace. You need to know how to judge a coin's true value and how to spot bargains, and gaining this kind of knowledge is a very tall order. The average person—however intelligent he or she may be—is going to have great difficulty even figuring out the value of an ordinary, run-of-the-mill collection, much less more sophisticated coins.

Mistake No. 3: *Failing to contact competent dealers for assistance.*

Whether you view yourself as a collector, an investor, a speculator, or perhaps a combination of some or all of these, you need to seek competent, independent advice before buying or selling coins with significant value. One source of such advice would be a grading service, and in Chapter 3, I explained in detail how to use these services to your advantage. But you need to go beyond merely buying certified coins and getting your own coins authenticated and graded; in fact, the expertise required to succeed may actually involve outsmarting the grading services on occasion. You need to seek out experts who can guide you in your numismatic pursuits—people who possess exceptional ability to analyze the marketplace . . . who may have worked for a time at one of the grading services . . . who may have authored books about coins . . . who are inner-circle dealers. Above all, you need to find someone who is able to maintain an arm's-length distance from your transactions.

I wouldn't suggest that my firm, Scott Travers Rare Coin Galleries, Inc., is the only dealer that you can trust. However, I do believe that the policies followed by my firm provide a good example of what you should be seeking in a numismatic consultant or advisor. My fundamental policy is not to maintain an inventory of coins. It's my belief that dealers who maintain inventories cannot keep an arm's-length distance from clients' transactions. If I had a $2-million inventory and someone came to me with $50,000 to spend on coins, I might be tempted to tell that individual, "You should buy some of these coins from my stock." Instead, I act as a broker when clients come to me to purchase coins: I seek out the coins they request, getting the clients the best possible terms and receiving my payment in the form of a nominal commission. Here's another suggestion: Seek full disclosure, whenever you buy a coin, on how much the dealer paid for that coin. Don't simply accept a verbal assurance; ask to see a receipt. With many transactions, I make it a point to provide written disclosures of the purchase price for my clients so there is no question exactly what I paid for every coin.

How can you find the kind of advisor you need? One way is to scrutinize numismatic periodicals and newsletters. Look for dealers who have contributed articles to these publications, or who are sought for quotes in other writers' articles and columns. Also make note of dealers who are interviewed as experts on television and radio programs. Don't be unduly impressed by dealers who have many club affiliations—many fancy-looking initials after their names; multiple memberships do not necessarily indicate expertise and independence of thought. Of course, there are also experts who don't really fit this profile, and yet would make marvelous advisors. One name that comes to mind is that of John Albanese, the founder of the Numismatic Guaranty Corporation. Albanese has never written a book and isn't in the limelight as a frequent contributor or source of expertise in the media—yet, he possesses one of the most brilliant minds in the numismatic field, particularly in the area of grading. You really need to develop an intuitive feeling for who would best serve you—who would truly be good, decent, and honorable dealers and advisors.

Mistake No. 4: *Having expectations that are too high.*

Many people enter the coin market with unreasonably high expectations. One reason for this, I suspect, is the widespread publicity generated over the years by the Salomon Brothers' annual survey of investment vehicles, which consistently rated rare coins among the best performers. The survey was discontinued under pressure from federal regulators, but many coin sellers used it at the time as a major selling tool—and some still do, citing past reports. Continued use of previous Salomon data is especially misleading, given the coin market's generally dreary performance in the years since the survey was discontinued.

You need to be realistic about your potential return when you purchase coins. It's unrealistic to think that you can plunk down $10,000 today and have your investment grow to $20,000 within three years, or to think that you're assured of a 20-percent return every year. It's also unrealistic to think that you can simply put your coins away and forget about them for the next five years—or even the next five months—and then come back and find they have magically doubled or tripled in value. As I explain in other parts of this book, many of the most profitable opportunities in the coin market today involve arbitrage—cracking a certified coin out of its holder and getting it recertified at a higher grade by a different grading service. These opportunities require constant awareness of market conditions and quick action. Successful arbitrageurs watch the market closely on a day-to-day basis; they certainly don't make money simply by sitting on their assets. Similarly, you need to act fast to capitalize on upward spikes in the market. Let's say gold bullion rises in value sharply and your gold coins increase in value by 40 percent from one week to the next—or 20 percent from one day to the next. To realize a profit, you need to sell those coins immediately; if you wait a week, or even a day, the price may recede and wipe out your paper gains.

It doesn't pay to wear rose-colored glasses when you make an investment in coins. Overly high expectations are an invitation for disappointment. Like pride, they inevitably come before a fall.

Mistake No. 5: *Placing yourself at the mercy of the dealer.*

The coin market is an easy-entry, easy-exit place to do business. As a consequence, it is possible to become a coin dealer without really being especially knowledgeable about either the marketplace or coins themselves. To put it bluntly, many dealers are bluffing, including some dealers who appear at first glance to be experts. Their knowledge is far more shallow than it seems to the casual observer. This can be difficult for the non-knowledgeable investor to discern, since these phony "experts" do have at least a little knowledge, and that can dazzle the neophyte who knows even less about the marketplace.

You need to avoid these phonies, and to do that you need to be able to identify who they are. Arm yourself with knowledge, for knowledge is truly power. Subscribe to price guides. Go to coin shows. Attend public auctions. And take careful note of everything you see. At auctions, for example, look at the coins beforehand and try to figure out what grades they really are (irrespective of the catalog descriptions) and how much they should bring, then compare your estimates with the actual prices realized. That's a wonderful educational experience.

Above all, don't let any dealer—phony or otherwise—call the shots for you. Don't just go to a dealer, hand him a check, and say, "Here's $50,000; treat me fairly." Learn about the marketplace so that you can not only identify knowledgeable dealers but work with them closely in structuring your portfolio or collection. The more you know, the better off you'll be—not only in obtaining the right kind of coins but also in negotiating their price.

Mistake No. 6: *Getting caught up in fads.*

There's always a great temptation to buy an item that's "hot." Following the crowd is easier than thinking for yourself. The trouble with fads, however, is that generally they lose their appeal—and value—all too soon: It's an all-too-easy transition from "fad" to "fade." One example of this was the 1995 doubled-die Lincoln cent, an error coin characterized by doubling of the letters in some of the inscriptions on the obverse (or "heads" side) of the coin, especially in the word LIBERTY. This coin stirred a sensation when its existence was first disclosed in March 1995, and soon eager buyers were paying upwards of $200 apiece to own an uncirculated example. Before long, however, more and more pieces began to turn up as people scoured rolls and bags of 1995 cents in search of this supposed rarity. By the end of the year, many thousands of examples had been found, and the price had plummeted to less than 10 percent of its early-year high. The lesson is clear: Stay away from fads—or at the very least, wait until the dust settles before buying such a coin. Those pennies from heaven could turn out to be engraved invitations to investment hell.

Mistake No. 7: *Expecting to get what you paid from coins that have decreased in value.*

Emotions often get in the way of common sense. When you buy a coin for $5,000 and it plunges in value to only $500, common sense tells you that this coin is a bad investment and you might be better off selling it before it decreases in value even more. Your emotions cloud your judgment, though: Because you paid $5,000, you have an emotional resistance to selling it for only $500 and suffering a $4,500 loss. You need to seek advice from an uninvolved, unbiased expert—someone who has no emotional attachment—when pondering the sale of such coins.

I've seen numerous cases where emotions overrode good judgment when people were confronted with buy-and-sell decisions involving coins. This happened frequently, for example, during the Wall Street boom of 1995, when high-flying stock prices created opportunities to dispose of bad coin investments advantageously. Because their profits from stocks were so high, people with coins that had gone down in value could have sold those coins at a loss and used that loss to offset part of their stock-related gains for tax purposes. This would have enabled them to recoup at least a portion of their money. But many chose not to do so, clinging to the coins emotionally—and irrationally—because they couldn't bring themselves to admit they had made a mistake. They did this even though it was clear, in many cases, that the coins had a much better chance of going down further in value–from $500 to only $300 or $200, perhaps–than of ever rising again to anything approaching $5,000.

Mistake No. 8: *Asking too much for your less desirable coins and too little for your prize specimens.*

This mistake illustrates one of the major reasons why I like public auctions as a way of selling coins. Often, when selling coins directly to a dealer, people will underestimate the true market value of their rarer, more desirable coins and give the dealer an asking price significantly below the amount they should–and could–expect to receive. Naturally, the dealer will agree to pay this. They're more likely to have overpaid, however, for the less desirable coins, since these coins are more common, more available, and more subject to market manipulation. Thus, while the rare coins probably went up in value after they bought them, these less desirable coins may have stayed the same or even gone down. The result is an interesting psychological phenomenon: After being satisfied with too small a profit on the rare coins, they tend to stick to their guns with the less desirable ones and demand to get at least what they paid for them, even though they may not be worth that much. This time, of course, the dealer declines. All too often, these people end up selling their really nice coins for a song and keeping their less desirable coins because they couldn't get their inflated asking prices for them.

Public auctions are the antidote for this problem, because they provide a setting in which *all* of a seller's coins–rare and common alike–receive the proper exposure among a broad group of prospective buyers. However, there are times when marketplace conditions or personal emergencies require a quicker sale than traditional public auctions would permit. My own firm offers an excellent alternative called the *lightning sale.* The format is similar to that of a public auction, but the time frame is greatly compressed; indeed, the lightning sale creates a competitive environment almost on the spur of the moment. When coins are consigned for sale in this fashion, my company assembles a representative group of bidders from among important buyers known to have an interest in such material. An early date is set for the sale, and additional consignments are accepted up until the night before that date. It has been my experience that results at lightning sales parallel those at traditional auction sales: Extraordinary coins bring extraordinary prices, and lesser coins bring prices reflective of market conditions. In both instances, the sellers are better served than they would be if they sold the coins outright to just one dealer, with all the attendant perils, pitfalls, and potential mistakes.

Mistake No. 9: *Buying coins that are low-end or unattractive.*

As I explained earlier in this book, coins are graded on a continuum. Not all coins of a certain grade level are equal within that group; among coins graded Mint State-65, for example, there are high-end 65s and low-end 65s. When I worked as a grader at the Numismatic Guaranty Corporation of America, we used the letters A, B, and C to denote the various sub-groups within a given grade level. An "A" coin was a high-end piece, very nearly qualifying for the next-higher grade. A "B" coin was right in the center of the continuum. And a "C" coin was a low-end piece, close to the next-lower grade. You should steer clear of low-end coins. A low-end certified coin won't have a "C" on its holder, branding it as such like a scarlet letter; the holder will carry only the numerical grade level. By using common sense, though, you should be able to spot most low-end coins. If a coin looks unattractive to you, chances are it will look that way to other people, too. If you see an obvious scratch in a grade-sensitive area, it's a problem coin—and problem coins are difficult to sell. Don't buy low-end coins just because a dealer gives you a discount. Even if you get a steep discount now, you'll pay for it—and may pay dearly—later.

Mistake No. 10: *Refusing to sell certain coins sight-unseen at certain times.*

This is a significant mistake. What often happens is that people will read about premium-quality coins in one of my books, or educate themselves some other way on this subject, then go out and purchase such coins, just as we experts recommend. For instance, they may buy Mint State-65 generic gold coins that are super high-end pieces—almost MS-66s—by handpicking magnificent specimens and paying a premium of possibly 10 percent. So far, so good; purchasing PQ (for "premium-quality") coins is a good idea. What may happen, however, is that gold will surge in value and generic gold coins will go up 50 percent or more almost overnight: Coins that were selling for $1,000 apiece may soar to $1,500 within a very short time. And instead of selling their premium-quality coins at the newly higher price level, taking their handsome profit, and running to the nearest bank, the owners of these coins will hold out for the extra 10 percent that they paid going in; instead of selling quickly for $1,500, they'll insist upon $1,650 or more, even though the premium factor isn't being given special weight in such a hectic marketplace. Instead of getting a bonus, they're more likely to blow their entire opportunity, for while they're hemming and hawing, the bullion price may well recede to its previous level, pulling the prices of gold coins down along with it. There are times when you need to forget about the premium you paid for those PQ coins and the time you spent tracking them down. If you can reap big profits by selling your coins quickly at sight-unseen price levels, you need to swallow your pride, sell those coins at once, go to the cash window, and start celebrating.

Mistake No. 11: *Buying generic silver coins because they are so much cheaper now than they were at the height of the market in 1989.*

A lot of people conclude that coins are great bargains at current market levels, as this is written in 2000, because they are so much cheaper than they were at the coin market's last major peak in May 1989. The contrasts are certainly striking; if you pick up a copy of the *Certified Coin Dealer Newsletter* from 1989 and look through the listings, you can't help but shake your head at how far many prices have fallen. In quite a few cases, coins that were selling for $20,000 in 1989 are worth only two or three thousand dollars as of this writing. But it would be wrong to assume that just because certain coins have plummeted to a mere 10 percent of their 1989 highs, those coins are necessarily gilt-edged bargains. In fact, quite the opposite may be true; rather than being greatly undervalued today, they simply may have been grossly overpriced at their market peaks.

Generic silver coins, in particular, rose to heights in 1989 that really weren't justified, now that we re-examine their marketplace performance with the benefit of 20-20 hindsight. A textbook example is the 1881-S Morgan silver dollar. In the late 1980s, this was one of the hottest coins in the marketplace, and thousands of buyers were only too happy to pay close to $1,000 apiece for specimens graded Mint State-65 by one of the major coin certification services. The coin was extremely popular with investors because it characteristically comes with sharp detail and brilliant, eye-popping luster. It was popular with sellers, including direct-mail marketing firms, because it was so readily available in pristine mint condition and thus could be used to sustain a major promotion requiring many hundreds of examples.

Market-watchers knew in 1989 that coins such as this were far from rare. Only later, though, did their true commonness come into sharp, clear focus. Since 1989, many thousands of additional 1881-S silver dollars have been certified in grades of Mint State-65 and higher by the top grading services. The certified populations of other generic silver coins also have grown by leaps and bounds. During that same period, most of the investors who coveted such coins in 1989 have deserted the coin market. Thus, these coins now offer exactly the opposite of what you would expect from a good investment: Their supply has risen dramatically, and demand for them has shrunk. Clearly, then, there isn't any basis for comparing the prices of generic silver coins today with the levels they enjoyed in 1989; it would be like comparing apples and oranges. The prices are dramatically lower today, it's true, but the coins to which they apply aren't really the same.

Mistake No. 12: *Expecting to enjoy the same negotiating power during a rally or bull market.*

Even people who educate themselves to the ways of the marketplace—who listen to experts' advice and follow it carefully—may find themselves at sea if the market gets hot all at once and prices begin to soar. The reason for this is what Maurice Rosen, publisher of the award-winning *Rosen Numismatic Advisory,* refers to as the "market-premium factor." In effect, the coin market has a built-in mechanism to reflect rising values during times when prices are moving up. Let's say a certain coin is listed at $1,000 in the weekly price guides. If the market is hot, you'll probably have to pay more than $1,000 for that coin, despite what the price guides say. That's because it's already on its way to a higher listing—perhaps $1,200—in the following week's guides. If the market is rising, you'll have to pay a premium; conversely, if the market is slipping, you ought to be able to get that coin for a discount. The coin market is extremely value-sensitive, and the value of a coin may very well be different at any given moment from what it was a month ago, a week ago, or even an hour ago. To understand this phenomenon more fully, read Chapter 4 of this book, "The Secrets of Coin Pricing."

Mistake No. 13: *Misjudging what is rare and what is not.*

People who are new to the field frequently draw incorrect conclusions about the true rarity and value of certain coins. Often, they are misled—deliberately or otherwise—by dealers who may not be very much better informed than they. To a new collector or investor, a set of coins including a Morgan silver dollar, a Mercury dime, and a Buffalo nickel might look like something of considerable value, just because these coins are now obsolete—especially if the coins are in a high level of preservation. Experienced collectors know that all these coins are readily available, especially if they're common-date pieces. Some of them, in fact, are as common as grains of sand on the beach. Even coins with much more limited mintages aren't necessarily great rarities. A good illustration is the high-relief Saint-Gaudens double eagle, or $20 gold piece. This 1907 coin is scarce, to be sure; only about 11,000 examples were produced. But it's what I would call a generic rarity: For those who have the money, plenty of examples are available. You need to get a feel for what is truly rare and what is not. You can get this kind of knowledge by attending auctions and studying auction catalogs and results, talking with dealers and other experts, reading the population and census reports issued by the leading certification services, and generally keeping abreast of everything that's occurring in the marketplace.

Mistake No. 14: *Storing your coins improperly.*

Coins need to be stored in a dry, stable environment. Moisture is a coin's deadly enemy; it can help set in motion a chemical reaction that will permanently damage the surface of the coin and drastically reduce its market value. It's also important to chemically neutralize the surface of a coin, or degrease it to remove impurities, before you place it in storage. And choosing the right holder is yet another crucial consideration: Pliable plastic "flips" made of polyvinyl chloride, or PVC, can wreak havoc on your coins, for example, and cardboard 2-by-2's can bring your coins in contact with flecks of loose paper that will lead to unsightly carbon spots. All too many people spend large amounts of money acquiring the right coins, only to see their investment go right down the drain because they didn't spend the modest sum of money required to store them properly. For further information on proper storage of coins, read the section on "Storage Risks" in Chapter 2 of this book.

CHAPTER 7

SECRETS OF THE PROFESSIONAL GRADERS

This chapter begins with an interview with a veteran dealer who reveals secrets. Interviews then follow with: David Hall, founder of the Professional Coin Grading Service (PCGS), Newport Beach, California; and John Albanese, founder of the Nu-

Figure 7-1. *An expert professional coin dealer examines and grades coins at a convention.* The nuances of coin grading can be daunting even for the most seasoned professionals.

mismatic Guaranty Corporation (NGC) of America, Parsippany, New Jersey. Albanese sold his interest in NGC in 1999, and this interview was conducted in 1995. All three men were patient and cooperative in answering some very tough questions.

TELL-ALL INTERVIEW WITH A VETERAN COIN DEALER

Jesse Lipka (Numismania Coins, P.O. Box 847, Flemington, NJ 08822. Tel. 908-782-1635) says that over the last decade he has done "millions and millions" of dollars' worth of business as a rare-coin dealer. Lipka is a familiar figure at coin conventions across the nation where he displays high-grade numismatic rarities worth many thousands of dollars apiece. This interview is a milestone for the rare-coin marketplace because traditionally dealers such as Lipka, who succeeded in the clubby, cliquish underbelly of the bourse floor, would closely guard the secrets that Lipka has so courageously revealed. In our interview, we touched on diverse topics ranging from state quarters to the problems of doctored coins at grading services. The opinions expressed are Lipka's and do not necessarily reflect the views of the author or publisher.

SCOTT TRAVERS: What do you think about coins as an investment?

JESSE LIPKA: Coins can be a very good investment, but only if you become really knowledgeable. Right now, there's a big emphasis on all this modern stuff. That's great for making money if you're manufacturing slabs and selling it to the public who can afford to buy things in the Internet market for a few hundred dollars. But true classics are always going to be the name of the game. And actually, there's a great opportunity right now, because the economy's really humming but all the professionals seem to be geared up toward the cheap coins on the Internet and a lot of the classic rarities haven't gone up and probably represent a great value. I mean, the very greatest rarities have certainly gone up—you know, the 1804 dollars and the 1913 nickels are worth as much as they've ever been.

TRAVERS: What do you think about the state quarters as an investment?

LIPKA: Well, I think it's great that state quarters have polarized the numismatic market and attracted so many new participants to our wonderful hobby. However, anybody who pays big money for proof or Mint-state state quarters in 69 and 70 is going to [lose big money].

TRAVERS: How long do you think these quarters will be popular and, by extension, bring along the U.S. rare-coin market in its popularity? This is a ten-year program. Has it already peaked? Is it going to peak in two years? Is it going to build? What do you think will happen?

LIPKA: Well, I just think that by 2010 it will definitely all be over. I think that it's a wonderful way to get people involved, but we have to switch them to real coins, to rare coins, once they are involved because basically they're just making hundreds of millions of these [state quarters] and the public is saving them in perfect condition. Therefore, I think the future of investing in them is bleak. If you want to make money on state quarters, make that money right now.

TRAVERS: Let's talk a little bit about some of the ways people are making money right now with modern coins. What's being done with modern coins?

LIPKA: People are taking large quantities of modern coins, assigning them a minimum grade at whatever minimum grade it takes for them to be able to profitably market them, sending them to a grading service and only paying grading fees for those coins which make their minimum grades. As a result, they can manufacture coins that might only be worth $25 to $50 but do it profitably, because they're not having to pay grading fees on those coins which don't make that particular grade.

TRAVERS: What's the approximate cost of a "minimum-grade" coin [submission] at a grading service?

LIPKA: Six to eight dollars.

TRAVERS: Are people making money right now other ways with modern coins, such as buying 50 States quarters in quantity and buying them at face value or slightly above and then selling them for several hundred percent more than that a short period of time later?

LIPKA: People are doing that. But everybody's on to it. The best opportunity for the state quarters was the first two issues, the Pennsylvanias and the Delawares. But right now, everybody's kind of on to that, so people are hoarding them by the bags. If you have any of that in stock, you should sell it right now and make your money *now,* because in the future people are going to realize just how many hundreds of millions of these coins exist in the highest possible grades.

TRAVERS: What do you think about the very dramatic increases in value of some of the modern Mint products—things that have gone from $30 to $300 over the last six to ten months?

LIPKA: I think that it's a flash in the pan. You should make your money right now. These are not the types of things to hold for a long term. I have been very amused recently by the claims over the double-denomination quarter/dollar Sacagaweas. There's something that's been overlooked by the numismatic press, and by everybody I've talked to about this. The fact is, here is a very, very expensive error that has no date. Now, when I was a kid, I learned that one should avoid errors that have no date. And because the obverse is that of a state quarter and the reverse is the Sacagawea, they have eight years in which to manufacture more of these. And the only way you can tell what year it's from is by the die variety and what year it possibly came out because these coins have no date. They're going to be using this obverse till 2008; they're going to be using this reverse possibly till long after that.

TRAVERS: All right. Let's talk about more conventional coins as investments, and the grading services, such as PCGS, NGC, and ICG. As you know, in the previous edition of *How to Make Money in Coins Right Now,* which came out in 1996, I had interviews with David Hall and John Albanese and we talked about the consistency of NGC and PCGS, respectively. What's your view of the consistency today at grading services?

LIPKA: As bad as ever. If you can get hold of a deal that was an original, fresh deal that's only been through a grading service once, odds are very much in your favor that there will be available upgrades. And of course, as all of your readers know, the best way to make money right now is to resubmit something to a grading service and get a higher grade. Then your profit is instantaneous.

TRAVERS: What have you seen recently relating to grading services that would convince you of their consistency or lack of consistency?

LIPKA: I see that there's more different grading services in business, and because they're seeing far more modern coins than anything else, they've lost their touch on the real coins—on classics. They're just not seeing as much of this stuff anymore. A lot of it has already been graded. Almost all of the old-time collections have already been graded and dispersed and the crack-out artists have already gotten hold of these after they've been through the first time and maxed them out. It takes a quantity of coins crossing your desk every day to be truly sure, truly consistent. I don't believe that the grading services have the ability to be truly consistent on real coins when they're spending 95 percent of their time grading state quarters in Proof-70.

TRAVERS: I don't think this has really been discussed before by anybody. You're basically saying that the graders of some of the leading services, in your personal opinion, might be a little stale right now.

LIPKA: I believe that. Also, we're at a point where both PCGS and NGC—none of these graders have been in the marketplace now for a number of years. When PCGS and NGC first started, they were employing graders who were playing both sides of the fence—people who were possibly dealing by day and grading at night. I think that kept them really sharp, because they had to put their own money on the line. Even after both services had gone to full-time graders for a couple of years, they still had the memories of being a dealer fresh in their perspective, fresh in their minds. But now, both PCGS and NGC have been using full-time graders for ten years or more. I believe that these people have lost their perspective. I believe that they just don't know what it is to put their own money on the line, and they're just—the ramifications of the grades that they put on are . . . They really can't see it from the other side of the fence.

TRAVERS: So how has that affected the accuracy of the grades given to real coins, classic coins, early collectible coins graded by the leading services?

LIPKA: Basically, I think that on many given days, the grading services are grading scared. When their complaints get to such a level and their submission volume goes low, then they overreact the other way. As a result, it leads to inconsistent grading over the long term.

TRAVERS: What have you seen recently that would bear this out—that was dramatically inconsistent or, in your opinion, just wrong?

LIPKA: Well, I have seen ... at one time, my success ratio on these crack-outs was 80 to 90 percent. I believe when you last interviewed me [in 1995] for this particular book, I had stated that my success ratio was down to 50 percent. These days, my success ratio is 20 to 30 percent, yet I'm more conservative, sharper, and more careful with my selections, and it's because the grading services are grading scared. They are more afraid of ridicule, of having to buy something back off the market, than they are of losing their submissions, or having declining submissions. I think that it's·been so long since they've had to put their own money on the line to correctly guess grades that they're no longer on the cutting edge.

TRAVERS: Talk about not being on the cutting edge, let's talk a little bit about coin doctors and coin doctors being on the cutting edge and the ability of grading services to be a step ahead of the coin doctors.

LIPKA: I tend to think it's the coin doctors that have always been a step ahead of the grading services.

TRAVERS: How about right now?

LIPKA: Well, the thing is, grading services have forced coin doctors to improve their techniques. In other collectibles such as art, such as paper money, people who are restoring material and doctoring material to fool their clients are really only having to fool their clients. Only in coins do doctors have to fool the experts to get their items sold. Necessity is the mother of invention, and these coin doctors are superb and use very, very subtle touches. Once upon a time, originality was valued, but now grading services have realized that coins that are white and bright are going to sell in any grade holders, so that's what they've encouraged. And the wonderful, original, beautifully toned coins that were marketable 15 years ago when coin dealers had to educate the public and a typical coin dealer was a coin expert, not a commodities dealer, it had a vogue because today's typical coin dealer—the person purveying slabs—is a commodities broker. They never really learned coins from the bottom up.

TRAVERS: How much income can a good coin doctor make per year?

LIPKA: If he can stay ahead of the services, unlimited. If a coin dealer with a certain technique can fool a grading service and he gets too greedy and all of a sudden the service sees thousands of coins that look the same way, they're not fools. They're going to figure it out. So if you're too greedy, you're going to get caught. So anybody who has a good technique is going to have to send in the coins a few here and a few there. Otherwise, they're going to get caught. If stuff that seems original just keeps coming in, hundreds of coins a day, you know, very shortly the grading services are going to recognize that this is possibly greed-influenced and as a result, they're going to shut it down.

TRAVERS: How prevalent is coin doctoring?

LIPKA: I guess I probably see it as more prevalent than, say, a collector might because being a large-volume wholesale dealer, I run into a lot of material and into a lot of people that are likely to want to [tamper with the appearance of] coins. But you know, if you buy a coin that's really nice for the grade and just has brilliant eye appeal, I don't think it's a big problem. I think that if a coin has been enhanced to . . . if a coin has been doctored to enhance its appearance, as long as it's not some technique that's going to cause long-term damage to the coin, it's not really relevant. An enhanced coin is going to be resalable; it can be resold.

TRAVERS: Using a ballpark number for all the coins that you see in shows—we're talking about over the last couple of months—what percentage of coins would you say have been doctored and found their way into holders?

LIPKA: It depends on your definition of "doctored." I would say probably 5 to 10 percent, if dipping and brightening are not doctoring. The services want white, bright coins, so people doctor to create white, bright coins. If dipping is not doctoring, then . . .

TRAVERS: What percent of the very high-value coins have been doctored, not including dipping as part of doctoring?

LIPKA: I would say in the 10 percent area. I think that one should look at as many coins as possible and get a feel for what really is original. When some auction company comes out with one of these seventy-five-year-old untouched collections, if you really want to learn you should go and look at those types of collections because then you'll know what original coins are and then you'll know what you're looking at when you see coins that are in holders in a dealer's inventory. Knowledge is attained simply by paying attention.

TRAVERS: What kind of coins are most likely to be cracked out as lower-grade coins, and which are more likely to get the higher grade?

LIPKA: Well, clearly, anything in an old holder. The grading services change their holders, it seems, every other year and obviously any coin that's been graded a long time ago might grade higher by today's standards. Standards aren't necessarily looser today, but grading services are more likely to max out an important coin, at least, that they haven't seen before or can't recall seeing before.

TRAVERS: Getting back to dipping, how can one of my readers tell if a coin will be able to *take* a dipping? What's your best professional advice from your years of experience in dipping coins?

LIPKA: After even my years of experience in dipping coins— and my confidence level should be far higher than that of a mere novice—I still make mistakes. Therefore, it's a very delicate situation, and one should be very, very cautious in dipping coins. One should show them to a full-time professional who has dipped thousands of coins before, before dipping. Also, right now, the services are on such a kick about white coins that you can get PCGS and NGC to dip your coins for you. If they're willing to take the risk, you might as well let them. Then your coin can only go up in grade and can't go down. And if it does go down, they at least claim that they will compensate you the difference.

TRAVERS: Let's get a little primer on how to identify doctored coins. Let's talk about the most common doctoring and alteration techniques and some of those kinds of coins that still slip by the services.

LIPKA: Well, gold, I believe, is the most doctored of the metals. There's one technique that some weeks after the coin is doctored, the coin has a bluish cast. One should avoid gold coins with bluish casts. Also, there are certain doctored coins that were doctored six, eight, ten years ago that while they were doctored, they still weren't graded by today's possibly looser standards. I have bought coins that were doctored in older holders to remove all the doctoring that was on them and still achieved a higher grade as an undoctored coin today.

TRAVERS: How can my readers identify coins that have putty on them or coins that have been thumbed?

LIPKA: One . . . let's see . . . thumbing gives coins a certain appearance. One can fool around with a few common $20 silver dollars and get an idea of what this appearance might be.

TRAVERS: Try and describe it as best you can.

LIPKA: Obviously, thumbing will create a slightly unnatural look, an unnatural haze of the high points. And so, with putty, the best way to identify doctored coins is to know what the original ones look like.

TRAVERS: What will [coins with] putty look like?

LIPKA: There are thousands of kinds of putty and they can all look different, and sometimes they change after a period of time. They've been puttying coins for twenty or more years. I have an acquaintance who bragged to me once that he went to a store and bought sixty different types of putty just to experiment on his coins. Therefore, there is no signature look that puttied coins might have, because as many different chemical compounds as exist, there could be different kinds of putty.

TRAVERS: Does putty today still fool grading services?

LIPKA: No, grading services are on to putty.

TRAVERS: What is the process today that the grading service would still be likely to grade a coin with that coin having had something done to it?

LIPKA: Well, the fact is, if I had some process that could fool grading services [so] that I could make a lot of money, I'd be fooling around with my coins and not giving interviews at this minute.

TRAVERS: (Laughs.) Well, you must have seen some things slip through [so] that you can come to some conclusion.

LIPKA: A lot of things that slip through aren't things that are definitely bad; they're things that are questionable. Because if they're definitely bad, the services ... they're trying to protect [themselves]. They're not going to put something that's obvious in a holder.

TRAVERS: What do you think about the accuracy of population and census reports?

LIPKA: Well, clearly they're inaccurate. Recently, a large accumulation of PCGS tags that I had acquired over a three-year period ... my father was trying to help me out and he tossed them out, thinking that they weren't worth anything, not realizing that not only would PCGS pay me fifty cents per tag in exchange for walk-throughs, but that my tags were incredibly valuable because I had tags from many, many finest-known coins. But I love my father with all my heart, so all I can do is get angry for a little while and go on to the next deal.

TRAVERS: How many tags did you have?

LIPKA: Probably a couple of thousand. I believe there were important tags in there.

TRAVERS: Important tags?

LIPKA: I did call up John Dannreuther regarding this terrible accident, and he said that over time that he was going over the pop report series by series, and if one coin was sent in multiple, multiple times by a submitter, that he would delete a lot of the additional appearances. So I'm not sure whether it's going to happen, but I'm trusting that eventually the pop reports will become more accurate. I believe that PCGS with John Dannreuther really, really cares about its pop report. I believe that NGC tends more to view its pop report as a sideline service;

it doesn't have quite the importance that PCGS places on its pop report, because I know of certain NGC coins that are out there that I can't even find in the pop report.

TRAVERS: Right now at this very moment in time that this interview is being conducted, July 23, 2000 . . . apparently, those pop reports are not all that accurate, considering that you had many finest-known coins that were resubmitted and the pop reports, I suppose, reflect multiple coins existing for great rarities.

LIPKA: But you can't really assume that all the pops are wrong because lots of coins only get sent in once and that's it, and generally I do return my tags. This was just an unfortunate occurrence.

TRAVERS: What do you think about the accuracy of the *Bluesheet–The Certified Coin Dealer Newsletter*?

LIPKA: The *Bluesheet* and all pricing data is accurate on things that trade constantly. It's very easy to ascertain the exact valuation of an 1881-S dollar in MS-65 because they trade every day and there's millions of them in existence and it's always easy to find out, using a computer, what the highest possible bid is and what the lowest possible ask is. The problem is, you get some rare coin, something that trades only every few years, and it's impossible to know what the market is. The market's what you can get somebody to pay for it, which is impossible to determine without really being in the thick of the market, without really having the feel of the people out there who are looking for it. The more esoteric an item is, the more difficult it is to evaluate—and that's true in coins, it's true in art, it's true in paper money, it's true in all collectibles, and all goods.

TRAVERS: What impact are the Internet and on-line auctions having on our field, and what do you think about it?

LIPKA: I think it's a wonderful thing. I think it opens up numismatics to everybody. When I was a kid, I saw rare coins as a closed clique, and I wanted to be in that clique so badly that I battled for many years, finally getting into the heart of the business. But today, I think that it's a much more even playing field because of the Internet and because of slabs.

TRAVERS: What do you think about the quality of the unslabbed coins offered by on-line auctioneers on the Internet?

LIPKA: I have not personally . . . I would only buy a coin sight-seen. There are occasions when I would buy a slabbed coin unseen if I have a client for it, or if I know something about the market that I can make an instant profit on it. But generally, 99 percent of the time, I want to buy only sight-seen coins.

TRAVERS: What's your opinion of coins that are uncertified that are being sold in regular catalogs? Is there a danger there of coins that have been doctored or altered that have not been able to make their way into grading-service holders being offered raw?

LIPKA: It depends. I mean, if something's in an estate sale and there are coins that some guy collected forty years ago and they've never had an opportunity to be certified, that's one thing. But in some of these auctions that sell raw coins, the only reason a dealer would sell some coin that's worth over two or three hundred dollars uncertified is because it won't make the grade that they want to sell it as. Any other explanation simply is irrational. If I have a coin that's worth two thousand dollars . . . if I'm selling it raw, it's because it won't certify in the grade that I need to make money, and that's why I avoid selling raw coins altogether because it's so obvious. On the other hand, many dealers make a living off naïve clientele, and they'll believe anything that they're selling.

TRAVERS: Are grading services helping the business, giving back to the business, employing intelligent, decent people who are supportive of the business and are going to help us grow into the new Internet marketplace that we've always desired to be, or is there something different than that going on?

LIPKA: I believe that there are individuals at the grading services that love numismatics and want things to be—you know, want to further numismatics and want to give back to numismatics. I also believe that the grading services have sucked hundreds of millions of dollars out of the coin business and put them into their stock portfolios. I believe that the grading services today, if they were to make a million dollars in coins, they wouldn't be going out and spending that money on coins or on anything coin-related. I believe it would be going into their stock portfolio, and I think that overall they're taking out more than they're adding. Which is not to say that they have evil intent or anything, but you know, if I can figure out a way to make a million bucks buying and selling coins and paper money, I'm probably going to take that million bucks and buy coins or paper money. I believe that if the grading services make a buck, it's gone from the industry forever.

TRAVERS: If you could make two recommendations to the grading services for ways of giving something back in exchange for what they have taken in, what two suggestions would you have for them?

LIPKA: I don't believe there *could* be a fair exchange. I mean, they can educate people—and I believe the major grading services do want to educate people. But considering the millions they've made off this hobby, there's no way they can give that back.

TRAVERS: Are you disappointed in what grading services have done for the hobby?

LIPKA: It was inevitably going to happen. I believe that certainly numismatics is a far bigger industry today than it would've been had no grading services ever come forward.

TRAVERS: Forgetting the size of the industry and setting that aside, do you think that overall we would be better off today without grading services than with them? Or are we better off with the services than without them?

LIPKA: I think we're better off with the services. I think that before services, numismatics was very cliquish and it was very difficult to get yourself into the clique. I remember as a kid finding gem coins and being unable to sell them for MS-65 because I wasn't in the right clique to sell to the people who were the correct marketers. It took years of pounding the pavement to get into that clique, to get to the point where marketers wanted to buy coins from me. As a result, people who bought gem coins often were forced to sell them for choice money because they had no way of accessing people who would pay, you know, who would buy a gem coin for gem money. I think that slabs and the Internet level the playing field. I think overall, slabs are probably a good thing. One bad thing about slabs is, if a coin changes after some doctor [alters its appearance], it stays in the holder forever. The services say they want to get the overgraded coins off the market, but obviously that would cost them money and I don't believe that that's their real intent. If they can dip a coin for you without taking any undue risk on their own part, they will. But if there's any risk at all, you're going to get the coin back undipped.

TRAVERS: Do you have confidence personally in the future of the U.S. rare-coin market, and are you expanding your inventory of rare coins?

LIPKA: I have tended, over the last two years, to increase my position in the rare paper money market. I believe that coins as a fully mature market are very close to full maturation. I believe that every series has been picked apart, to where a lot of numismatics has been overdone. A lot of the angles—I mean, right now, there must be a hundred books out there on Morgan dollars. Every die variety has been explored ... people are splitting hairs to find reasons to collect this stuff. While I believe that if you buy classic rarities, you're always going to be OK, I think it's very hard to find a little niche in coins that nobody else has already thought of. And if you can find such a niche, you might be able to hype it and make it seem important, but it's not really going to be important. As a result, I'm looking for other areas in numismatics other than mainstream coins that have yet to be fully developed. I believe that rare American legal-tender paper money is one such area, and I've been concentrating on that over the last several years.

TRAVERS: Where do you think grading services will be in three to five years?

LIPKA: I believe that there may be more in three to five years than there are now, and unfortunately more and more they're deriving their income from modern coins and things that are truly not important and have limited long-term prospects.

TRAVERS: I want your overall analysis of the positive attributes of PCGS, NGC, and ICG. Why don't we limit it to a couple of positive attributes of each of those services, starting with PCGS.

LIPKA: Well, PCGS coins are the most salable of any grading service. I believe that they have the financial strength that they're going to be around for a long, long time. And I believe that. All of the services have a standard. PCGS, by and large, at least, does stick to its standard and perhaps of the three major grading services, as a result they are the most predictable.

TRAVERS: OK . . . NGC.

LIPKA: NGC has at least a couple of graders that really love coins and really, really love numismatics—and NGC has more graders that actually made a living as rare-coin dealers. I also am impressed with NGC's error attribution. And, of course, NGC is conveniently located.

TRAVERS: OK, ICG.

LIPKA: ICG's best attribute is that they give grades to eye appeal. The types of coins that ICG will max out are types of coins that will sell in any holders. I believe that ICG has the best future on the upside of any of the three services. I think that Keith Love is going to do everything in his power to create a viable product and create value for consumers.

INTERVIEW WITH DAVID HALL
(FOUNDER, PROFESSIONAL COIN GRADING SERVICE [PCGS])

SCOTT TRAVERS: What do you think of PCGS's consistency?

DAVID HALL: I think that it's reasonably consistent but not as consistent as I would like it to be. There's always somewhat of a subjectivity, and there's always those 5 or 10 percent—I'm not sure exactly what the right figure is—of coins that are liner coins that some days are 63 and some days are 64.

TRAVERS: It sort of seems as if the whole industry—at least the part of the industry that revolves around grading services—is based on the ability of a handful of people at each service.

HALL: They have a tremendous impact in a certain aspect of the coin market. And in that regard, Ron Howard is one of the most powerful men in the market.

TRAVERS: How does it make you feel that there are people out there trying to second-guess the graders at PCGS?

HALL: It certainly wasn't why we started PCGS. But I guess they're sort of like arbitrage traders in any market. And I think in the big picture, the arbitrage people—"crack-out artists," I guess you'd call them in the coin market—don't really have a significant impact on the direction of the market.

TRAVERS: PCGS looks at a coin, and perhaps the coin is worth $10,000 as a 65 and $2,000 as a 64, and it's kind of splitting hairs between whether it's called 65 or 64. If you call it 65, you've created wealth—you've given possibly $8,000 to the submitter. On the other hand, if you call it a 64, in a sense you're taking wealth away. How does that make you feel?

HALL: Well, again, we didn't start PCGS to feed this arbitrage that's developed over minute differences in grade. I accept that it's part of the business. And in my mind, I think it's actually overemphasized. I think that the crack-out arbitrage artists don't do as well as they say they do. I sometimes review coins; I'm not a grader, but I sometimes review coins just to sort of see what's going on. And in my mind, the arbitrage crack-out artists take huge risk, and they lose as often as they win.

TRAVERS: Let's talk about those coins that are resubmitted—the coins that are right-at-the-edge coins, the ones where they could be the lower grade or the higher grade. How can somebody outguess the experts? What do your graders look for when they're sitting there in their rooms grading the coins?

HALL: You're asking me a couple of different questions. First is, what do the graders look for. And the graders basically look at the same thing that all coin dealers look at when they're grading coins. For Mint State coins, they're looking at strike, luster, the amount of marks, and the eye appeal of the coin. The coin that does the best at PCGS is the coin that has great eye appeal. One of the sayings in the grading room is that eye appeal adds a little and forgives a lot. So good-looking coins will do the best at PCGS.

TRAVERS: What kinds of coins are most likely to be cracked out as lower-grade coins and are most likely to get the higher grade?

HALL: The coins that are most often cracked out, at least by the professionals, are those that have the biggest spread between the grades—those with the biggest financial incentive to crack out.

TRAVERS: And the lowest downside on the lower grade?

HALL: I think that most coin dealers are huge risk-takers and don't properly assess the downside. I think a lot of them don't even think about it. It is my experience that most coin dealers aren't that sophisticated.

TRAVERS: What do you think about dipping?

HALL: I think that silver coins, in particular, can be dipped and you can't tell whether they're dipped or not. Now, they can be *over*-dipped, and the luster gets stripped away. Dipping is cumulative.

TRAVERS: How can someone tell if a coin will be able to take a dipping?

HALL: First of all, you have to decide what the object is. Most coins have more to lose than gain by dipping. So if a coin looks original and has a little color, that's a plus—certainly at PCGS. And there would be no reason to dip that coin. Only if perhaps there's a minor fingerprint—say, on a proof Walking Liberty half dollar—or a little bit of haze in the field. That coin could possibly—possibly—improve in appearance if it had a light dip. What you're looking for is maybe light discoloration, light haze, a light fingerprint—light, light, light, light, light. Little, little—something small. If a coin is heavily toned, in some cases it digs into the surface of the coin. That coin is going to look horrible after you dip it, so you're going to go from bad to worse. Encrusted, mottled, yucky toning—just deal with it; don't dip the coin. It's 10 to 1 that it will turn out better.

TRAVERS: What are the coins that are most likely to be on the edge, where PCGS isn't sure—where a grader like Ron Howard might actually sit there and labor over the coin and say, "I'm just not sure. Should I call this a 64 or a 65?"

HALL: As he does! I don't know what you're telling your readers, but I want to stress that in my opinion, professional crack-out artists have a difficult time. Yes, they win. Yes, some of them make a very good living at it. They are extremely talented rare-coin graders. It is, in my opinion, a total and complete waste of time for a novice to try to make a hit cracking coins out or sending them in for regrades.

TRAVERS: What coins would Ron likely labor over and say, "Should I call it 64 or call it 65?"

HALL: Coins that are on the line. A coin that's a very high-end for the grade that it's in. And how do you tell? You have to be a professional coin grader. You have to just have 20 years of experience and have looked at a hundred million dollars' worth of coins and won and lost a lot of money buying and selling coins. I do have a rare coin firm, and believe it or not, we really don't crack coins out.

TRAVERS: You *never* crack coins out, or you just generally don't?

HALL: Occasionally, we'll send in coins through the PCGS re-grade service, maybe 5 or 10 coins a month.

TRAVERS: You own a coin firm. Do you *ever* grade coins at PCGS?

HALL: No.

TRAVERS: What coin types do you think people would have the greatest crack-out advantage with?

HALL: This may sound incredible, but I've never really thought of it in those terms—that a particular type is easier to make, so to speak, than the others. I know there are *some* coins that are really, really *hard* to make, and all you have to do is just look at the population report. You'll see, for instance, that a $2½ Indian in MS-67 is going to be hard to make. Therefore, if you have a $2½ Indian in MS-66, it's probably pretty foolish to try to get it to grade MS-67.

TRAVERS: Let's talk about some of the more obvious scores. How about coins in older holders, both from your service and from NGC. Coins graded maybe in 1987. Magnificent, brilliant cameo proofs in 65 holders that people might be able to crack out and get 66 or 67 on because you graded under a tighter standard in 1987. I mean, it's no secret that the standards today at both services are not what they were in 1987.

HALL: I disagree with that a little bit. I think that what was happening in '86 and '87 was, the graders were extremely reluctant to grade coins above 65. It was impossible to get a 67, 68, or 69. But in terms of coins that are 63 and 64, there are some people who will pay premiums for old-holder deals.

TRAVERS: I just had one walk in the door—all in PCGS 63 holders. Very old holders. They were graded 63. I'm reasonably certain most of those coins will grade 65. Many of them will grade 64. Some will grade 66. They were all graded in, I think, 1986 and '87.

HALL: It depends on the old-holder deal. I've seen old-holder deals that are embarrassing. In fact, through our guarantee resubmission program, we occasionally buy back coins in old holders.

TRAVERS: So are there any particular coins that you think back in 1986 were more tightly graded? Type coins, for example, that were brilliant, that are in 65 holders.

HALL: I think in general, stuff that is in 65 and 66 holders— again, I think the real difference is the total reluctance in '86 and '87 for graders to grade coins 67 and 68.

TRAVERS: Let's talk a little bit about the problem of coin doctoring. Why don't you talk a little bit about how PCGS has put together an educational grading set of doctored coins.

HALL: Well, we have as part of our grader reference set several boxes—and there's two things. There's counterfeit coins, and then there's doctoring. And we have reference examples of both. Some of our friends who are dealers—every time they buy a counterfeit coin, they'll send it to us for our reference set. In terms of doctoring, sometimes when we make a mistake and have to buy it back through guaranteed resubmission, rather than reselling the coin, we'll put it in the reference set to make sure that we don't make that mistake again. So after a 10-year period we have a nice group of about 40 or 50 coins, and we display them at coin shows a couple of times a year to give people a little education as to what exactly to look for and what doctored coins actually look like. And it's real hard to show pictorially what coin doctoring looks like. It's real hard without actually looking at the coin to really describe what it looks like. But if you put one that *is* next to one that isn't, there's a difference and it's clearly discernible.

TRAVERS: Let's give a little primer on how to identify a doctored coin. Let's talk about the most common doctoring or alteration techniques.

HALL: For a puttied coin, it won't have the typical luster, the typical shine to it. It will look subdued—but not subdued like a coin that is subdued over time. It'll look almost kind of gunky. You can smell bleaching, if that's done to a coin, but that's not so widespread anymore. Epoxy is usually used on proofs, and it's so overly bright—especially where it shouldn't be, like over planchet flaws and hairlines and stuff—that I don't think epoxy is a big problem. The two major issues are artificial toning and then adding stuff to the surfaces. As for thumbing, this is a variation of the puttying. It's where you add a little body oil to a coin to maybe dull the luster over an area that has marks. Artificial toning is a very subjective look that's hard to describe. But if you look at original toned coins for 20 years, they have a certain way the colors look. If you look at an artificially toned coin, it's the wrong color, the wrong combination of colors, the colors aren't smooth as they run into each other.

TRAVERS: How about advising people to look beneath the surface to see whether a coin is artificially toned?

HALL: I don't think that's a way to tell whether a coin is artificially toned or not, because a nicely toned coin can have scratches, nicks, marks, planchet flaws underneath the toning.

TRAVERS: How big a problem do you think doctoring is, and artificial toning is, for coins that are sold at public auctions?

HALL: Well, if they're third-party certified, most of the more recognized third-party services do a fairly good job of catching the doctoring. And certainly, PCGS has a grading guarantee that takes care of mistakes when they *don't* catch it. It's a huge problem for the grading services in that we're constantly bombarded with it. For the consumer, we're the buffer in between. For non-third-party-graded coins—coins that you would buy raw at public auction—unless you're buying them from an old-time collection . . . say, the Eliasberg Collection . . . I think that at least 50 percent of all coins sold raw have been doctored. Basically, it's a way for the dealers to dump their no-grades.

TRAVERS: What percentage of coins that have been doctored do you think have made their way into your holders?

HALL: That's hard to say, and it really depends on what you define as doctoring, and what is acceptable and what isn't acceptable. Blatantly doctored coins, I think the percentage would be very, very low. If a person were to just thumb lightly the surface of a silver dollar, often the best experts in the world can't even tell it's been done. You almost wonder why the doctors do it.

TRAVERS: And if they *can* tell, you might still put it in a holder anyway because it's generally accepted in the marketplace?

HALL: Right. If it was real light. And a thumbed coin can sometimes look exactly like a coin that you would pull out of an original mint-sewn bag, with a little bit of moisture haze or whatever. So it depends on the severity of the doctoring. Blatantly doctored coins, I think a very, very, very low percentage get through.

TRAVERS: How about coins with very light puttying? Would PCGS knowingly put some of those in holders once in a while if it were extremely light and not likely to interfere with the appearance that much?

HALL: If we think that it's actually been puttied, we won't do it. If we think that, well, there's a little haze on the coin—is it real or not?—and you can't tell, then haze is a negative in terms of eye appeal and it would be given an appropriately lower grade. But knowingly? If we knew that a bunch of coins had been lightly hazed, we wouldn't put them into holders.

TRAVERS: On a coin which has been thumbed, is it possible for the coin to deteriorate after it's in the holder because what's used for thumbing—the body moisture—can react with the coin and later lower its level of preservation?

HALL: It could. But if a person very lightly thumbs it, you couldn't even tell it's been thumbed. I don't think it's a big issue, because we're basically talking about silver coins. A copper coin would, of course, be much, much different. In terms of the deterioration in the holders, it is true that some coins change—some naturally, some unnaturally—and that's why PCGS has a grading guarantee and we stand behind our product. We want the consumer to be able to buy PCGS coins with confidence and know that if there *is* a mistake—and we certainly admit that we're not perfect—that we'll take care of it.

TRAVERS: Do you think it's a liability to you that you guarantee the grade of copper coins? They really do turn color in the holders.

HALL: Yes, some do. And we look at it as a cost of business. We've been doing this 10 years, and it's averaged about $20,000 a month; maybe four or five coins a month come back and they're mistakes and we buy them back.

TRAVERS: Wasn't there a Proof-69 Indian cent that you certified and the coin grew a spot after it had been certified?

HALL: $50,000! It's in the grading room—in the grader reference set. And on the holder, we have typed: "The $50,000 fingerprint."

TRAVERS: Do you think that this could pose some type of a financial burden on you sometime in the future?

HALL: No. Maybe we were gambling a little at first. Maybe we were a little arrogant about our ability at first. But we now have a 10-year track record. And in fact, our auditors actually make us put a certain amount of money in reserve to take care of guaranteed resubmission buy-backs. And it's based on our approximate $20,000-a-month average.

TRAVERS: Three graders on each coin. What percentage of the time would you say that the graders agree with what the final grade is?

HALL: Where all three would be the same grade? Seventy percent. A good grader is 70 percent.

TRAVERS: What type of grading percentages would you say your graders have?

HALL: It depends on the series. The easiest coins for graders to grade are Morgan dollars, and you can be 80 to 85 percent correct if you're a real good grader. The hardest coins to grade are probably low-grade type coins. By low-grade, I mean low-grade Mint State type coins. The hardest of all would be early type coins in circulated grades—but then you have an argument over what you consider correct. If a person grades a coin VF-30 and the final grade is VF-35, is he wrong? But with type coins, 65 to 75 percent—and they're probably the hardest.

TRAVERS: Give me a guesstimate: What percentage of coins do you think people have cracked out of PCGS holders?

HALL: I would say for coins that have a big spread, 50 percent. Cheap coins, extremely low. Bullion gold, very low. This is from a total of 4,318,357 submittals.

TRAVERS: Out of that number, what would you say is the percentage—just a guesstimate—the percentage of those coins that people have cracked out and resubmitted?

HALL: Well, large numbers of those coins are inexpensive silver dollars and bullion gold. So let's say there's 2 million of those. And then there are real cheap coins. I would say there's been several hundred thousand coins cracked out—anywhere between 200,000 and 500,000. But the thing is, it's not so much the number of coins; it's the fact there are certain coins that can be resubmitted 20, 30, 40 times just because they're high-spread coins that are high-end examples of a grade that have a good look. With that kind of coin, a guy might submit it five, six, seven, eight, nine, ten times. He sells it; some other guy submits it five, six, seven times. It just has the look.

TRAVERS: What does that do to your population reports?

HALL: When the people don't turn in the tags, it skews the reports. We actually keep track of the high submitters and try to harass them to do that.

TRAVERS: What do you think about the *Bluesheet*—the *Certified Coin Dealer Newsletter*?

HALL: I think that with what a lot of us did—and I'm the guy that started all of this—there was a flaw in our thinking, and the flaw was the lack of capital in the marketplace. A bid-based system does not work. I think the only thing that would really work for coins—or any other collectibles—is an electronic trading system based on ask prices. As it is now, the bid prices for coins can be based on things that have nothing to do with the coins' value. For instance, a guy goes on vacation and takes down his bids. It could be as simple as that. A couple of coins come on the marketplace, a guy needs some money—and he hits a bid. Does that mean the coins are worth less, or a guy was just desperate and had to sell an MS-65 Barber half because he needed some money? The way coins are traded does not have a direct relationship to their value. It's backwards.

TRAVERS: Where will grading services be in three to five years?

HALL: Well, we've talked about the problems of grading services. Let's talk about the one thing that grading services do: In any marketplace where the seller represents the quality of a product and the quality has something to do with price, you need a buffer. You need a third-party arbitrator on that quality issue. And that is what grading services do. And they do it successfully—not perfectly, but they certainly do it successfully, and there is no reason for the consumer to abandon that idea. And PCGS has taken that idea to other marketplaces, and particularly sports cards, and the consumer is embracing it incredibly. And the reason is, it works for the consumer. So there *will* be grading services in the future.

INTERVIEW WITH JOHN ALBANESE
(Founder, Numismatic Guaranty Corporation of America, Inc. [NGC])
Note: Albanese sold his interest in NGC in 1999

TRAVERS: How did NGC come about?

ALBANESE: With a checkbook. I was one of the initial founders of PCGS, and at the time I was tired of traveling to 30 or 40 coin shows every year. I had gotten married and we were starting a family, so I wanted to do something where I could settle down.

TRAVERS: Did you dislike what the other service was doing, or did you just feel that you could do better?

ALBANESE: I thought I could do better, number one. At the time, I really wasn't aware of the amount of coins we would get; doing a business plan, I was thinking we'd get 5,000 coins a month, and I would have been happy with that. As it turned out, the industry boomed shortly after we opened NGC. In 1988, coins took off again.

TRAVERS: What did you do about grading standards back then?

ALBANESE: I think we did the same thing we do now:

Whether it's popular or not, we really grade according to what we think the coins are worth. In other words, it's sort of instinctive as a coin trader—as a coin wholesaler—that if you pick up a Saint-Gaudens and in your mind it's worth $1,000, you grade it 65, because that's where the market will accept it, as a 65. If you grade it 64, it'll obviously be cracked out. If you grade it 66, even though technically it might be a 66, it doesn't sit well with coin dealers, because here's a 66 that's only worth $1,000. I'm not saying that we always market-grade coins, but it's very important that the grade you assign a coin corresponds to the value—at least be close to the value. Otherwise, the market won't accept it.

TRAVERS: How about the grading set? Is that still used?

ALBANESE: It's still used, but it's not used that frequently. It's not something that we usually use. Unfortunately, with the coins that are hard to grade—like a 1795 half cent where you're trying to decide between 61 and 62—you really can't go to a grading set. Other services brag that they have the biggest grading sets, but it doesn't do us much good to have 20, 1880-S Morgan dollars in a grading set, because we pretty much grade those very easily. What we really would need in the grading set would be the tougher coins—the early coinage and things like that—and it might cost $10 million to put together a set like that.

TRAVERS: What do you think about NGC's consistency?

ALBANESE: I think we're the most consistent service out there.

TRAVERS: It seems as if the whole industry is based on the ability of a couple of people—based a good deal on the way John Albanese, Mark Salzberg, and Jeff Isaac perceive the market value of a coin to be. How does it make you feel that people are out there trying to second-guess the graders at NGC—people who are world-class experts in their field?

ALBANESE: I wouldn't say it makes me feel either good *or* bad, really. It's sort of unfortunate that that's the case. It has taken away the independence of some other firms. There are still people fighting grading services; they had things their way for many years. And that's fine. However, the grading services were formed for a good reason—to do away with the blatant overgrading that took place in the 1960s, 1970s, and early 1980s. A coin doesn't have to be graded in order to be a good deal. If you're a knowledgeable collector and you know how to grade, you don't need a grading service.

TRAVERS: Don't you feel as though you're a creator of wealth? You look at a coin, NGC looks at a coin, and it's worth $10,000 as a 65 and $2,000 as a 64 and it's kind of splitting hairs between whether it's called 65 or 64. If you call it 65, you've created wealth—you've given possibly $8,000 to the submitter.

ALBANESE: That's true. But on the other hand, you could also take away $8,000. I'm not crazy about it. Again, NGC tries to assign a grade which corresponds to the value.

TRAVERS: Talk about your personal feelings, though. How does that make you feel when you look at that coin, when you're grading it, knowing that splitting the hairs could mean 8,000 bucks one way or the other?

ALBANESE: I don't think we really look at it that way when we grade a coin. We don't look at it as being worth this in this grade or that in that grade. Most coins are pretty easy to call. I can sit down with 20 coins in front of me and tell you how they grade, and you would probably agree very quickly with 18 of them. We might have a discussion about two of them.

TRAVERS: But those aren't the ones that are resubmitted— the ones that are easy to call. The ones that are resubmitted, where you're talking about wealth-building for somebody—where you're talking about creating wealth or taking it away—are those right-at-the-edge coins, the ones where they can be the lower grade or the higher grade. Give us some secrets here. How can somebody outguess the experts here?

ALBANESE: I think if anything, at least from a buying standpoint, if you're going to give the benefit of the doubt to a coin, it has to be a nice-looking, eye-appealing coin. There *are* some coins that we see even today where we'll say, "Hey, this is a 65," but it's ugly—it has ugly toning. And we might penalize it and call it 64.

TRAVERS: Suppose someone's looking to crack out coins. If they're looking to take a coin that's technically a 64 but has great eye appeal, great aesthetic appeal, satinlike luster, dripping with luster perhaps—what should they look for? What should they do? What kinds of coins are most likely to be cracked out as lower-grade coins so they can get the higher grade?

ALBANESE: From what I hear and what I see, it's generally people buying the uglier coins that are technically 65 but ugly, and taking a chance and cracking them out and dipping them. They might have a 65 when they're finished, they might have a 61. Who knows? But that seems to be where, if you're knowledgeable, you can usually tell—depending on your degree of knowledge—whether a coin will dip out nicely.

TRAVERS: Try to describe as best you can, using the most vivid adjectives, what a coin should look like if it will dip out properly—and what it might look like if it won't be able to take a dipping.

ALBANESE: Actually, it's somewhat more complicated than that. You have to understand the issue. You have to know what date the coin is, first of all. Some coins that are very prooflike might show hairlines more readily. That might be more of a dangerous coin to dip. If you have a toned coin that's prooflike, it might be dangerous, because the surfaces are so delicate. Whereas if you have a coin with somewhat of a crusty surface, like an 1892 quarter or an 1865 quarter or something like that—with a crusty, granular surface, where the fields are much tougher—you have a better chance there of the coin dipping out nice.

TRAVERS: Give me a list of a few coins that you think people would do best in cracking out. What are the coins that are most likely to be on the edge, where you're not sure? What do you sit there and labor over and say, "I'm just not sure . . . do you think I should call it a 65?"

ALBANESE: I don't want to create a circumstance in your book where people read the book and start cracking out coins and dipping them because, to me, that's very dangerous. Only an experienced professional should do it—and even professionals lose a lot of money doing it. So I don't really want to encourage it, because it could be very dangerous to your financial health.

TRAVERS: Let's not talk about dipping then. Let's just talk about cracking coins out. What coins do you labor over?

ALBANESE: Generally, it would be a coin that's, let's say either a 65 or a 66—where maybe the coin is technically a 65½ or something, but it has incredible eye appeal.

TRAVERS: How many coins has NGC graded?

ALBANESE: It's got to be close to 2 million by now.

TRAVERS: And out of 2 million coins, give me a guesstimate: How many coins do you think have been cracked out?

ALBANESE: Maybe 50,000. I don't really know. Recently, a coin came in—an 1874 $3 gold piece in proof—and it was told to me by Jeff Isaac that he's seen the coin here at least 10 times in the last few months. It's a 64 coin, but it has a great cameo. It doesn't quite make 65 because it has too many hairlines, but it's close.

TRAVERS: Describe the difference. What would push the coin over into the 65 category?

ALBANESE: To me, 65 means gem, so it has to be a little bit special. It's almost like an emotional thing, being a 65. It's a gem—and this thing just had too many hairlines for us to call it a gem.

TRAVERS: What coin types do you think people would have the greatest crack-out advantages on?

ALBANESE: Well, it seems to me in the last few years, from what I've heard, the biggest scores I've heard of were generally people buying at auction proof gold coins with a film on them. In fact, this happened with the 1872 proof set. We caught hell for having graded it, but it was worth double after we graded it from what it brought in the auction. These coins had a fine, bluish film on them, and on the film there were little scratches—almost like grease marks. They looked like hairlines. But the dealers who bought them cracked them out and dipped them, and the coins came out fabulous. PCGS actually graded them even higher after we graded them. But the point is, there *are* gold coins at auction—these proof gold coins—that may not bring that much money because they appear to have hairlines on this bluish film. They're simply grease-marked. And the dealers dip them, and they make huge scores. On the other hand, if they're wrong—and sometimes the film is covering hairlines—they can also lose five figures on a coin.

TRAVERS: How about some other scores? How about coins in older NGC holders—coins from 1987 and 1988? Magnificent, brilliant cameo proofs in 65 holders that people might be able to crack out and get 66s and 67s?

ALBANESE: I don't have any knowledge of that. I've heard of it—but again, mostly it's people dipping the coins. It seems to me actually, if we've made any kind of changes in the last few years, we're a little bit tougher on darker coins. In the first few years, we were actually criticized for being too liberal on toned coins. Maybe that's true, maybe it's not—but it seems to me that without making a conscious effort, but after being criticized for years and years and years for being too liberal on toned coins, maybe we're now a little bit tighter on toned coins. And maybe we're a little bit looser on brilliant coins. Perhaps we were too fussy on a perfectly white Barber half dollar in proof; we would call it 65 if it had a slight hairline. Maybe we would 66 some of those coins today. On the other hand, if it were a toned Barber half in 66, maybe we would 65 it today.

TRAVERS: Do you personally or corporately submit coins to PCGS or any other grading service?

ALBANESE: No, I don't.

TRAVERS: You only buy the coins after they've been certified.

ALBANESE: Correct.

TRAVERS: What stories have you heard or seen on the bourse floor about coins that have been cracked out and upgraded—or, on the other hand, coins where people lost their shirts? And I don't mean dipped coins—just coins.

ALBANESE: It's kind of funny, because you hear all these stories. People who are outside the circle seem to exaggerate; they hear about a certain dealer making $20,000 on a coin or something like that. It seems to me that people hear these stories of these fabulous scores and these upgrades and things like that, but if you take maybe the 30 biggest dealers who would rely on that for a business in the last few years, maybe since 1990, I would suspect that at least 25 of them have lost at least three-quarters of their capital by doing this. So if they were that successful, if there were that many upgrades, these guys would be on a yacht right now—but they're not. To me, it seems very exaggerated, this upgrade business.

TRAVERS: What percentage of the time do your graders agree with the final grade? I mean your best graders.

ALBANESE: I think it's 90-plus percent. Because we're human, I think we all have [consistency] problems. I will look at a coin at 3 o'clock and then, when it's shown to me 10 minutes later, it doesn't look as good or it looks better. I think as far as humans go, we do the best job we can. If you're asking do we have a problem being 100 percent, of course we do.

TRAVERS: So if you look at a coin in the morning, it could be a 64, and then in the afternoon be a 63?

ALBANESE: That happens sometimes. It's scary. It's happened to me since I was seven years old, and I don't know what to do about that. Maybe we should just grade all of our coins at 8 o'clock in the morning and no other time; I don't know. I think we do the best job we can, humanly. But are we 100 percent consistent? Of course not.

TRAVERS: What if somebody has a coin they've bought on a retail basis and they feel it has been misgraded? What's the procedure?

ALBANESE: We get resubmissions every day. Whether the coins go up or down, we get these coins every day.

TRAVERS: What type of recourse do consumers have if they buy a coin that's in a 65 holder and they feel it's not a 65, it's a 63?

ALBANESE: You send the coin to an authorized dealer on a resubmission form, and NGC looks at the coin again. In fact, we've lowered about six silver dollars and better-date gold coins already today.

TRAVERS: And what happens? Do you pay the people money?

ALBANESE: Yes. We pay the difference between the two grades.

TRAVERS: What do you use as the basis for that?

ALBANESE: Generally, it's the *Bluesheet.* But sometimes, if it's a special circumstance, we use something else.

TRAVERS: How many coins a year would you say you do that with?

ALBANESE: I don't know. It's in the hundreds, I know that.

TRAVERS: Over the years, NGC has also changed its holders. Explain the different types of holders and why that occurred, and perhaps the dates.

ALBANESE: We just changed our holder again because we wanted it to be thinner. It was a little bit too thick. And we put holograms on the holders [as a security precaution] in, I guess, sometime in 1990. And that was the most major change we made.

TRAVERS: Do you think that by having several holders, that this kind of dates when a coin was graded?

ALBANESE: I guess it does, yes.

TRAVERS: Do you see a liability to you from silver coins turning color in their holders?

ALBANESE: Well, I don't know. The coins are toning, OK? Unfortunately, we can't control what has happened to a coin before we holdered it. If someone put their fingerprint on it, or somebody was breathing on it—we can't control that. If someone dipped it improperly—unfortunately, we can't control that. We do get maybe five coins a month that people claim have really toned in the holder. In fact, the other day, an arrows-and-rays half dollar came in that looked terrible. And it was in a 64 holder.

TRAVERS: But you're required, under your guarantee, to buy this back.

ALBANESE: In this case, a dealer owned it and he sent it to us and he wanted us to dip it for him. We dipped it, it came out beautiful, and it's fine. I think probably the coin, when we graded it three or four years ago, wasn't properly dipped.

TRAVERS: But what would happen, though, with coins—and there *have* been some, and I've seen some myself and I have some right here—silver coins with high grades that turn color in the holders and look horrible? Do you end up buying those coins back?

ALBANESE: We have in the past made up for the loss, yes. We have lowered the grade and given the coin back to the customer.

TRAVERS: So that's sort of a security blanket for a consumer against a coin deteriorating. A consumer who doesn't even like slabs can buy a $100,000 or $50,000 coin, and if it deteriorates in the holder and he bought it as a 65 and it then deteriorates to a 64, you would buy the coin back?

ALBANESE: Yes.

TRAVERS: You know they can deteriorate in the holders—they can and they have.

ALBANESE: Some have, although it seems to me in most cases—literally in 98 percent of the cases—the coins dip out fine. If a coin is nice to start with, it should dip out fine. But this is a very small percentage of the coins.

TRAVERS: Is the holder airtight, or under some circumstances will air be allowed in the holder?

ALBANESE: The holder's airtight.

TRAVERS: What are some coins that are difficult to grade?

ALBANESE: People say that the Indian gold is hard to grade. I personally don't find it hard to grade. But again, my tough material are these early coins.

TRAVERS: How about coin doctoring; what kind of a problem is that?

ALBANESE: It's a big problem. We must have no-graded about 50 coins today. A lot of coins came in with putty on them and polished surfaces. It's a problem.

TRAVERS: Are you taking any general precautions against coin doctoring?

ALBANESE: The best we can do is just not grade the coins. And that usually discourages people from doing it, from sending them in.

TRAVERS: How about some of the coins that were already encapsulated that were doctored in some way?

ALBANESE: It seems to me that there are times where a coin will come in and we're not sure if it's doctored. In that case, and if it's a liner 64/65 coin and we think it might have been doctored but we're not positive, we knock the grade down. If we know for certain it's been doctored, we definitely call it a no-grade. If we're not sure, we always knock the grade down.

TRAVERS: How about census reports? How should consumers be using those?

ALBANESE: Personally, if I'd have had it my way, I would have probably eliminated the census reports. I mean, it seems to me that at this point, we actually can't, because we'd be accused of hiding information. But it seems that some coins that are not rare get sold for a lot of money because of the census reports. And some coins that are truly rare—again, like this 1874 $3 gold piece—I don't know whether this dealer has sent the tag in so it gets taken off the census report, but it's possible that this really rare coin could show up as having 10 of them graded, even though there's only one coin.

TRAVERS: How many inserts are being sent back to correct the census reports?

ALBANESE: I don't know.

TRAVERS: Do you provide a financial incentive, such as paying fifty cents per insert, to get people to send their inserts back?

ALBANESE: I think PCGS was, and may have stopped. I'm not sure what they were doing. We never were. We have no problems getting inserts from dealers, because it's the right thing to do.

TRAVERS: What do you think about this onslaught of your grading of modern coins?

ALBANESE: We've had quite a few comments from collectors who were collecting certain series of coins and they wanted a complete set, and they couldn't do it with our product. So we did it as a matter of completion. For investment purposes, to me they're a joke. I don't consider modern coins a good investment.

TRAVERS: Where is the *Bluesheet* the strongest, and where is it the weakest?

ALBANESE: The *Bluesheet,* from what I understand, reports on sight-unseen transactions—so generally, it's more accurate on the coins with the most transactions. With a coin like a 1796 dime in MS-66, the *Bluesheet* means hardly anything. With an MS-64 $20 Liberty, it means a lot more. I don't know if it's totally off anywhere. If it's off anywhere, it's very hard for the *Bluesheet* to keep track of coins every week that may only trade twice a year. I disagree with the whole concept of a *Bluesheet,* anyway—sight-unseen trading. I disagree with that altogether.

TRAVERS: You're now dealing in coins?

ALBANESE: Yes.

TRAVERS: Is anyone else at NGC dealing in coins?

ALBANESE: No.

TRAVERS: Do you think that your dealing in coins poses a conflict?

ALBANESE: I have never seen it as a conflict. I don't submit coins for grading, so I don't see it as a conflict at all. If I'm here grading, the chances are zero that I will grade one of my own coins. I think it's actually helpful for NGC to have me here, because I'm in the market, and I can give them some perspectives on the market.

TRAVERS: Does it get tedious just sitting there and grading?

ALBANESE: No, I find that the day actually goes by very quickly. But some people—some personalities—really can't handle it. We have tested people before, in the old days, and some people just can't sit still for more than an hour. But I really don't have a problem concentrating for eight or nine hours a day, looking at coins.

TRAVERS: What do you think is going to be the role of grading services—certification services—even five years from now? Is it going to be increasing? Decreasing? What do you think will happen?

ALBANESE: I think it will probably be decreasing. A lot of coins have been graded already. I'm not saying more can't be graded, but it seems to me a lot of coins have been graded, and every day that goes by, there's fewer coins that will be graded. I can envision a time when the grading services are half the size, or a quarter of the size.

CHAPTER ✦ 8

THE COINS TO SELL RIGHT NOW

This is a landmark chapter—probably the most important chapter in this book, and perhaps the most important chapter you'll read in *any* coin book. Virtually every coin book on the market tells you how, when, and why you should *buy* coins, but very few offer specific advice on coins you should *sell right now*.

A case in point is my bestselling book *The Coin Collector's Survival Manual*. In that book, I provide extraordinary advice on how to sell coins, once you've made the decision to do so. But I never specifically tell the reader which coins to sell right now, or even offer detailed advice about the timing.

Interestingly, even numismatic newsletters rarely, if ever, tell their readers which coins they should sell right away. But this is not surprising, since most of the people who write these newsletters are coin dealers themselves and derive most of their income from selling coins. Their principal objective is getting people to buy more coins, not sell the ones they already have.

CHANGING STRATEGIES

In years gone by, the accepted approach to investing in coins was to buy good material and hold it as long as possible, confident in the belief that over the long term, prices would inevitably go up. But nothing is inevitable anymore—not that anything ever really was. The glory days of surefire price increases have faded into distant memories, and the gravy train of "guaranteed" profit has been sidetracked. The coin investment climate has changed dramatically, and this calls for drastic changes in coin investors' strategy as well. In fact, it calls for a number of *different* investment strategies regarding coins' retention or dispersal, depending upon the nature of the coins that are involved. Some coins should be sold—even at a loss. Others should be held. And others should be traded for different coins.

There's no time like the present to review your coin collection and formulate a plan for restructuring your holdings to reflect the market realities of today. And one of those realities, regrettable as it may be, is the undeniable fact that most investment coins are worth far less as this book is being written, in 2000, than they were at the coin market's last big peak, in May 1989.

Thousands of examples of the market's sharp decline can be found in every issue of the *Certified Coin Dealer Newsletter* (or *Bluesheet*), a respected weekly price guide to the current market values of certified coins—those that have been graded and encapsulated by one of the major coin certification services. Let's look at just a few of these, and then see how some very different lessons can be drawn from them:

- On May 26, 1989, the *Bluesheet* assigned a value of $500 to an 1880-S Morgan silver dollar certified as Mint State-65 by the Numismatic Guaranty Corporation of America (NGC). As this is written, that same coin is valued at only about $66.
- On May 26, 1989, the *Bluesheet* value for a no-motto Liberty Seated half dollar graded Mint State-65 by the Professional Coin Grading Service (PCGS) was $23,500. Today, that coin is listed at only $4,100.
- On May 26, 1989, the *Bluesheet* assigned a value of $4,060 to a common-date Saint-Gaudens double eagle ($20 gold piece) graded Mint State-65 by NGC. Today, that coin is valued at just $680.

All three of these coins plunged in value. But while this gives them something important in common, a person who owned all three coins would have to use very different strategies in selling each one to maximize his or her return.

THE NEED FOR CERTIFICATION

No matter which path you follow in disposing of investment coins, your first move should be to get them certified—if they haven't been already—by one of the major coin-grading services. If you acquired your coins in the late 1980s or thereafter, the chances are good that they were already certified when you got them. But if you bought them earlier, there's a strong possibility that they may be uncertified, or "raw," to use the common marketplace term for such material. If so, you need to get them graded and encapsulated in order to be sure of just what you have and maximize your chances to sell them or trade them advantageously. Even if your coins have already been certified, it may be desirable to resubmit them to a certification service; grading standards have changed since the late 1980s and they might well receive a higher grade today. You need to examine each previously certified coin to determine whether it might be a candidate for an upgrade. To do this, review the guidelines I provided in Chapter 3.

In theory, certification doesn't affect the grade of a coin; if a coin is Mint State-65, that should be its grade regardless of whether it's raw or in a grading-service holder. In practice, however, certification does make a difference in many potential buyers' perception of the grade, for it serves to reassure them that the coin is as described. Without this safety net, they might very well seek to purchase it at a price corresponding to a somewhat lower grade—and that could easily translate into a significant reduction in what you would get. That's why it's important to get your investment coins certified before you even begin to formulate plans for their dispersal.

GENERIC COINS

The 1880-S Morgan silver dollar is an excellent example of a *generic* coin. Coins in this category are available in large quantities, even in high levels of preservation. As a result, they have come to be regarded very much like commodities. This gave them great appeal to Wall Street brokerage firms and Wall Street–type investors when those outsiders entered the coin market in large numbers during the late 1980s. Their age,

Figure 8-1. *1881-S Morgan dollar graded MS-65 by NGC.* Common, generic Morgan dollars such as this date, along with other issues such as the 1880-S, have not been good investments. This old-holdered NGC coin might regrade MS-66 upon re-submission.

pristine quality, and high silver content made them seem scarcer and more valuable than they really were, and their availability made them easy to promote. All this drove their prices far beyond levels that were warranted.

Since then, generic coins have suffered a double whammy. The Wall Street crowd has deserted the coin market, effectively removing most of the demand that kept these coins' prices artificially high. At the same time, the grading services have certified many thousands of additional examples, thus expanding the supply exponentially. This is clearly a formula for disaster.

At first glance, generic coins appear to be real bargains at current price levels. That 1880-S Morgan dollar in Mint State-65 condition sounds like an absolute steal at $66; after all, it would have cost you $500 or more in 1989. This is one case, however, where you do have to look a "gift horse" in the mouth. Far from being a bargain, it's probably overpriced even now, at its new, lower level. And so are most of the other generic coins that used to be so popular—high-grade, common-date Peace silver dollars, Walking Liberty half dollars, and "Mercury" dimes, for example.

I strongly recommend that you divest yourself at once of all the generic silver and nickel coins you now possess—even if you have to take a loss in the process. You can sell them outright or, if you prefer, you can trade them for other coins. It's my considered judgment that despite their drastically lower price levels, these coins aren't going anywhere but down—in the short run and especially in the long term. Dwindling demand and expanding supply add up to dismal price performance.

HIGH-GRADE RARITIES

Many high-condition coins of legitimate rarity also have suffered a major loss of value in recent years. The no-motto Liberty Seated half dollar is a case in point. But unlike generic coins, these *high-grade rarities* remain genuinely scarce, and relatively few additional examples have been certified since 1989—especially in grades of 65 and above. The population and census reports issued by the major certification services confirm that supplies are still extremely small. The coins' loss of value stems from reduced demand, and that, in turn, reflects the departure of unknowledgeable investors from the coin market. A solid collector base continues to exist for these true collector coins, and it wouldn't take much additional demand to push their prices higher—perhaps dramatically so—within a short period of time. In short, they have enormous potential at their current depressed price levels, and they will be among the first— and biggest—winners if the coin market enjoys another boom.

If you have many generic silver and nickel coins at present in your collection, it would be a great idea to sell them—even at a loss—and use the proceeds to purchase high-grade rarities such as proof gold type coins. Or, as an alternative, you might trade them for such coins. (This approach can have beneficial tax implications, as I will explain shortly, although these benefits primarily pertain to cases where your coins have appreciated in value, not declined.) If your holdings are extensive and valuable enough, you might even consider converting them—through sale or trade—into one single spectacular high-grade rarity. Imagine the sense of pride you would feel in owning a classic raity with a known population of just a few dozen examples! This is one case where putting all your eggs in one basket could prove to be a very wise move. Besides making you proud, it also would be highly prudent, for while both may be stalled in the

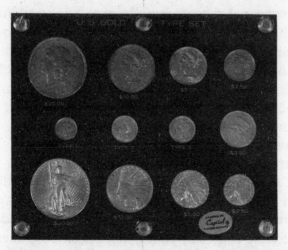

Figure 8-2. *Uncertified or "raw" 12-coin U.S. gold-type set.* These common-date generic coins appeal to investors because of the beauty of their designs and the fact that the coins are gold. *Photo courtesy Captial Plastics.*

basement right now, generic coins are clearly going nowhere, while high-grade rarities are poised to catch the very next elevator up.

GENERIC GOLD COINS

During the late 1980s, many investors—and many collector/investors, as well—purchased large quantities of generic gold coins. Often, these included common-date Saint-Gaudens double eagles in grades such as Mint State-63, or even Mint State-65, as in the case I cited earlier in this chapter. You don't want your holdings to be top-heavy in such coins, but they can be good for short-term action. No more than 30 percent of your holdings should consist of generic gold coins. Some people have nothing *but* generic gold in their collections, and if you're one of those people, you need to diversify and bring the percentage down.

Double eagles contain close to an ounce of gold, and if gold bullion were to rise in value dramatically, these coins' intrinsic value would enjoy a similar gain. In fact, they would go up in price even more percentagewise than bullion, since they would be perceived as having extra value as collectibles and this would be magnified in a hot market environment. Don't be misled, however, by temporary surges triggered by upward spikes in the bullion market, or, for that matter, by hoopla and hype in the coin market. Generic gold coins were clearly over-priced in the late 1980s, and the lower price levels of the mid-1990s were far more accurate gauges of their true market value. They're certainly worth a premium over the bullion price, but not the kind of premium they commanded in the overheated marketplace of 1989.

Many investment advisors recommend keeping a certain amount of gold, including gold coins, in your portfolio. My advice would be to keep a few—but only a few—generic gold coins as part of your holdings. If you have about a hundred Saint-Gaudens double eagles in your safe deposit box, keep a few of the better-date pieces and trade the rest for coins with greater potential, such as high-grade, low-mintage rarities.

LIKE-KIND EXCHANGES

If you prefer not to sell your generic coins (and other coins with low potential) outright, you might consider trading them for other coins that you believe possess greater potential. Tax laws permit *like-kind exchanges* involving rare coins. These are particularly useful in cases where your coins have gone up in value since you purchased them and you would face the prospect of being taxed on your gains if you were to sell them. By trading them for coins of similar value, you could defer the tax obligation on such gains.

Suppose you bought a coin for $1,000 and it went up in value to $5,000. Rather than simply selling the coin and having to pay taxes on your $4,000 profit, you could trade it for other coins whose current market value totals $5,000—coins that might be at the bottom of their price cycle now. Later, if those coins went up in value to $10,000, you could repeat the process. In fact, you could keep repeating it over and over for many years, all the while postponing your day of reckoning with the tax man.

Eventually, of course, taxes must be paid on any gains that are realized. But if you played your cards right, you could postpone the actual sale of the coins—and payment of the taxes—until you were retired and in a lower income tax bracket, thereby greatly minimizing your obligation.

In recent years, losses have been more common than gains for people investing in coins, so the tax-deferral advantage of like-kind exchanges hasn't been as useful as it was in years gone by. In fact, there are often circumstances in this kind of hostile market climate where it might be preferable from a tax standpoint to sell coins and claim a loss, rather than trade them. You should check with your accountant to see which approach is better for you.

A Tax-Slashing Strategy

Many people have a psychological aversion to selling their coins at a loss. They may say to themselves, "Hey, I paid $10,000 for these coins. I'm not going to sell them for $2,000; that's an $8,000 loss." Well-known coin dealer Michael R. Fuljenz of Universal Coin & Bullion Corp. in Beaumont, Texas, has come up with an interesting strategy that enables such people to enjoy the tax benefits of their loss without giving up the coins— at least not for very long. Fuljenz has advised clients in this kind of situation to sell such coins to their favorite dealer at the fair market wholesale value, then wait 30 days and buy the coins back—or purchase comparable coins—at the fair market retail value then in effect.

Let's say you paid $10,000 for a coin portfolio in 1989 and its fair market wholesale value today is just $1,500. Using the strategy formulated by Fuljenz, you could sell that portfolio to your favorite dealer for $1,500, enabling you to declare an $8,500 loss on your tax return for the year, and then buy it back 31 days later for perhaps $2,000. It's essential, Fuljenz says, to avoid what tax rules call a "wash sale"—that is, the sale and repurchase of the same investment within 30 days.

The IRS regulation governing this kind of transaction is Internal Revenue Code Section 1091. In applying this rule to transactions involving rare coins or precious metals, Fuljenz says, "It is clear that the ability to deduct a loss is dependent on the economic substance of the transaction." His company follows six standard procedures to ensure that its transactions meet the IRS test for having "economic substance." Here, in brief, are the steps involved:

- After viewing the client's coins, the company will buy them with no obligation for the seller to repurchase them, and will bear the entire market risk of loss or gain during the agreed-upon time period.
- The client must provide written or faxed agreement to bids presented by the company for these coins prior to December 31 of the current year.
- The company will give the client the opportunity to repurchase the same group of coins after 30 days, but the client is under no obligation to do so.
- The client will receive an invoice for the coins purchased by the company and have his account credited with the proceeds.
- The client must pay the company a 3-percent fee if the coins are repurchased after 30 days.
- The company will store the coins in a segregated safe, properly identified and fully insured, during the time they are in its possession.

I would strongly recommend that you check with your accountant or financial advisor before engaging in such a strategy. It's an interesting concept, though, and one that Michael Fuljenz—a highly astute dealer—has recommended to many of his customers.

FIVE TYPES OF COINS TO SELL

There are five basic categories of coins that you should consider selling *right now,* and each one calls for a different kind of strategy. Let's look at them one by one:

Coins That Have Increased in Value

In a rising market, it's often very difficult to judge just when to sell your coins. If you buy a coin for $100 and it jumps in value to $1,000, that might very well be a good time to sell it—

but then again, it might not be the *best* time: The coin might continue increasing in value to $2,000 if the positive forces at work in the market are strong and sustained enough. Should you wait to squeeze that last extra price increase out of the market and risk losing the profit you've already made on paper? My advice would be to take the money—sell the coin now—and run all the way to the bank. There's nothing wrong with taking a profit, and when coins have risen dramatically within a short period of time, you should go to the cash window and celebrate.

Of course, there's more involved in selling your coins advantageously than merely walking up to a window—or a coin dealer's counter—and picking up your money. You can sell them directly to a dealer if you wish, and this might work out well if you have a good rapport and a good working relationship with the dealer in question. But don't expect an optimal return if you simply walk in cold to a shop where you're a face without a name, or approach a dealer's table at random at a show. You'll pocket a profit, yes, if your coins have gone up significantly in value, but you may end up leaving a lot of your money on the dealer's table, or, to be more precise, in his or her wallet.

The ideal venue to sell rare coins is a grand-format auction where the coins are showcased to maximum advantage in an eye-catching catalog, the sale is widely publicized, and all of the major interested buyers are assembled in one room at the same time, or represented there by surrogates. All of this enhances the likelihood that the coins being sold in such a sale will bring top dollar. But selling your coins in a full-scale auction can be a lengthy process; months can pass between the time you consign your coins and the moment when the gavel finally falls, and if the market is volatile, your paper profits may shrivel by the time the bidding begins.

My firm, Scott Travers Rare Coin Galleries, Inc., of New York City, offers an alternative that combines some of the advantageous features of a full-scale auction with the benefits of quick—almost overnight—sale. This format, which I call the "lightning sale," is a modified form of competitive bidding which takes place almost at once, thereby all but eliminating the waiting risk associated with traditional auctions.

We assemble some of the most knowledgeable and influential coin bidders in the industry—the very same people you'd be likely to encounter at the biggest public auction sales—and give them an opportunity to examine the coins being sold. Then, at the consignor's sole discretion, we proceed with the sale at once. Competition is fierce, and prices tend to be strong for existing market conditions. Thus, consignors "lock in" their profits, so to speak, avoiding the risk that the market might fizzle down the line. What's more, successful bidders wire their payments the very next day, so instead of waiting months for their money, the consignors get the proceeds from the sale right away.

Another good way to sell your coins quickly while still securing exposure to a broad range of buyers is to place them in one of the telephone bid sales conducted by Teletrade, a New York State company which conducts such sales on a regular basis by means of a sophisticated computer system accessed by Touch-Tone telephones. These sales are limited to coins that have been certified and encapsulated by one of the leading grading services. For further information, contact Teletrade, 27 Main St., Kingston, NY 12401-3853.

Among the coins you should seriously consider selling right away are those you have been successful in getting upgraded by one of the certification services. Perhaps you had a coin that was certified as Proof-64 and you cracked it out of its holder and resubmitted it to the same service—or sent it to a different service—and it came back as Proof-65. That one-point enhancement in the grade might very well be worth several thousand dollars more in value, and that's surely something to celebrate!

In this case, I would recommend placing your coin in a grand-format auction. I've seen many coins graded Proof-64, or Mint State-64, that possessed truly remarkable visual appeal but were held back from a higher grade—initially, at least—because of some technical deficiency such as minor striations (or stress lines) on the reverse that were barely visible. It's altogether possible that bidders in an auction would look upon such coins as being premium-quality—perhaps even Proof- or Mint State-66—

if they viewed them without the limiting framework of the "slab" with a stated grade of 65.

Coins That Will Never Come Back in Value

Certain coins you have in your portfolio simply may have reached a dead end. Perhaps you have some high-grade generic coins whose populations have risen astronomically during recent years because of new submissions to the certification services. Given the enormous supply now available, you may see no hope that these coins will ever rebound to anything approaching their former value. Or perhaps your holdings include some random-quality coins that you perceive as having little or no chance of being upgraded if you were to resubmit them, even with grading standards looser. These coins may have lost a substantial part of the value they had when you acquired them, but, even so, you probably should give some serious thought to selling them right now.

Selling such coins at a loss would at least allow you to use that loss to reduce your federal income tax obligation. This could be a good way to offset your capital gains from more successful investments—perhaps including windfalls from stocks and bonds. Keep in mind, however, that capital losses are deductible against ordinary income only up to a maximum of $3,000. Coins that have dropped in value below your tax basis should *not* be traded. If you trade coins on which an outright sale would have resulted in a loss, that loss will be postponed, just as a gain is postponed through like-kind exchanges involving coins whose value has increased.

Coins You Are Finished With

There may be certain coins that you simply want to get rid of. You're through with them and never want to see them again! Perhaps you had a bag of 1,000 Morgan dollars and you picked out the 10 or 20 best pieces; now you've replaced those coins with less desirable dollars and you want to get the bag out of your way. Depending upon market conditions and your cash-flow situation, you might either sell that bag directly to a dealer who handles bullion or, alternatively, place it in auction. Either way, these are coins you should sell. It's just not productive to keep them around, and you could come out of the sale with many thousands of dollars to invest in other coins with much greater upside potential.

Another kind of coin that might well come under this heading is a certified coin you've resubmitted over and over again in an unsuccessful bid for a higher grade. Perhaps you have a coin graded Mint State-65 and it's worth $500 in that grade, but you've made a dozen fruitless attempts to get it bumped up to Mint State-66 because it would be worth five *thousand* dollars in that level. You've given up on the upgrade, and now you simply want to blow this coin out. Given your state of mind, that's exactly what you should do!

Coins You Want to Sell or *Have* to Sell

There are times when circumstances dictate the sale of certain coins. You may find yourself almost forced to sell them for financial reasons or other personal reasons.

Recently, a friend of mine confronted this kind of predicament. He had a magnificent 1909-S VDB Lincoln cent which had been graded Mint State-65 by the Professional Coin Grading Service, and he found himself facing a serious cash crunch. The coin was an extraordinary premium-quality piece and the market wasn't conducive to selling it at that time. Still, my friend was strapped for cash and absolutely needed immediate funds, so he sold the coin. You could find yourself in a similar unfortunate situation.

In selling a coin when you're under duress, by all means avoid telling potential buyers you have to sell it. Don't go to a coin show and let a dealer smell blood. Don't go to some fly-by-night dealer who's holding a liquidation sale in a room he took for the day at a local hotel. And don't go to a coin or collectibles shop where the people don't know you and let them persuade you to sell that scarce coin at a fire-sale price. There's no need to engage in panic selling. The marketplace today is much more sophisticated than it used to be, and many new options are available to sellers in must-sell situations.

If you're selling a whole collection and it has substantial value, you might be able to get a generous cash advance by consigning it to an auction company. Some of the largest coin auction houses in the nation offer this type of service. These companies have a public policy of giving cash advances for up to 50 percent of the estimated value of coins that are consigned to them for sale. However, this limit can often be stretched; I've known of cases where auction firms gave advances for up to 85 percent of the value of the coins in a consignment. Naturally, you would have to sign a security agreement and pay a standard interest rate on the money you received as an advance. But you would have the funds you needed right up front, and when your coins did go on the auction block, perhaps two months later, their sale would be taking place under highly advantageous conditions, thus helping to maximize your return.

Family Accumulations Acquired Secondhand

I've had firsthand experience with numerous instances where people with little or no knowledge of rare coins inherited extensive collections, or found large accumulations in an attic or some other family hoard. Often, this material consists for the most part of high-mintage, low-value sets issued by government mints, or private-mint medals that are pretty but definitely *not* worth a pretty penny.

THE ANATOMY OF A COIN TRANSACTION

When people with limited knowledge of coins—or no knowledge at all—inherit a collection or stumble upon an old accumulation in the attic, they often tend to view it as a single entity, rather than a mosaic made up of widely differing components. This can be a serious mistake, particularly if they treat it that way when they sell it. All too often, people will take such coins to a local dealer and sell them en masse, reasoning that this is the most convenient approach, and assuming that, in any case, they'll get the same price no matter what method of dispersal they use.

The fact is, different kinds of coins require different methods of sale in order to bring the seller the best return—or at least need to be sold to different dealers. And if you were to sell a collection or accumulation in a single transaction to just one dealer, he or she would probably use all or most of these methods in reselling the coins to others, and then the return would be maximized for that dealer, and not for you.

Let's say you came into possession of a large and diverse collection of coins, with many different kinds of material—everything from rare type coins to modern government proof sets. This may be hypothetical for the purposes of this book, but it could become very real for you or someone you know, if not right now, then somewhere down the line. Let's separate this collection into its major components and consider the best way to sell each one. In fact, let me go one step further and suggest a specific dealership which you, as a seller, might contact to get top dollar for each component. In each case, I'll select a dealer currently among the most active in that area—and also among those now paying the highest prices for such material.

WARNING: *These recommendations apply only at the time of this writing. Anyone with large holdings is encouraged to contact the author personally to be certain that these dealers are still active in these particular areas. This is a volatile marketplace, and active market-makers and large dealers often take turns at the helm of their respective areas of interest. You need to be certain that these dealers are still interested in such material—and even still in business—before sending any coins to them. I make these recommendations in good faith and based upon the facts as they are known to me now, but you are responsible for screening prospective buyers yourself before you sell your coins.*

Let's look at each area individually:

Bullion silver coins: If you were to find yourself with large quantities of pre-1965 Washington quarters or Roosevelt dimes in circulated condition—or even in Mint State condition, chances are that you would want to sell all or most of these coins. One of several renowned bullion dealers with a *national* reputation is Silver Towne Coin (Leon and David Hendrickson), P.O. Box 424, R.4, Union City Pike, Winchester, IN 47394, telephone (317) 584-7481. A very honest dealer in this type of material is Sal Germano, S. G. Rare Coins, Inc., 625 Lafayette Ave., Hawthorne, NJ 07506, telephone (973) 612-0520.

Key-date circulated coins: If you had a collection of key-date Morgan silver dollars in circulated condition, or a collection of circulated Lincoln cents that included such key coins as the 1909-S VDB cent, and you took those coins to a local dealer, that dealer might pay you 20 or 30 percent less than the bid prices in *The Coin Dealer Newsletter.* But that dealer probably wouldn't resell those coins to a consumer—a collector—for 10 percent back of the bid price and settle for a nominal commission. Chances are that dealer would turn around and sell those coins to a company actively pursuing such material and paying top dollar to get it—a company such as Littleton Coin Company, 653 Union Street, Littleton, NH 03561, buyer telephone (603) 444-1020. You should do likewise. And keep in mind that for a collection valued at more than $35,000, Littleton will send a representative to your home to appraise and acquire your coins.

Modern government proof sets and "mint sets": If you suddenly found yourself with hundreds of late-date U.S. proof sets and uncirculated coin sets (better known as "mint sets"), it would be a big mistake to cart those sets to a coin or collectibles shop near your home, plunk them down on the counter, and take the dealer's word—and check—for their value. In all likelihood, that dealer would try to buy those sets from you for 30 or 40 percent less than the prices listed in *The Coin Dealer Newsletter*—and he would then sell them for the *CDN* bid price, or even slightly more, by shipping them off to Michael Keith Ruben, 38 Yorkshire, Hilton Head Island, SC 29928, telephone (800) 635-2646. Ruben is among the biggest market-makers in modern proof and mint sets, and he might pay the highest prices. He will pay them to you instead of that local dealer if you send the sets directly to

Figure 8-3 (left and right). *1804 Stickney Specimen Class I "original" silver dollar, obverse and reverse.* This coin, from the collection of Louis E. Eliasberg, Sr., was sold at auction for $1.815 million in April 1997. The highest price realized for an 1804 dollar was $4.14 million in August 1999 for a specimen graded Proof-68 by PCGS. *Photo courtesy Auctions by Bowers and Merena, Inc.*

him. But he won't buy your sets unless you have a lot of them: He limits his purchases to material worth a total of *at least* $10,000. Call first before shipping anything.

Major rarities: Some dealers might keep major rarities in their inventories and sell them to regular customers, if these were among the coins in a collection that you sold to them. But chances are, many would consign such coins to a major auction firm for sale at a public auction. Auctions have long been the favored method of sale for truly rare coins because they provide the maximum exposure for these valuable but often esoteric items and bring together all of the interested buyers at a single time and place. There are many well-known national numismatic auction companies which receive my *highest recommendation,* such as Auctions by Bowers and Merena, Heritage Numismatic Auctions, Stack's, and Superior Galleries. As a practical alternative to a full-scale, grand-format auction, I also highly recommend my own Lightning Sales, which compress the time required to sell rare coins while still providing many of the advantages of an auction format. Anyone interested in learning more about this process can contact me at P.O. Box 1711, FDR Station, New York, NY 10150, telephone (212) 535-9135. A Lightning Sale is a competitive process, similar to a standard auction sale, through which people can sell their coins *almost immediately* in return for a nominal commission.

The value of competitive bidding was underscored recently when a woman from South Carolina decided to sell four gold coins that her father had given her years ago, telling her they would always be worth something. She needed money to pay the college tuition for her only son, so she went to some local coin dealers near her home and asked what they would give her for the coins. These local dealers offered her $200 apiece, for a total of $800. After thinking it over, she decided that the best way to find a coin dealer was by going to the library, instead of going through the Yellow Pages, so she went to the local library, picked up a copy of my book *The Coin Collector's Survival Manual*, found my phone number inside, and called me up. To make a long story short, I submitted these coins to NGC for certification, all four received grades of Mint State-65, and the woman ended up getting more than $20,000 for them at one of my lightning sales. That's $20,000 for a group of four coins that this woman was very close to selling for just $800 a few weeks earlier.

The lesson is clear: Competition will enable you to maximize your return when you're selling coins of high value. It isn't as crucial—and may not really matter at all—in selling more common, less valuable coins; with those, the going price is fairly well established, and the key is finding an active buyer who needs and wants your material. With higher-priced coins, however, the market value at any given time may often be a gray area—or there may be a fairly broad price range—and having several dealers vie for the right to buy them will frequently result in a higher return.

Consider the case of the woman from South Carolina. The local dealers probably viewed her four gold coins as Mint State-63 specimens and offered her Mint State-60 prices, figuring they would make a tidy—but not outrageous—profit by selling them at 63 prices. My professional opinion at the time was that the coins would be graded no higher than Mint State-64. But because they were so original and had full, vibrant mint luster, NGC graded them 65, even though they had a few scratches. The winning bidder for all four coins at my Lightning Sale was Jesse Lipka of Numismania in Flemington, New Jersey, and the underbidder was Heritage Capital Corporation of Dallas, Texas. Both Heritage Capital and Jesse Lipka are active buyers, but with rarer, more valuable coins, I suggest creating an active environment and not just selling to one particular active buyer. With a gray-area coin, there could be a relatively broad value range—say, anywhere from $1,500 to $4,000. In that kind of situation, buyers—even highly reputable dealers—tend to like to pay a price at the lower end of the range. But when these items are put up for competitive bidding, the dealers usually end up paying a price at the upper end of the range, whether they like it or not. So competition can be extremely healthy for you—the seller—when you are dispersing scarce or rare coins worth thousands of dollars apiece.

Generic, fungible silver coins: High-grade, common-date silver coins—and generic nickel and copper coins, as well—should *not* be sold at auction; the commissions are too high for such material. If you find yourself with large numbers of these coins—1881-S Morgan silver dollars graded Mint State-65, for example—a good place to sell them might be Heritage Capital Corporation, Heritage Plaza, Highland Park Village, Dallas, TX 75205-2788, telephone (800) 872-6467.

Generic gold coins: Generic gold coins require a somewhat different selling strategy from generic silver coins because their high intrinsic value gives them special appeal to a different kind of buyer. One of the most active, most reputable, and best-paying buyers for large quantities of generic gold coins is National Gold Exchange (NGE), 14309 North Dale Mabry Highway, Tampa, FL 33618, telephone (813) 969-4111. The person to contact is Mark Yaffe. Heritage is an equally strong buyer in many cases when it comes to generic gold coins. And Heritage maintains overseas buying offices. If you're selling generic gold coins certified by the Numismatic Certification Institute (NCI)—and, in *some* cases, PCGS and NGC generic gold coins—a good buyer to contact is Sal Germano, S.G. Rare Coins, Inc., 625 Lafayette Ave., Hawthorne, NJ 07506, telephone (973) 304-0520. If you have a quantity of *generic* type coins graded by NGC, in many cases the highest sight-unseen buyer will be NGC's founder himself, John Albanese. You can contact him at John Albanese Numismatics, P.O. Box 1776, Far Hills, NJ 07931-1771, telephone (908) 781-9101.

CHAPTER 9

THE COINS TO BUY RIGHT NOW

Every time gold bullion moves over $400 per ounce, prices seem to immediately jump up—especially for the top-quality gold coins.
—David Hall, founder and president of PCGS

Time is of the essence when it comes to making money in coins. But buying coins *right now* to turn a profit doesn't necessarily mean running out and buying them right this minute—and it doesn't mean you'll see the profit instantaneously either. When I use the expression *right now,* I really mean a general period of time—the next several weeks . . . the next several months . . . possibly even the next couple of years.

The fact is, *right now* means *right this minute* more with some coins than with others. When I say *right now* with some coins, I mean today. When I say *right now* with others, I mean next week. And with still other coins, when I say *right now* I mean they'll be big winners only if the price of gold goes up $100 an ounce.

There are three separate categories of coins to buy *right now* that we will be considering in this chapter. First are "crack-out" coins—certified coins that you can crack out of their holders and realize a profit from almost literally *right this minute* (and a handsome profit, at that!) by getting them recertified at higher grade levels. Second are coins that have fallen sharply in value—sometimes by thousands of dollars—but possess good potential for bouncing back; I'll tell you how to pick the right ones. The final group of coins that you should buy *right now* will be the ones whose value would get a tremendous boost if gold were to rise $100 or more within just a short span of time.

CRACK-OUT COINS TO BUY *RIGHT NOW*

I outlined the reasons for cracking out certified coins—and explored the potential risks and rewards—in Chapter 5, "Realizing a Profit Right Now." Briefly, you can often make quick, substantial profits by removing a high-end certified coin from its holder, resubmitting it to one of the major grading services, and getting it upgraded to the next-higher level. If you were successful in getting a coin upgraded from Mint State-64 to Mint State-65, for example, you might be able to sell it for hundreds—even thousands—of dollars more, since small differences in grade frequently are accompanied by very large differences in price.

Now, I'm ready to make some specific recommendations on crack-out coins that you should consider buying *right now*. In drawing up this list, I sought the expertise of Jesse Lipka, one of the nation's leading crack-out coin dealers, who does business in Flemington, New Jersey, under the corporate name Numismania. In an exclusive interview, Jesse shared with me secrets he has gleaned from cracking out thousands of coins.

Jesse's company grosses millions of dollars per year, and most of his profit used to come from successful crack-outs. Up until 1994, he said, his success rate in getting crack-out coins upgraded was phenomenal. He would go to a convention, buy coins that he considered good candidates for upgrades, and the overwhelming majority would in fact be recertified in the next-higher grade.

A Harder Game to Win

As a sign that times are changing, even the great Jesse Lipka admits that his success rate in getting crack-out upgrades is down today to about half of what it once was. The game has got-

Figure 9-1. *Indian $5 gold piece obverse graded Mint State-63.* The coin was purchased as a premium quality MS-63, but was later certified as an MS-64.

ten tougher—and this should be fair warning to those of you who think you can get a coin upgraded with little or no trouble and make yourself a quick return of several thousand dollars. If Jesse Lipka, one of the very best crack-out artists in the business, is enjoying a success rate of only 20 percent—even with his uncanny knack for picking winners and his full-time involvement in the game—then you can be pretty sure that your rate will be substantially lower.

Jesse is very selective when buying coins today at conventions. His game plan, he said, is to purchase premium-quality coins for which he has to pay little or no premium. This is very similar to what Jim Halperin recommends, as I reported in Chapter 5. With the game getting tougher, Jesse has become more conservative: Nowadays, he told me, he has to have a really strong conviction that a coin will be upgraded before he puts himself in a risk position.

Winning may be harder, but the game is still worthwhile, for the fruits of victory can be very sweet indeed. And you can improve your chances of winning by patterning your purchases after the experts. With that said, let's examine some of the crack-out coins that you should be buying *right now*.

Premium-quality Indian $5 Gold Pieces Graded Mint State-63

The coins in this list are not necessarily presented in the order of their importance. It so happens, though, that my first recommendation is also the No. 1 choice—by far—of crack-out artists across the country. Jesse Lipka confirmed this, and so did other dealers who play the crack-out game but aren't as courageous as Jesse in agreeing to be named.

Indian Head half eagles and their smaller companions, Indian quarter eagles, differ from all other U.S. coins in that their designs are incuse, or sunken below the surface, rather than raised above it. This makes them quite difficult to grade—and that, in turn, results in inconsistency by the graders: These coins are much more likely than raised-relief coins to receive different grades the second time around. Beyond this, there is a very substantial difference in the market value of Indian half eagles between the grades of Mint State-63 and Mint State-64, giving crack-out dealers a high degree of incentive to resubmit coins graded MS-63. As of this writing, in August 2000, Indian $5s certified by the Professional Coin Grading Service (PCGS) are valued at $715 in 63 and $1,900 in 64. Those certified by the Numismatic Guaranty Corporation of America (NGC) are worth about the same. What's more, the downside risk is relatively small: If, by chance, you cracked out and resubmitted an MS-62 coin and it came back as an MS-61, the coin would still be worth about $300.

This particular crack-out play is actually fairly easy, as long as you begin with really premium-quality 63 coins. You need to find a coin with blazing luster and minimal marks. Many times, you may get a coin that's right on the line—a 63 coin that's super high-end for the grade, where the grading services just aren't sure. In many other cases, you may get a coin that was graded in the services' early years, when their standards were slightly stricter—a coin in an old holder from 1987 or 1988. If you find such a coin and resubmit it, you're going to do quite well. But most of the upgrades we're seeing today with MS-63 Indian $5s involve coins that were graded only a short time ago—coins that in a sense were just graded.

Mint State-65 Saint-Gaudens Double Eagles

My second pick is actually the marketplace's No. 2 pick as well. The magnificent Saint-Gaudens double eagle (or $20 gold piece) always has enjoyed enormous popularity; this is widely

Figure 9-2. *Mint State-65 Saint-Gaudens double eagle.* This premium quality 1927 example, in an old PCGS holder, exhibits swirls of vibrant mint luster upon impeccable surfaces. Upon resubmission, it would likely be graded MS-66.

viewed as America's most beautiful coin. That beauty is showcased to maximum advantage in upper Mint State grades such as Mint State-66—and crack-out dealers are dazzled by a different kind of allure when they see the large price spread that now exists for "Saints" between the grade levels of MS-65 and 66. As this is written, common-date Saints graded by PCGS and NGC are valued at $700 in MS-65 and twice that much—$1,400—in MS-66. And as in the case of Indian $5s, the downside isn't really all that great: These coins are worth about $500 in Mint State-64, so the loss in a one-point downgrade would be only a couple hundred dollars, whereas you'd double your money with a one-point upgrade.

The chances of getting an upgrade are relatively good, assuming that you choose a nice premium-quality 65, and you shouldn't have any problem getting such a coin regraded as at least a 65. If anything, the services are liberal in their grading of PQ Saints. Nice examples dated 1927 and 1928, in particular, seem to receive the benefit of the doubt because these coins are typically well-struck and eye-appealing. Prospects for an upgrade are enhanced by the fact that the services have become less strict in some respects in grading Saints. A rub or marks on Liberty's breast no longer are viewed as detracting, for example, as they would have been even a few years ago. And the services have grown less finicky about any marks on the sun on the obverse. When PCGS and NGC first began operations, they paid very close attention to the sun, viewing it as a critical grade-sensitive area. But nowadays, Jesse Lipka reports, the services are all but ignoring the sun. As a consequence, there are numerous Saints with minor imperfections in this portion of the design that you can crack out of 65 holders and readily get upgraded to 66.

EARLY GOLD TYPE COINS GRADED MINT STATE-62

Gold coins produced in the U.S. Mint's earliest years, from 1795 through 1839, are rare and coveted collectibles, and the price differential from one grade to the next can be many thousands of dollars. Getting an upgrade with one of these coins isn't easy; the certification services are keenly aware of the money that hangs in the balance, so they tend to be very conservative. If you are successful in getting one, however, the reward can be enormous. And the coins with the best potential for winning such an upgrade are those graded Mint State-62.

Let's consider two examples of the profits you might reap. As of this writing, a Draped Bust $5 gold piece with a small-eagle design on the reverse—a coin type minted from 1795 through

Figure 9-3. *Super premium quality 1795 small eagle $5 graded MS-62 upgradable to MS-63 or MS-64.* An exceptional cameo contrast between the frosted devices and golden-pond-like fields contribute to the coin's premium quality status. Resubmission will possibly yield a grade of MS-63, with a "shot" at MS-64. The MS-62 sight-unseen value is $33,500; the MS-63 sight-unseen value is $74,000.

1798—is worth $33,500 in MS-62, as graded by either PCGS or NGC. In MS-63, the price more than doubles to $74,000. A Coronet $10 gold piece dated 1838 or 1839 is listed at $17,500 in MS-62. The price increases to $32,000 in MS-63.

In many cases, the standards at the services in regard to gold coins are slightly looser now than they were two or three years ago. That loosening may be just a quarter of a point, but that's a significant difference for coins that are near the line from one grade level to the next—quite possibly enough to push a coin up from MS-62 to 63. If you find a really nice PQ early gold coin that was graded 62 several years ago, you might be able to get it upgraded to 63 and make a quick profit of tens of thousands of dollars. The odds are against you; the graders know what's at stake and err on the side of caution with such coins. But you could make a killing with just one win.

PREMIUM-QUALITY MINT STATE-64 INDIAN $2½ GOLD PIECES

The Indian quarter eagle has the same incuse design as the half eagle of this type and is hard to grade for precisely the same reason. With this smaller coin, however, the best crack-out play is in a somewhat higher level of preservation: getting an upgrade from MS-64 to MS-65. In PCGS holders, common-date Indian $2½s are valued at $610 in 64 and $1,700 in 65. The corresponding prices for NGC-graded specimens are $600 in 64 and $1,600 in 65. The downside is about $200 if one of these coins gets regraded as only 63—but the upside is more than $1,000, making this an excellent gamble.

Incuse gold coins are undeniably difficult to grade; in fact, Jesse Lipka goes so far as to assert that the certification services are inept at grading them. These half and quarter eagles were really made much differently from all other U.S. coins. But after having graded tens of thousands of these coins, the services have become more adept than they were just a couple of years ago. In general, I would recommend resubmitting any premium-quality MS-64 Indian quarter eagles that were graded originally prior to 1994. After that, the grading became more consistent and accurate.

Although the downside risk from a one-point lower grade is

quite acceptable, you also should be aware of a second—much more serious—kind of risk: the real possibility that the coin you crack out of its holder may have been doctored. You might very well pay $600 or more for a so-called premium-quality Indian $2½—a coin with vibrant luster and exceptional eye appeal—only to discover, after cracking it out, that someone had finagled with its surfaces. A few years back, before the grading services got wise to the trick, skilled coin doctors would take an epoxy resin, mix it with gold filings, then use this substance to fill in the scratches on an otherwise attractive Mint State-60 Indian quarter eagle. They did this so well that the services didn't detect it, and presto!—an MS-60 or MS-61 coin with a big gouge on the cheek was transformed just like that into what appeared to be a premium-quality MS-64, or even an MS-65. You need to be alert for this, because the downside risk is enormous. You could crack a coin out of its holder thinking it would receive an upgrade to 65, and instead get it back with a form letter saying it's not gradable. As long as doctored coins are in a service's holders, the service is responsible for compensating you for its mistakes. Once you crack them out, though, the loss becomes yours, and all you have left, in effect, is not much more than what the coins are worth as precious metal.

Bust Half Dollars Graded About Uncirculated-58

Bust half dollars—large silver coins issued by the U.S. Mint from 1796 to 1839—are perennially popular with collectors and investors alike. Nice Bust halves are always in demand and easy to sell, even in higher circulated grades. For this reason, many have been certified in grade levels from About Uncirculated right through the Mint State range, and that has created interesting opportunities for profitable upgrades.

Frequently, an otherwise eye-popping Bust half dollar will be graded only About Uncirculated-58 because of light rub (or friction) on the high points; the graders will reason that this is evidence of wear, however slight, and that they cannot assign a Mint State grade. At other times, however, the services will give MS grades to attractive Bust halves even if they do exhibit very slight rub. I have even heard of instances where grades

Figure 9-4. *Bust half dollar graded About Uncirculated-58 that appears to be a Mint State-64.* This is just the type of coin that would upgrade to MS-64 upon resubmission: It has peerless color and surfaces, with just the slightest trace of friction on the highest points.

as high as Mint State-66 have been given to coins with almost imperceptible—but nonetheless detectable—rub.

Jesse Lipka told me of one case where he bought a Bust half dollar graded AU-58 by NGC, cracked it out of its holder, resubmitted it to NGC, and got it regraded as Mint State-64. I wouldn't expect an upgrade from AU-58 to MS-64—or MS-66—very often, but if you succeed in getting one, you'll pocket a tidy profit. In fact, you'll do quite well even if you get that AU-58 coin upgraded to MS-62. At this writing, certified Bust halves are worth $200 in AU-58, $500 in MS-62, $1,000 in MS-63, and $1,550 in MS-64. You should look for a coin with attractive, original luster, where the surfaces are beautiful and unimpeded and which is being graded AU-58 only because it has a light rub. That kind of coin could easily be upgraded to MS-62, and might even get a higher grade than that.

COINS THAT WERE CERTIFIED BY ONE OF THE MAJOR GRADING SERVICES DURING ITS FORMATIVE PERIOD

By their own admission, PCGS and NGC were much stricter in grading coins—especially in very high levels—during the time when they were first doing business. As PCGS's founder and president, David Hall, puts it, the graders were much less willing

Figures 9-5 & 9-6. *Early NGC (left) and PCGS holders.* The NGC holder is a publicity photograph. In the actual holder, the coin's reverse appeared beneath the NGC logo.
Photos courtesy Numismatic Guaranty Corporation of America, Inc., and Professional Coin Grading Service, respectively.

to give out grades above Mint State-65. They were frankly afraid of those higher grades during the services' very early stages. If you can locate coins that were certified during those years, you stand an excellent chance of getting upgrades. And it's possible to distinguish coins that were graded then by checking the holders (Figures 9-5 and 9-6). PCGS holders have been modified since then, and NGC didn't add imbedded holograms to its holders until it had been in business several years.

Your best bet is to stick with premium-quality brilliant coins. With these, you will be almost sure of upgrades much of the time. Jim Halperin confided that with brilliant coins that were certified by one of the major services from 1986 to 1988, his success rate at getting upgrades has been almost 100 percent, although he has had to resubmit some coins more than once in order to get them. Jesse Lipka helped one prominent collector get upgrades on many coins prior to the sale of a notable collection of Liberty $10 gold pieces, which took place as part of a Heritage Numismatic auction in Long Beach, California. After

Figures 9-7 & 9-8. *Newer NGC holder reverse (far left) has a hologram of NGC and the ANA. The slightly older NGC holder has just the NGC logo. Newer PCGS holder reverse (right) has a hologram of PCGS and the Professional Numismatists Guild (PNG). The slightly older PCGS holder bears just the PCGS logo.* A number of leading experts contend that some coins graded and encapsulated in the older holders might have been graded more conservatively than their recently graded counterparts and today might qualify for upgrades.

helping the collector assemble the coins in the first place, Lipka selected 110 specimens to crack out and resubmit to PCGS, largely on the basis that they had been graded originally during the early years of third-party certification. Fifty-five of these coins—fully half—received upgrades. And all 11 coins that were housed in NGC holders crossed into PCGS holders—with not a single one going down in grade.

One word of caution: Recently, toned coins have been penalized by the services. If you are dissatisfied with the grade that you receive on such a coin, you should send it in again. There is a dramatic difference of opinion regarding toned coins at the present time, and you might very well get a much better outcome the second time. Better yet, don't even crack toned coins out of their holders—especially if the holders are early ones; toning was viewed with favor in the services' early stages, and toned coins graded then might well come back today with lower grades. By contrast, brilliant coins are very much in favor now; attractive, problem-free examples of these are universally seen as being desirable. These are prime candidates for crack-outs and upgrades—all of which could be highly lucrative for you if you play your cards right.

Insights from a Crack-Out Expert

Jesse Lipka plays the crack-out game about as well as anyone in the business, and he has made some interesting observations along the way. According to Jesse, NGC is more likely than PCGS to become excited when it gets a group of flashy, original coins, and it tends to reflect this by grading such coins optimistically. On the other hand, he said, NGC may penalize a gem coin if it is submitted in a group that also includes inferior coins. Jesse said PCGS is much more concerned with a coin's technical qualities. For that reason, he said that it sometimes overgrades coins which comply fully with the technical requirements for a grade but which don't have much pizzazz and may even be unattractive from the standpoints of luster and eye appeal. These unappealing coins, Jesse said, are hard to sell and end up getting sold at a discount.

I asked Jesse to tell me the crack-out that gave him the greatest satisfaction. After pondering the question, he pointed to his purchase of an 1873 doubled-die Indian Head cent, a coin which many feel is the king of Indian cents. He purchased the coin for $19,500 in a PCGS holder with a grade of Mint State-64 Red-Brown. He cracked the coin out of this holder and submitted it to NGC, which then graded it Mint State-65 Red-Brown. Leaving it in its new NGC holder, he then sent it to PCGS for consideration as a crossover—a process by which a coin in one service's holder is transferred to a different service's holder at the same or higher grade without having to be cracked out before submission. (For details on the mechanics of submitting coins for certification or crossover, see Appendix A—"How to Submit Coins to Grading Services.")

Lo and behold, the coin crossed over, ending up in a PCGS holder with a grade of Mint State-65 Red-Brown. Remember, this was the same coin PCGS had graded originally as Mint State-64 Red-Brown. With the coin now certified a full grade level higher, Jesse then sold it for a tremendous profit. To make this success story even sweeter, the dealer who bought it had *passed* on it when it was still in a Mint State-64 RB PCGS holder and it was offered to him for less than what Jesse originally paid.

BEAR-MARKET BARGAINS

The second group of coins that you should be buying *right now* consists of what might be called *bear-market bargains*. Many rare coins are selling today for just a small fraction of what they were worth at the market's last big peak in the late

1980s, and these have the potential to be tremendous winners when the bears give way to the bulls.

It's true that as this is written, the market remains depressed. But bad times aren't permanent; even the Great Depression of the early 1930s gave way to full recovery in time. And when the slumping coin market does get back on its feet, the prices may go up every bit as fast—and every bit as far—as they went down in the first place when the roaring bear market took hold.

When a coin plunges in value from $10,000 to $2,000, that's bad news indeed for anyone who paid $10,000 to obtain it. It's marvelous news, however, for anyone who wants that coin and *didn't* pay the price when the market was at its peak. In short, it's a great opportunity. There are untold thousands of great opportunities in the current coin marketplace. Be wary, however, of generic silver coins such as common-date Morgan silver dollars, Walking Liberty half dollars, and Mercury dimes in high levels of preservation. These coins have gone down in value tremendously, to be sure—but the number of pieces available has actually gone *up* significantly because of new submissions to the certification services. What's more, demand has diminished because so many investors—prime customers for these coins—have left the marketplace. These are coins to avoid at all costs, even if those costs seem incredibly cheap.

Rare Values

The market is replete with wonderful bargains today. As a matter of fact, *most* collectible coins are sensational values. You need to be sure, however, to purchase coins best suited for your particular game plan. If you're looking to maximize long-term potential gain, stick with coins that offer genuine rarity. If you're seeking shorter-term profits, take a closer look at generic gold coins. Unlike generic silver coins, these offer a realistic expectation of profit under certain market circumstances, as I will explain later in this chapter.

I've chosen three coins to illustrate the bargains that you can find today in truly rare coins. All are proofs—predominantly 19th-century proofs—and all are legitimately scarce and desirable coins, with small existing supplies and significant demand. In each case, I'm quoting the going market values in various levels of preservation at the market's last big peak, in mid-May 1989, and at the time this is written seven years later. The prices correspond to sight-unseen specimens; levels would be higher for premium-quality coins.

- *Proof nickel three-cent pieces:* In May 1989, these coins were selling for $1,750 in Proof-65, $3,650 in Proof-66, and $7,650 in Proof-67. Today, they're priced at just $410 in Proof-65, less than $700 in Proof-66, and $1,200 in Proof-67. I consider these exceptional buys!

  The Proof-67 merits particular scrutiny. An on-sight coin would have cost you eight or nine thousand dollars in May 1989 and, for a somewhat scarcer date, the wholesale price would have been $10,000. Today, that scarcer-date piece can probably be obtained for just $1,200. That's less than one-eighth the price it was bringing seven years ago. And it's every bit as rare and desirable now.

- *Proof Shield nickels:* In May 1989, these were listed at $1,875 in Proof-65, $4,100 in Proof-66, and $8,650 in Proof-67. Today, they're $525 in Proof-65, $730 in Proof-66, and $1,600 in Proof-67. Seven years ago, a premium-quality Proof-67 specimen would have cost you 12 or 14 thousand dollars. Today, you can get it for less than $2,000. That's a remarkable deal!

- *Proof Liberty nickels:* In May 1989, these cost $1,525 in Proof-65, $3,600 in Proof-66, and $10,750 in Proof-67. Today, they're just $420 in Proof-65, $675 in Proof-66, and $1,325 in Proof-67. Again, these are stunning values!

A List of Potential Winners

When David Hall talks about rare coins, people listen. David was a major figure in the coin market even before he founded PCGS in 1986, ushering in the Age of Certified Coins; for many years before that, he had been a prominent dealer. Since that time, his stature has grown even more. And people who buy and sell coins hang on his every word when he comments on any aspect of the marketplace.

At the time this book was nearing completion, David issued a statement giving a bullish assessment of the market and its direction. Rare coins, he said, "are hot again." He added: "We are actually in the initial states of what could be a major bull market."

Around that same time, David and I discussed the market's outlook in greater detail, exchanging candid views on which coins might be the best performers. We came up with a list that I will share with you now. It includes both regular-issue U.S. type coins and U.S. commemorative coins, and the price range is broad, stretching all the way from $120 to $15,000 as this is written.

COIN	GRADE	WHOLESALE VALUE 8/00
Two-cent piece	MS-65 RD	$1,000
Three-cent silver	PR-65	1,000
Capped Bust 25¢	MS-65	11,000
Liberty Seated 25¢	MS-65	1,300
1854–55 Liberty Seated 25¢ with arrows beside the date	MS-65	6,300
Trade $1	MS-65	7,000
1920 Pilgrim Tercentenary 50¢	MS-65	
1936 Long Island Tercentenary 50¢	MS-65	250
1918 Illinois Centennial 50¢	MS-65	300
1925-S California Jubilee 50¢	MS-65	650
1936 Delaware Tercentenary 50¢	MS-65	275
1934 Texas Centennial 50¢	MS-65	120

For people on limited budgets, David Hall recommended three "ultra bargains": common-date MS-66 Mercury dimes with full bands in the fasces ("40 bucks or so—an incredible deal") . . . slightly better-date Buffalo nickels—any dates in the 1930s other than 1937-P and 1938-D—whose going market price is under

$100 . . . and inexpensive pre-1982 commemoratives. For big-budget people, Hall said, "The world revolves around proof gold, and proof gold is an unbelievably good long-term deal. If we were to see any move in the gold bullion market that created more activity in the coin market, proof gold prices could easily double in value," he predicted.

Hall encourages collectors to assemble coins in sets, describing this as "a good long-term strategy." However, he considers it inadvisable to pursue coins in extremely high levels of preservation. "If you want to make money right now," he said, "don't get involved in what I call the gaga grades . . . condition rarities, fairly common coins in 69, 68, even 67 condition. Whether you're buying inexpensive coins or expensive coins, don't go for the wild grades."

Golden Opportunities

Gold bullion and rare coins have a symbiotic relationship. They complement each other well, and people with an interest in one of them tend to find the other appealing as well. In the 20-plus years since Americans regained the right to private gold ownership in 1974, strength in gold bullion has often gone hand-in-hand with similar strength in rare coins. The most dramatic example occurred in 1979 and 1980, when gold's amazing surge to $850 an ounce coincided with the coin market's most spectacular boom.

In recent years, the relationship between gold bullion and rare coins has been more a case of misery loving company. Both have been in the doldrums throughout the 1990s, and both are well below the price levels they scaled in the booming 1980s. But both are overdue for a turnaround, and if that upturn occurs in the bullion market first, it's likely to spread to the coin market, too, in short order. And if history is any guide—as it almost always is—a surge in the price of gold will be magnified when its impact hits the coin market.

If Gold Went Up $100 an Ounce

As this is written, gold is trading for about $270 an ounce, and its value hasn't changed much for many months. But experts see a realistic chance that given the right combination of economic circumstances, possibly including a sharp downturn on Wall Street, the yellow metal's price could easily reach the $500 range within a short period of time. And that could be an enormous boost for the coin market. I am convinced that if gold does go up $100 an ounce, many rare coins—and even some not-so-rare coins—will jump in value. And that could create tremendous opportunities for those who take advantage of the marketplace.

There is ample historical precedent for gold to go up dramatically and quickly. Just look at what happened in 1979 and 1980, when it surged within a year from $236 an ounce to $850. Even in recent years, amid the general stagnation, there have been periods when gold rose appreciably in short but significant spurts before dropping back to a dead calm. When that occurs, we see an almost immediate impact on coins which are bullion-sensitive—bullion-type coins and generic gold coins. I described this phenomenon in detail in Chapter 5. If the increase in gold bullion is sustained, the impact spreads to other gold coins with only incidental bullion value. And finally, it is felt by the marketplace as a whole, including coins with no precious metal at all.

During such periods, gold coins which possess numismatic value tend to rise in price even more sharply than the rise in gold itself. Like ripples in a pond when someone casts a stone, they grow ever larger as they spread.

Generic Gold

As I explained in Chapter 5, generic gold coins are an excellent short-term play—a way to reap handsome profits almost literally *right now*—if you buy them at a time of market inactivity and sell them when the price of gold is moving upward fast. Attractive Mint State specimens of common-date gold coins with a numismatic aspect—Saint-Gaudens $20s, Liberty $20s, and Indian $5s, for example—will magnify and multiply the price increase enjoyed by gold itself.

Under such circumstances, David Hall believes the coins most likely to yield big profits *right now* are Saint-Gaudens $20s and "almost all the Liberty gold" in grades of MS-64 and 65. "The generic gold issues will be the first to feel it and they'll feel it very quickly," he told me. "If gold went up 50 bucks, the price for MS-65 Saints could double." Hall sees it as "a relatively safe play" to buy generic gold when the market is dormant and set it aside for sale when things heat up. "You know, it's a pretty volatile world that we live in," he remarked, "but it certainly looks like a pretty safe bet."

The Impact on Rare Gold Coins

Generic gold coins such as common-date Saint-Gaudens double eagles are looked upon as collectibles, to be sure, but their precious-metal content is also a major factor in their value. Thus, it makes sense that a rise in the price of gold would have a direct impact on the value of these coins. I cited specific examples of this in Chapter 5. There's less apparent reason, though, why similar increases—or even more spectacular ones—should take place in the prices of rarer-date gold coins already selling for multiples of their precious-metal value. Yet we have seen such increases time and again. And we have even seen them, in brief but impressive bursts, when gold flexed its muscles only in passing.

"Every time gold bullion moves over $400 per ounce, prices seem to immediately jump up—especially for the top-quality gold coins," David Hall pointed out. "If gold makes a significant move above $400, prices could rise an additional 20 percent to 30 percent from current levels. If gold gets over $450 an ounce, prices could easily rise 30 percent to 50 percent. And if gold can get to $500 and stay there, prices could rise 50 percent to 100 percent on virtually all top-quality rare coins."

What would this mean in dollars and cents? Let's consider the no-motto Liberty $5, so named because it lacks the motto, "IN GOD WE TRUST." In Mint State-63, this genuinely rare coin type has a current market value as this is written of $5,600, or more than 20 times the value of the gold it contains. Based on David Hall's estimate, if gold were to go up $100 an ounce, we might very well see this coin rise in value to as much as $9,200. An MS-64 example, now $7,500, could shoot up to more than $17,000.

The impact would be felt by major rarities, too. In fact, they could enjoy an even bigger boost because they are so sensitive to even the very slightest rise in demand.

When rare collector coins react in this way to a rise in the price of gold, it's largely a matter of marketplace psychology. Bullion-market activity creates a positive climate for the coin market, too, and the newly kindled enthusiasm feeds upon itself. In a very real sense, it soon becomes a self-fulfilling prophecy. The strength in precious metals provides a security blanket, reassuring buyers and making them more receptive to purchasing coins as well. We then see this strong new demand acting upon supplies that are really much scarcer than most people ever realized. And this, in turn, drives prices sharply higher, attracting even more attention and bringing even more new buyers into the market.

A Spillover Effect

If a $100 rise in the price of gold bullion were sustained, the effect would soon spill over into Mint State type coins, proof type coins, and other rare coins not even made of gold, and, in many instances, not even made of precious metal.

- Proof-65 Barber quarters, worth about $1,200 as this is written, could very well go up more than 50 percent—to the $2,000 range—under such a scenario. Keep in mind, these coins were worth many thousands of dollars in the late 1980s.
- Proof-65 no-motto Liberty Seated quarters, now selling for $3,500, could jump almost overnight to $5,000 or more.
- Coins which are highly sensitive to changes in the population and census reports—coins graded Mint State-67 and 68 and Proof-67 and 68, for example—also are very sensitive to movements in bullion prices, and would rise in value significantly in response to a meaningful rise in the price of gold. In fact, this could prove to be the most profitable area of the marketplace if gold were to go up $100 an ounce and sustain the gain.

● Traditional U.S. commemorative coins—those issued prior to 1982—would feel the impact, too. As of this writing, beautiful white Mint State-65 examples of many of these coins are priced at $500 or less. In 1989, some of these coins carried price tags of $2,500, $3,000, or even $4,000. If gold went up $100 an ounce, the excitement could propel these coins to several times their current market value. Within a matter of weeks, they could easily become $1,500 or $2,000 coins.

Coin Dealers' Role

Coin dealers play a highly pivotal role in energizing the coin market when there is a surge in the price of precious metal. They do this, in part, by alerting their clients and getting the ball rolling, so to speak. But they are active participants—and crucial ones, at that—in the whole process. Indeed, they are the ultimate consumers of many coins, and because so many coin dealers buy and sell gold in bullion forms as well, they serve to cross-pollinate the interrelated coin and bullion markets. We saw graphic evidence of this during the white-hot coin market boom of 1980. Coin dealers made enormous sums of money trading in gold and silver at that time, and many of them plowed

Figure 9-9. *Cameo Proof-68 Morgan dollar graded by NGC.*

those profits right back into coins. That fueled the boom and drove up rare coins' prices even more.

An Overdue Boom

The *rare* coin market is overdue for a boom. Twelve years have passed since the market began its downturn, and that's a long time for traffic to be essentially one-way. There's reason to believe, though, that when the turnaround does take place—as it surely will—the slump's prolonged nature will make the upturn even more intense. Experience has shown that when similar deep recessions have occurred in other markets, such as stocks and real estate, the pent-up demand has made things fizz even more when the cork was removed.

A boost from gold bullion would be an enormous catalyst in bringing about a coin boom. We got a sneak preview of this in 1992 and again in 1993, when gold rose significantly for short periods and coins tagged along for the ride. Both times, shrewd buyers who purchased generic gold coins for quick short-term action were able to cash in their chips. During those two flurries, gold type coins rose in value sharply. Unfortunately, though, the gains didn't last long, and as soon as people saw a dip in bullion prices, they dropped coins, too, and the bubble that seemed so promising simply burst.

A Word of Caution

Despite recent gains in some market areas, rare coins remain at bear-market price levels as this book is written in 2000. Buying them at these levels could turn out to be a marvelous idea if gold goes up in value—especially if it rises $100 an ounce— and if the bears finally leave the scene. We could see coins appreciate tremendously once the market turns the elusive corner.

But I would be remiss not to add a word of caution: Although it is not far-fetched to suggest that gold might rise by $100 an ounce or even more, it's also quite possible that a gain of this type might be short-lived. If we do see this type of increase, I urge you to view it not as the time to buy even more gold-related coins, but rather as the time to cash out some of the ones you already have. Grab your profits and sit on the sidelines for a while—waiting for gold to come *down* $100—before you start buying again.

The generic gold game is not a risk-free play, as some people learned when gold staged its rallies in 1992 and 1993. At that time, playing this game was almost like trying to catch a falling knife. Some people did it successfully—but a lot of others got bloodied. Some got hurt, as well, attempting to board the bandwagon after it was already under way. And some lost pieces of their financial "luggage" when the rally stopped short and prices went skidding.

No one can say for sure where gold may be headed, but it's reasonable to believe that it may rise sharply in value within the next couple of years—possibly even within the next few months. And those who hope to hitch their wagons to that star should start preparing their hitching posts now. Once the bandwagon hits the open road, we're liable to be in for quite a ride.

POPULATION AND CENSUS REPORTS

In years gone by, a coin's availability was measured by simply checking its mintage figure—the number of examples produced by the U.S. Mint of any given coin in any given year and at any given mint. There were some exceptions, to be sure; certain silver dollars and gold coins were scarcer than their mintages would suggest, for example, because many pieces had been melted over the years. But most buyers and sellers were familiar with these exceptions and, by and large, dealers and collectors accepted mintage figures as accurate reflections of available supplies.

Since the rise to prominence of independent grading services during the 1980s, the marketplace has been given a new set of tools for measuring the supply of a given coin: the population and census reports issued by the leading grading services. These reports, pegged primarily to Mint State and proof coins (the kinds that account for the overwhelming majority of grading-service submissions) show the certified population of every U.S. coin graded by each service—the cumulative number graded and encapsulated by PCGS, NGC, and ANACS. By checking the monthly *Population Reports* issued by PCGS, the corresponding *Census Reports* put out by NGC, and the twice-yearly *Population Reports* from ANACS, buyers and sellers can see at a glance the cumulative grading activity of these companies—the total number of coins of any given type certified by each service in each of the major grade classifications.

Interpreting Population Reports

In a sense, population and census reports are fine-tuned versions of the mintage reports issued each year by the Mint. They zoom in from the wide-angle shot of a coin's total mintage to offer a close-up look at the relative numbers available in specific grade levels—primarily in the Mint State range and in proof. But whereas mintage figures establish an outer limit for a given coin's supply—a figure that will shrink as time goes by and coins are lost or melted—the population and census figures tend to grow in time as more and more examples are submitted to the services and certified.

You should be suspicious of any coin whose certified population has grown by leaps and bounds in recent years. You should be doubly suspicious if the coin is a type that appeals primarily to investors, for recent years have witnessed a sharp decline—not a gain—in coin-buying activity by investors. Perhaps the best examples of coins with this double whammy are common-date Morgan dollars graded Mint State-65. These shimmering silver dollars are just as attractive as ever, and they certainly seem like bargains at current market levels: They're priced at less than one-fifth of the figures they commanded in the late 1980s. But two fundamental changes have occurred: Far more examples have been certified since then, and far fewer people are buying them today. In short, supply is up and demand is down—and that's a sure-fire formula for disaster.

Unfortunately, population and census reports are seriously flawed. Their usefulness is compromised by the fact that they fail to distinguish between coins being submitted for the first time and those being resubmitted—perhaps many times—in quest of an upgrade. For this and other reasons, the figures simply cannot be relied upon. In a sense, the close-up pictures they give us of market activity are badly out of focus—and this is too bad. Clear, sharp pictures would be worth not only a thousand words, but perhaps many thousands of dollars.

CHAPTER 10

THE U.S. MINT AND ITS ONSLAUGHT OF "COLLECTIBLE" COINS

Certain coin dealers stand out above the rest because of the volume of business they handle, the name recognition they enjoy, the longevity they have built up, or perhaps a combination of all these factors and others as well. Bowers and Merena

Figure 10-1. *1989 Bicentennial of the Congress half eagle.* The U.S. Mint sold these for as much as $225 each during the year of issue. In August 2000, these coins weren't worth much more than their gold bullion value: $90. *Photo courtesy U.S. Mint Press Kit.*

Figure 10-2 (left and right). *2000 Massachusetts States quarter struck at the Denver Mint.* This type of coin, now available in pocket change, has caused a national collecting frenzy among over 100 million Americans.

Galleries, Heritage Rare Coin Galleries, and Stack's all fall into this exclusive group.

Which of these well-known firms is the world's largest coin dealer? The answer is none of the above. None of them, in fact, comes even close. That distinction belongs to a man better

Figure 10-3. *Coin-convention booth of album manufacturer H. E. Harris & Co. attests to the popularity of the states quarters and Sacagawea dollars as collectibles.* Millions of albums and folders that house these coins have already been sold.

known to people around the planet for just about anything but: the venerable symbol of the U.S. federal government, Uncle Sam.

As a result of the 50 States quarters program and the Sacagawea dollar, more than ever the United States Mint has become a towering presence in the coin market—though strictly as a seller, never a buyer. Each year, the Mint routinely sells hundreds of millions of dollars in premium-priced coins and coin sets to a broad cross-section of the American public, including not only established coin hobbyists but also noncollectors with little or no knowledge about rare coins. Then again, the coins being sold by the Mint are seldom truly rare; on the contrary, they are almost always struck in very significant numbers, well beyond the level that experienced collectors deem scarce, much less rare.

It's true that the supply equals the demand, at least initially; the Mint produces these items—notably proof sets and commemorative coins—in quantities equal to the number of orders it receives. Those orders, generated by a huge mailing list and slick marketing gimmicks, used to far outstrip the core collector base for such material—until Americans started "collecting" the states quarters.

Experience has been an interesting teacher in this area, as the value of these products tended to fall for many years—often to just a very small fraction of the prices at which they were issued. However, with the release of the states quarters and Sacagawea dollars—and all of the Mint products that go with them—many of these once lackluster "investments" began to appreciate in value substantially. A number of recently released proof sets, in particular, have seen their values soar several hundred percent.

This is not to say that all modern Mint products are good investments. A phenomenon with surprising parallels to the coin boom of the early 1960s (see the Introduction) took shape in 1999 as a frenzy of collecting activity surrounded the release of state quarters. Once-shunned modern coins suddenly became the darlings of the coin marketplace as new collectors snapped up available Mint products that had been released over the last several years. The boom in modern Mint products is truly a

Figure 10-4. *1952 Proof Set*. Earlier proof sets such as this one have appreciated in value smartly over the years. *Photo courtesy Captial Plastics, Inc.*

craze, as much of the purchasing is being done by uninformed accumulators. But most importantly, these coins aren't rare: In some cases, millions were minted, and most have been preserved and are still available in their original high grade. Rules of thumb of coin investment that I have repeated time and again are: *Coins which are common now will remain common for the foreseeable future. Coins which are scarce can become rare. And coins which are rare often become rarer.*

Figure 10-5. *1981-S Proof Set*. The later-date proof sets are still a mixed bag in terms of price performance. Despite phenomenal performance by some sets, many late-date proof sets remain losers.

A veteran dealer interviewed in Chapter 7 recommends that you cash out of your position in state quarters Mint products, but he forecasts that the frenzy could last until 2009. So enter this speculative market at your own peril.

"Collectible" coins sold by the U.S. Mint fall into four major categories: proof sets, uncirculated coin sets (also known as "mint sets"), commemorative coins, and premium versions of the American Eagle gold and silver bullion coins. Let's take a closer look at each of these.

- Proof sets are annual coin sets containing one proof—or specimen-quality example—of each regular U.S. coin being produced for circulation that year. The Mint produces proofs by taking special, highly polished planchets, or coin blanks, and striking them multiple times at slower speed and with higher pressure than what it uses for standard-quality coins. The resulting coins emerge with mirrorlike surfaces and very sharp detail, and often with attractive frosting on the devices, or raised portions of the design. The Mint also offers silver proof sets, in which three coins—the dime, quarter, and half dollar—are made from a 90-percent silver alloy instead of the usual clad copper-nickel. Until being discontinued in the mid-1990s, two other options were the "Prestige set" and "Premier set," which contained the regular (nonsilver) proof coins plus a proof example of one of the new commemorative coins being issued that year. (Prestige sets had more elaborate packaging than Premier sets.)
- Mint sets, like proof sets, are issued each year—but they differ in two key respects. First, the coins in a mint set are a business-strike quality—that is, they are equivalent to the coins that are produced for circulation, although the Mint reportedly strives to include superior pieces in these sets. Second, a mint set contains one example of each different coin from each mint that issued that coin during the year. Thus, if cents are being struck at both the Philadelphia and Denver mints in a certain year, the mint set for that year will include two different cents—one from each mint.

- Commemorative coins are coins produced specifically to honor some noteworthy person, place, or event or mark some special occasion. Typically, they are issued in just a single year and in limited quantities, and are sold to collectors and interested noncollectors for a price in excess of their face value. United States commemorative coins are divided into two categories, "traditional" and "modern," according to the time frame in which they were produced. "Traditional" commemoratives are those made by the U.S. Mint from 1892, when the program started, through 1954, when the Treasury Department suspended it because of recurrent abuses. "Modern" commemoratives are those produced by the Mint since 1982, when the program was revived following a hiatus of nearly three decades. Unfortunately, as I will show, the modern series also has been plagued by abuses.

- American Eagle bullion coins have been struck by the Mint each year since 1986. They were authorized by Congress as U.S. alternatives to existing bullion coins, such as South Africa's Krugerrand and Canada's Maple Leaf. By definition, a bullion coin is one whose price is based on the value of the metal it contains, rising or falling in direct and immediate response to rises or falls in the value of the metal itself. For example, the price of a one-ounce bullion gold coin is determined by taking the current market value of one ounce of gold and adding a small surcharge to cover the costs of producing and distributing the coin. In addition to the regular American Eagle coins, which are made in business-strike quality, the Mint has also offered special proof versions of some or all of the coins. These are sold at premiums well above the value of the metal they contain, based upon the premise that their high quality and limited mintages give them added worth as collectibles.

PROOF SETS' PRICE PERFORMANCE

For many years, U.S. proof sets were a marvelous buy. From 1950 through 1964, the Mint sold these sets for $2.10 apiece, and they never failed to rise—and stay—well above that level in the resale market. Many collectors ordered multiple sets from the Mint every year, keeping one or two for themselves and selling the rest at an immediate and often substantial profit. As word got around about this, even noncollectors started buying proof sets every year and stashing them away as a "guaranteed" form of investment. They looked upon this as part of their retirement nest egg, or perhaps as a way to help put their children through college in years to come.

In truth, those proof sets did provide good value for those who acquired them directly from the Mint, and all of them continue to be worth substantially more than their $2.10 issue price. For the most part, however, subsequent proof sets haven't fared nearly as well. The Mint suspended production of these sets in 1965 because it needed all of its equipment to combat a nationwide coin shortage—and when it resumed the program in 1968, the sets had a much higher price tag and much lower potential as an investment. The Mint more than doubled the issue price of the sets, from $2.10 to $5 apiece, thereby wiping out (and taking for itself) the immediate profit buyers had enjoyed in earlier years. Adding insult to this financial injury, the precious-metal content provided by previous proof sets was now greatly reduced: The dime and quarter no longer contained any silver, and the half dollar had only 40 percent. Up to 1964, all three coins had been 90 percent silver. Thus, proof set buyers were paying a lot more but getting much less in return. The 1968 proof set did enjoy a speculative surge at the start, during which pent-up demand pushed its price well above $5 in the secondary market. But the bubble soon burst and even today, more than thirty years later, the set is still worth little or no premium over its issue price.

Since then, the Mint has raised the issue price of its regular proof set six more times. It provided something meaningful in return on only two occasions: in 1973, when it boosted the price from $5 to $7 to cover the inclusion of a new coin, the Eisenhower dollar, and in 1999, when it included all five statehood quarters for that year, rather than just a single 25-cent piece as in previous years. There also was a hidden price increase in 1982, when the Mint kept the price the same despite the removal of the Susan B. Anthony dollar, whose production had been halted the previous year. In 1999, with the introduction of the states quarters program, proof set sales went through the roof—despite the increased issue price of $19.95 for the complete nine-coin set. (The Mint also offered a five-coin proof set containing just the statehood quarters for an issue price of $13.95.) The year 2000 proof set consists of the cent, nickel, dime, five quarter dollars, the half dollar, and the Sacagawea dollar. And this time, the Mint actually added something (the new "golden dollar") without raising the price. The 2000 proof set was expected to have a total mintage of 3 million or more—well above the levels of recent years, reflecting public interest in the statehood quarters and, to some extent, the new dollar coin. In 1999, the Mint also offered a nine-coin silver proof set for $31.95. It was expected to do likewise in 2000, but no announcement had been made as of late October 2000.

Are hobby leaders still trashing modern proof sets as "common" and "poor investments"?

"There is strong potential for both the 1999 and 2000 proof sets as an investment," says David L. Ganz, past president of the American Numismatic Association and author of *The Official Guidebook to America's State Quarters* (House of Collectibles, mass-market, 2000). "Collectors and accumulators in 2005 who start collecting this series will have to go back to Year One and Two. There are 105 million people collecting these coins right now, and if even 1 percent collect these sets, the prices will go out of sight."

Proof sets produced since 1968 have been far less successful in the secondary market than their predecessors, with the exception of proof sets from the mid-1990s to date. Every single proof set prior to 1968 still commands a premium over its issue price, while many sets from 1968 onward are still worth *less than* issue price today.

The proof set craze has caused a number of sets from 1995 to date (as this is written in August 2000) to experience very solid upward adjustments. The chart here illustrates just how dramatic some of those gains have been.

ONE YEAR PRICE* COMPARISON OF SELECTED
U.S. PROOF SETS, 1995–1998

PROOF SET	JULY 23, 1999 VALUE	JULY 21, 2000 VALUE
1995-S	$38.00	$75.00
1995-S Silver	40.00	112.00
1995-S Prem. Silver	37.00	120.00
1996-S	7.00	9.00
1996-S Prem.	120.00	210.00
1996-S Silver	24.00	50.00
1996-S Prem. Silver	27.00	55.00
1997-S	24.50	30.50
1997-S Silver	23.00	112.00
1997-S Prem. Silver	28.00	120.00
1998-S	18.00	20.00
1998-S Silver	24.00	40.00

*Prices listed are "bid" prices as recorded in *The Coin Dealer Newsletter.*

MODERN COMMEMORATIVE COINS

For many years, modern U.S. commemorative coins were a big loser in the resale market. The primary reason is obvious: U.S. commemoratives issued since 1982 have been overpriced consistently by the government. Much of the blame for this lies not with the Mint but rather with Congress, which inevitably orders the Mint to tack hefty surcharges onto the prices of these coins and turn the money over to various "worthy causes." Typically, Congress mandates surcharges of $7 per coin on commemorative silver dollars and $30 per coin on half eagles (or $5 gold pieces). These charges amount to enforced contributions to the causes for which the coins are issued, such as the U.S. Olympic movement and the World Cup Soccer program. They also inflate the coins' issue prices well beyond the levels at which they otherwise could have been sold. Traditional U.S. commemoratives—those issued prior to 1955—also were sold at a premium, it's true, and also raised funds for organizations associated with their issuance. But during that era, the premiums were much smaller, often amounting to only two or three times face value.

Modern commemoratives often bring somewhat more than issue price in the resale market during the period just after their introduction. But supply soon overtakes demand as more and more of the coins are shipped to their buyers. There have been few sellouts to date, for until recently, Congress established mintage limits well above the levels it could—and should—have anticipated. At times, in fact, the limits have been ludicrously high. For instance, Congress authorized up to 10.5 million coins in three different denominations for the 1992 Olympic Games, and the Mint ended up selling fewer than 1.5 million. A similar scenario occurred the following year, when 10.75 million coins were authorized for the World Cup Soccer Games and fewer than 1.5 million were sold. In that case, the Mint even claimed to have lost money because of overproduction and other outlays tied to expectations of much higher sales.

Even with the success of the state quarters program, many modern commemoratives still are turning in lackluster performances. There have been some notable exceptions, but these two-dozen or so "winners" are not representative of the entire series. Many people have focused on the impressive gains of certain issues—and the performance, for coins which are so common, is admittedly fascinating. For example, in a one-year period (1999–2000), the 1997 Jackie Robinson four-coin set doubled in value, from $450 to $900.

The chart here illustrates how ten top modern silver commemorative coins performed over a one-year period (1999–2000).

ONE-YEAR PRICE* COMPARISON OF SELECTED MODERN COMMEMORATIVES, 1996–1998

MODERN B.U. SILVER DOLLAR COMMEMORATIVE	JULY 23, 1999 VALUE	JULY 14, 2000 VALUE
1996-D Wheelchair Athlete	$55.00	$135.00
1996-D Tennis	48.00	93.00
1996-D Rowing	48.00	120.00
1996-D High Jump	48.00	120.00

* Prices listed are "bid" prices as recorded in *The Coin Dealer Newsletter*.

MODERN B.U. SILVER DOLLAR COMMEMORATIVE	JULY 23, 1999 VALUE	JULY 14, 2000 VALUE
1996-S Community Service	65.00	200.00
1996-D Smithsonian Anniversary	37.00	65.00
1997-P Botanic Garden	25.00	28.00
1997-S Jackie Robinson	24.00	39.00
1997-P Law Enforcement	30.00	70.00
1998-S Black Patriots	30.00	62.00

The bottom line for buyers of modern U.S. commemoratives has been that, despite the extraordinary price performance of some of these issues, for many the resale value is far less than what the Mint charged for the coins in the first place. In 1987, for example, the Mint charged $200 for a $5 gold piece celebrating the 200th anniversary of the U.S. Constitution; at this writing, thirteen years later, that coin can be purchased in the secondary market for $90. In 1990, the Mint charged $25 for a silver dollar marking the 100th anniversary of Dwight D. Eisenhower's birth; today, that coin can be bought from a dealer for just $10. Nor are these isolated cases: In the long term, many modern commemoratives issued by the Mint (well over one hundred different coins so far) have plummeted below, and often well below, the issue price.

Professional numismatist Harvey G. Stack told a House of Representatives subcommittee in July of 1995 that in selling such coins to the public, the Mint should affix a warning label similar to the surgeon general's notice on cigarette packages. "These are not rare coins," Stack declared. "The only thing rarer than these modern commemoratives will be finding someone to give you a profit when you try to sell them." Then-Mint Director Phillip N. Diehl also appeared before the House subcommittee that day, and startled critics of the commemorative coin program with a frank admission. "The record is absolutely clear: These coins are not good investments," Diehl acknowledged. He said that they are authorized by Congress, and issued by the Mint, not as potential sources of profit for their purchasers, but rather as "keepsakes" and "mementos." In yet another eyebrow-raising comment, he told the gathering: "We compete with T-shirts."

Judging from the sorry track record of some of these modern commemoratives, T-shirts represent a better buy; at least their buyers have something to wear. All too often, purchasers of some of these commemoratives seem to be *losing* their shirts, at least in a figurative sense (and certainly in a financial sense). Beth Deisher, the savvy editor of the weekly hobby newspaper *Coin World*, told the same members of Congress that the secondary market for modern U.S. commemoratives is "weak to nonexistent." Said Deisher: "If a collector chooses to liquidate, it's difficult to find a buyer, and he or she can reasonably expect to receive from 50 to 65 percent of purchase price for an entire set of modern U.S. commemoratives."

TRAPS SET BY THE MINT AND HOW TO AVOID THEM

The U.S. Mint has been careful to avoid using the "I-word"—*investment*—in advertising and brochures soliciting orders for proof sets, commemorative coins, and other "collectibles" in its growing product line. There can be little doubt, however, that these coins are represented as good values. "Keepsakes" and "mementos"—the words used by former Mint Director Diehl himself—are, after all, widely perceived as items well worth owning and passing on to future generations, at least in part because of their intrinsic worth. It's cynical for the Mint to suggest that profit motive does not play a major part in many buyers' decisions to purchase its products. On the contrary, Mint officials like to cite survey results showing that many buyers consider these products to be good investments. And if buyers had purchased only the coins shown on the charts in this chapter, those purchases actually might have turned out to be good investments. Unfortunately, however, these isolated winners are the exceptions, not the rule. Likewise, the proof sets from the mid-1990s to date which have surged in value in the marketplace of 2000, in the months just before this is being written, remain very much in the minority among U.S. proof sets of the last third of a century. Of the proof sets issued since 1968, the great majority still carry the stigma of being poor investments, and many are still selling below their issue prices—without even allowing for the inroads of inflation.

The lesson is clear. People shouldn't buy coins—from the Mint or anyone else—until they learn enough to make an informed judgment. Uncle Sam is the nation's biggest coin dealer, and his coins don't come with a price guarantee any more than any other dealer's.

CHAPTER 11

MYTHS AND FALLACIES AND BANKRUPT CONVENTIONAL WISDOM

It isn't always wise to accept conventional wisdom. All too often, people place blind faith in sage-sounding dictums that seem like solid truths but are, in fact, merely myths and fallacies beneath their false veneer of respectability.

This is true with coins, just as with everything else. And frequently, the myths that masquerade as wisdom in the field of numismatics are teachings that have been heard for many years. Long repetition has given them an aura of inevitability—even infallibility. But no matter how many times it is repeated, a myth remains an illusion, and that's a fancy way of saying it's a lie.

Recognizing fallacies isn't always easy. Some enjoy wide currency and thus convey a sense of false security. Even common sense may not be a perfect guide in helping you distinguish fact from myth. Still, it is essential to exercise good judgment—basic common sense—in making important decisions regarding coins. And above all, it is vital to keep an open mind: Question, analyze, and evaluate everything—even so-called axioms that seem at first glance like the gospel truth.

Here are some examples of the myths that mislead the unwary in today's coin marketplace:

Myth No. 1: *Certified coins assigned the same grade are worth the same amount of money.*

This is simply not true. As I explained in Chapter 3, coin grading is performed on a spectrum or continuum. Some coins rank at the high end of a grading bracket, very nearly qualifying for the next-higher level; others fall at the low end and just miss dropping to the next-lower level; and still others land right in the middle. It would be naïve to assume that buyers and sellers would view—and value—these coins precisely the same. Logic dictates that a high-end Mint State-65 coin, being almost a full grade better than a low-end 65 coin, should bring a higher price, and in practice it does: The difference in market value between two such pieces frequently amounts to many hundreds of dollars. It takes sophistication and a keen knowledge of grading to spot the difference at times, but other times the contrast may be quite obvious.

The people who write price guides and create the pricing structure have given serious thought to listing coin values—for certain grades, at least—by showing a range of prices, rather than using a one-price-fits-all structure. Let's say a certain coin is listed at $900 in the grade of 64 and $2,000 in 65. It would probably be more accurate to list a price range of $700 to $1,400 for the 64 grade, and $1,600 to $3,000 for the 65. The point is, a coin's desirability—and value—can jump dramatically not only from one grade to the next, but also within a given grade. Coin grading is not an exact science. It's an opinion—an informed opinion, yes, but an opinion nonetheless. And people who grade coins are craftsmen, not scientists. So in analyzing a grade to determine what something is worth, we need to proceed with flexibility, not precision, and give weight not only to the big picture but also to the small but meaningful nuance.

Myth No. 2: *Certified coins are almost always traded sight-unseen.*

The advent of certified coins in the late 1980s was followed by the establishment of the Certified Coin Exchange, a trading network on which "slabbed" coins changed hands routinely on a sight-unseen basis, very much like commodities. This conveyed the impression that *all* certified coins could—and would—be traded in this manner and reinforced Wall Street's interest in rare coins. The fact is, however, that even when coins were hot in the late 1980s, only certain coins were commoditized in this fashion. The system was practical only for coins which exist in sufficient quantities to be readily interchangeable—or in trading terminology, to be *fungible.* Morgan silver dollars graded Mint State-65 fill this bill; so do Walking Liberty half dollars in high levels of preservation. But with these and other series, only common-date pieces were—and are—considered to be fungible and traded sight-unseen.

Even at the market's peak, most certified coins were bought and sold sight-seen; in other words, their buyers demanded to see them first. In the weak market environment of the 1990s, buyers have been even more discriminating, and even more insistent on examining everything first before plunking down their hard-earned cash. A numerical grading system may be an excellent guide, but personal taste has always played a basic, crucial role in coin-buying decisions, and undoubtedly always will. Likewise, coin dealers know it's to their advantage to show off their merchandise when it's attractive, and thus resort to sight-unseen trading only when disposing of lower-end coins. This should make you wary of accepting any offer to purchase your coins sight-unseen: A sight-unseen offer is pegged to the bottom-most coins within a given grade, not to coins a cut above the rest.

Myth No. 3: *Price-performance data confirm that rare coins are a marvelous investment.*

In 1978, Salomon Brothers, Inc., the respected Wall Street brokerage house, began including rare coins in its annual surveys of popular investment vehicles. To the delight of the nation's coin dealers, these surveys found coins to be among the very best performers being tracked; in fact, they showed that over the long haul, rare coins had outperformed stocks, bonds, real estate, and other more traditional forms of investment. Soon, these reports were being trumpeted loudly not only by legitimate coin dealers but also by less reputable sellers drawn to the field by the lure of quick profits. This, in turn, set the stage for some serious reversals of fortune—individually and collectively; as new investors made ill-advised purchases from seemingly omnipresent telemarketers, they helped sow the seeds for the downfall of the coin market as a whole. Initially, however, the wide dissemination of the Salomon surveys' findings created the impression among the general public that rare coins were indeed a great investment, and many continued to cling to that belief even when coin prices plunged and remained deep in the doldrums for years thereafter.

The fact is, many coins *were* good investments at the outset of the Salomon Brothers' studies; in the coin and bullion boom of 1979 and 1980, high-grade coins enjoyed an astronomical rise in market value. And many had experienced healthy gains already during the 10-year period preceding coins' inclusion in the surveys (a period Salomon covered, retroactively, by using historical data). Unfortunately, though, the Salomon survey of coins was flawed from the very outset because its conclusions were based on a "market basket" of coins too small and too narrowly drawn to accurately reflect marketplace conditions as a whole. The 20 coins in this basket consisted overwhelmingly of collector-type coins in Mint-State but less than gem condition— hardly representative of a market where the action, throughout the 1980s, was in very high-grade investor-type coins. What's more, there was not a single gold coin among the 20, despite the significant role played by gold coins in the marketplace.

By the early 1990s, abuse of the Salomon surveys had caused such serious problems that the Federal Trade Commission pressured the firm to remove rare coins from its studies. It was probably just as well: By then, it was amply clear that far from being great investment vehicles, many rare coins had been doing dismally.

Beyond the inadequacies of the Salomon Brothers studies,

price-performance data tracking rare coins inevitably reflect another major deficiency that renders them highly misleading, if not downright meaningless: They fail to give proper weight—and often give no weight at all—to changes in grading standards that occurred during the period they are covering. Well-known market analyst Maurice H. Rosen of Plainview, New York, has documented this problem in great detail. Rosen has amassed compelling evidence that grading standards industry-wide tightened dramatically in the mid-1980s, effectively reducing the grades of many coins several levels—or even more—below the ones assigned in earlier years.

We're seeing the opposite phenomenon today: Grading standards have actually *loosened* somewhat at some of the certification services, so coins that were processed prior to the change may now be *undergraded* in relation to the companies' current standards. This can have the effect of making a given coin—or even the overall marketplace—seem to be doing worse than it actually is. Let's say that in 1989 you bought a coin that PCGS had certified as Proof-64 and you paid the going price of $3,000. Today, the price in Proof-64 may be only $1,000, so on paper you seem to have lost $2,000. But that coin might very well be Proof-65 by current grading standards at PCGS, and if it had been a premium-quality 64 coin in 1989, it might even merit a Proof-66 grade today. In that event, it might be worth close to what you paid for it—say, $2,500 or so—if it were removed from its 1989 holder, resubmitted to PCGS, and graded by today's looser standards. For details on recent changes in coin-grading standards, I suggest that you read the fourth edition of my book, *The Coin Collector's Survival Manual* (Bonus Books, 2000, $18.95).

The lesson from all of this is crystal-clear: Price-performance data can easily be manipulated to support whatever point the company or person disseminating the data is trying to make. Rare coins can indeed be an excellent investment—even in adverse marketplace conditions—if their purchase is approached with imagination, prudence, and a well-conceived strategy. But price-performance data, in all too many instances, don't confirm a thing except the devious nature of their compilers.

Myth No. 4: *Coins are attractive as long-term investments.*

At one time, it was accepted as a basic truism that if you acquired desirable coins at a fair market price, stored them properly, and held them long enough, you would reap a handsome profit. But that was then, this is now—and yesteryear's blueprint for guaranteed success is at best a chancy strategy today. The coin market nowadays is more speculative and volatile than it was in the good old days, just a generation ago, and it's hard to predict with any degree of accuracy what's going to happen even a few months or weeks down the line, much less 10 or 20 years.

One reason for the change is that coin collecting isn't a growth industry anymore. Every available measuring stick suggests that it peaked as a hobby in 1964 and hasn't come close to regaining that level of interest. Consider, for example, the weekly circulation of *Coin World,* a newspaper published by Amos Press of Sidney, Ohio, which enjoys a reputation as the coin hobby's journal of record. In 1964, *Coin World* reached its all-time high distribution of 175,000 copies per week; as this is written 36 years later, its circulation is less than 100,000. The steady growth in prices that people took for granted a generation ago was based to a large extent on the steady, continuing growth in the hobby's collector base. Now that the base has shrunk, the upward pressure on prices is diminished. It's really a simple case of supply and demand.

Then, too, we are seeing a much different breed of coin buyer today. In fact, investors in general are much more sophisticated, not only when it comes to buying coins, but in terms of investments as a whole. They no longer feel as threatened by the specter of inflation, or by the possibility that the dollar may be devalued. They're shielding themselves against such concerns by sheltering their wealth in stock and mutual funds. Faced with the prospect of inflation, investors in bygone years might have gone to a coin dealer and said, "Here's $100,000. I want to buy coins and precious metals and hold them for the duration." Today's investors call their broker instead and say, "Transfer X amount of dollars from my ABC growth-stock fund to a gold

coin market hit a spectacular top at the start of 1980 before falling back to a bottom in 1982.

The market hit a top again in 1986, and under normal conditions it would have begun sliding thereafter, possibly bottoming out in 1988 or '89. But artificial stimuli kept the boom going and made it even stronger. First came the advent of certified coins in 1986 with the establishment of PCGS, which in turn was followed closely by the founding of the rival NGC. Then came the influx of Wall Street money, lured by the prospect that certified coins would make it easy to buy and sell coins much like stocks. Up to that point, the coin market's booms and busts had always come in response to what Maurice Rosen calls "economic justification"—inflation pushing coin prices higher, for example, and disinflation pushing them down. But this time, the boom was artificial, and just as it's not nice to fool with Mother Nature, it also can be risky to tamper with natural rhythms in marketplace economics. When the overlong market boom finally hit its top in May 1989, it gave way to a bust that proved to be longer and deeper than anyone imagined at the outset.

As this is written, the market is doing well, thanks in no small measure to widespread interest generated by the statehood Washington quarters. But beyond the short term, its future is by no means crystal-clear. What does seem clear is that regular market cycles are unlikely to return in their previous form. Too much has changed, not only within the coin market itself, but also in the wider investment marketplace. Investors today are much better informed and much more discriminating than their counterparts of the past, and they have a much broader selection of money-making vehicles to choose from—an immense supermarket shelf of financial products. They're unlikely to follow blindly when promoters tout coins as incredible investments; they'll demand to see tangible evidence—and that may not be easy to provide, since coins' price-performance record has now been tarnished. Unless and until the coin market gets on track again, the emphasis is likely to be on short-term trends and short-term gains, not the long-range picture that gave coin buyers such comfort and security in the past.

Myth No. 7: *A rare coin's value varies in direct proportion to its population.*

Low mintages and high prices often go hand in hand. Thus, it's not surprising that people see big dollar signs when they come across coins with small numbers next to them in the population and census reports issued by the certification services. These reports, published periodically, list the number of pieces graded by the companies for each different date of each different coin in every grade.

Often, low figures in population reports do indeed point to coins of great rarity and value. But rarity is not the only significant factor in determining how much a coin is worth. Demand is important, too: Coins may have extremely low populations and yet command surprisingly modest premiums if the number of people pursuing them is similarly small. Then, too, numbers can and do lie. Far from suggesting great rarity, a low population actually might reflect extreme commonness: A high-mintage modern coin, for example, might have a low population in one of these reports because so few people found it worthwhile to send any in for certification. Because their premium value is so small, coins such as this aren't worth the bother and expense of being certified.

Myth No. 8: *Population and census reports are 100 percent reliable.*

Population reports are helpful and informative, but at times they can be thoroughly misleading. Perhaps the biggest reason for this is the fact that they don't discriminate between resubmissions and totally new ones. Right from the very inception of the certification services, people have been cracking coins out of their plastic slabs and submitting them again in search of a higher grade, and each time a coin is resubmitted, it's listed in "pop" reports as a new submission.

The incentive can be great for resubmitting a coin, especially one with claims to a higher grade. To illustrate the point, suppose you had a magnificent Morgan dollar that seemed to qualify easily as Mint State-65 but came back instead as Mint State-64 because of a tiny scratch on the reverse. And suppose that coin was worth $200 in Mint State-64 but the going market price was $1,000 in 65. You'd surely crack it out of its MS-64 holder and resubmit it—several times, if necessary—in hopes of getting a grade of 65. The potential financial windfall would more than cover the cost of many such resubmissions.

Does it make sense to resubmit coins? Absolutely. Does it make sense to rely upon census and population reports as accurate barometers of coins' true rarity? Certainly not. All too frequently, resubmissions skew these reports.

Myth No. 9: *You always should buy the highest-grade coin you can afford.*

This rule of thumb has been around so long, and sounds so convincing, that it seems almost blasphemous to question it. And many times, it's actually good advice: Historically, high-grade coins have usually outperformed their lower-grade cousins. I tend to recoil, however, from absolutes. I don't like rules that include the word "always"—with the solitary exception of "Always get your money's worth."

It's true that high-grade coins tend to produce the best returns. But this isn't always the case, and what is wise at one point in time may be ill-advised at another. It would have been very wise, for example, to purchase supergrade coins in 1986 and '87, when coins in very high levels of preservation—levels such as Mint State-67 and 68—were bringing just modest premiums above similar coins graded Mint State-65. These coins could have been sold in 1989 for substantial profits. But 1989 was a very bad time to *purchase* supergrade coins, and lower-grade pieces would have represented far better values, judged on the basis of 20-20 hindsight. Looking back, it's clear that by and large, coins graded Proof-63 have held their value since 1989 far better than coins graded Proof-67 and 68.

I'm bothered, as well, by yet another aspect of the drumbeat insistence on always buying only the very best: It tends to put a damper on the coin collecting activities of those who are young or otherwise in no position to spend large sums of money. It seems to suggest that youngsters just getting started in coins should spend their limited funds on one or two high-grade pieces, rather than settling for lower grades and filling more holes in their coin boards. To me, that's not the way for new-comers to get started in the hobby.

Myth No. 10: *Certified coins always represent the best deal.*

This is just not so. In the first place, grading and pricing are two separate issues, and although certification may give you re-assurance regarding the grade of a coin, it doesn't guarantee that you're getting a good deal. No matter how accurately a coin may be graded, you'll get a lousy deal if it isn't fairly priced. I dis-cuss this point in detail in Chapter 4.

Beyond this, nobody's perfect—including the grading experts at the certification services—and more than a few of the coins housed in these companies' "slabs" are overgraded or otherwise problem-plagued. Some, for example, were artificially toned be-fore being submitted to the services in order to enhance their apparent level of preservation, and somehow eluded detection by the experts. Getting stuck with one of these coins certainly wouldn't be a good deal. The companies have been diligent about buying back their mistakes, and their graders are getting better all the time, so the number of new mistakes has declined dramatically. Still, the marketplace has to deal with all the mis-takes of the past—and there are many.

Myth No. 11: *The "slabs" used to house certified coins are vacuum-sealed and contain no air.*

This is a common misconception. For the most part, the coins encapsulated in plastic by the certification services aren't vacuum-sealed but sonically sealed. NGC's founder, John Al-banese, explains that sonic sealing is accomplished by using high-pitched sounds to convert energy into heat, and then using that heat to fuse together the hard plastic holder's two halves. Vacuum-sealing wouldn't be practical, Albanese says, because it would require pressing the plastic right up against the coin, much as plastic wrapping is pressed against frozen turkeys in a supermarket, and that would damage the coin. Thus, while they are airtight, coin slabs are not air-free.

Myth No. 12: *Coins perform well only in inflationary times.*

Inflation is certainly good for the coin market; it stimulates interest in coins and other investment vehicles—such as gold and silver bullion—that tend to serve as hedges against erosion of wealth in inflationary times. We saw a classic example of this in 1979 and 1980, when double-digit inflation triggered a massive exodus from traditional investments into tangible assets, including coins. But not every coin boom has come about because of inflation or inflationary fears. The boom that occurred in the late 1980s, for instance, was fueled by Wall Street's newfound interest in rare coins. Inflation had little or nothing to do with it. Thus, while inflation can be a big boost for rare coins, it isn't a prerequisite for a boom.

Myth No. 13: *Gold coins are always a better investment than silver, nickel, or copper coins.*

There's an undeniable aura of glamour about gold coins. The beauty, allure and high intrinsic value of gold itself imparts a mystique to these coins, making them seem superior somehow to coins made of less noble metals. The fact is, however, that while they are more valuable intrinsically, gold coins are subject to the same perils and pitfalls as all other coins when it comes to investment potential. Investment-related decisions should be made without regard to metallic composition, or, for that matter, intrinsic value. Rarity and quality, supply and demand—these are the ingredients that go into determining a coin's investment potential and its numismatic value at any given time. And when coins are judged by this set of standards, gold is not all that glitters.

Myth No. 14: *Toning on silver coins is akin to rust on iron.*

Self-styled experts on coin chemistry have perpetrated the myth that silver coins with beautiful natural toning are actually damaged goods. One went so far as to liken such coins to rusty cars. This assertion is outrageously inaccurate and misleading. Far from damaging silver coins, the lovely natural toning that develops over time actually serves to protect the coins' surfaces. What's more, its aesthetic appeal enhances the coins' value in the eyes of knowledgeable numismatists.

The process that causes silver coins to tone is altogether different from the one that causes iron to rust. My father, Harvey C. Travers—a chemical engineer with a master's degree from the Massachusetts Institute of Technology—has carried out extensive studies on this subject, and here's what he has to say about it:

> *When moisture reacts with iron, there is an all-out destructive attack of the metal. However, silver is relatively inactive and does not react with oxygen in the air, even at high temperatures. It reacts with certain chemical compounds, notably those containing sulfur, if a catalyst is present—moisture, for example. But even then, the reaction stops short of an all-out destructive attack. In the case of silver coins, the sulfur causes a coating to form on the surface of the metal, but far from being destructive, the coating is actually protective. If it develops quickly and tends to be unsightly, we call it tarnish; if it happens more slowly and attractively, we call it toning.*
>
> *Unlike iron, which loses metal when it rusts, silver is not eaten away—that is to say, corroded—by this limited chemical reaction. When iron rusts, it spalls and loses metal; when silver tones or tarnishes, there is no loss of metal.*

CHAPTER 12

SECRETS OF CHERRYPICKING

There's something deeply satisfying about picking up a bargain—in coins as in anything else—by outsmarting somebody else, particularly when that somebody is supposed to be an expert on the subject. People who pursue hidden bargains in coins are called *cherrypickers,* and their ranks have been expanding in recent years. So have their rewards, and you can grab a share of those rewards by following the guidelines provided in this chapter by leading authorities.

Success in cherrypicking is directly proportional to the effort you put in, for in almost every case, people who spot bargains are able to do so because they have done their homework and know more about a coin than the person selling that item. In years gone by, "cherrypicker" had a more general meaning; a buyer was said to have cherrypicked a dealer's inventory if he went through the dealer's coins and picked out the very best pieces—or *cherries.* Nowadays, the term is applied primarily to someone with specialized knowledge of die varieties. Typically, a coin will be underpriced today because it is a scarce or rare variety and the seller—not realizing this—has marked it at the price corresponding to a common or "normal" variety.

Valuable varieties can range from very obvious ones, such as the dramatic double images on the obverse of the 1955 doubled-die Lincoln cent, to subtle, almost indiscernible ones—

perhaps one mint mark stamped above another, where only a strong magnifying glass will reveal that there is something out of the ordinary. Other potentially valuable varieties include coins with overdates, repunched dates, repunched mint marks—and even engraving errors. Early U.S. coinage was particularly rich in varieties because the Mint's equipment and methods were far less sophisticated. Also, it was common practice at that time, for reasons of economy, to continue using dies when a calendar year ended by punching the new year's date over the old.

J.T. Stanton is a preeminent authority on cherrypicking die varieties. He is co-author, with Bill Fivaz, of a best-selling hobby guidebook called *The Cherrypickers' Guide to Rare Die Varieties,* which contains descriptions and photographs of more than 400 valuable coin varieties that might very well be encountered at common-variety prices. He also is the publisher of *Cherrypickers' News,* a bimonthly newsletter offering reports on important new finds and updated price information. (The book is available for $19.95 plus $3 postage and handling. Subscriptions to the newsletter are $19.95 for six issues. To order either one, write to J.T. Stanton, P.O. Box 15487, Savannah, GA 31416-2187.)

Stanton recommends that anyone considering a cherrypicking expedition first stock up on knowledge by reading one of the many books available today on specific coin series and also by joining CONECA, the national club for collectors of error coins and varieties. (Membership in CONECA costs $15 per year, plus a first-time application fee of $5. Inquiries should be sent to 9017 Topperwind Court, Ft. Worth, TX 76134-5501.) "Don't expect to find rare varieties right away," Stanton cautions. "If they were easy to find, they wouldn't be rare or valuable. It may take months or even a year before you find your first rare variety—but once you find that first one, you'll be hooked!"

With valuable coin varieties, one picture may be worth even more than a thousand words—or, for that matter, a thousand dollars. J.T. Stanton has generously shared some of his high-quality photographs vividly illustrating varieties you should be looking for (Figures 12-1 to 12-6).

Figure 12-1. This 1971-S proof Lincoln cent with a doubled-die obverse retails for $1,000, compared with the 75¢ value attributed to the unremarkable specimen. *Photo courtesy J. T. Stanton.*

Figure 12-2. Repunched dates can be subtle or very pronounced. This 1894 Indian cent will command a price over $1,000, compared with $150 for the unremarkable example. *Photo courtesy J. T. Stanton.*

Figure 12-3. An overdate is one date that was punched into a die over a different date. This 1887/6-O Morgan dollar will bring as much as $7,500, according to cherrypicking authority J.T. Stanton. *Photo courtesy J. T. Stanton.*

Figure 12-4. Rare variety: 1942-D Jefferson nickel, D mint mark over a horizontal D mint mark. This repunched mint mark makes this coin worth as much as $750, according to Stanton. The unremarkable coin is valued at $30. *Photo courtesy J. T. Stanton.*

Figure 12-5. An "over mint mark," similar to an overdate, is one mint mark punched over a different mint mark. This 1950-S/D Washington quarter is a good example. Values can reach several hundred dollars for an otherwise common coin. *Photo courtesy J. T. Stanton.*

Figure 12-6. A "blundered die" is a variety that can cause a coin to have an unusual appearance, such as that exhibited by this 1870 Indian Head cent's denticles below the date. Digits were punched in that area. Varieties are known with date punches in many different areas. *Photo courtesy J. T. Stanton.*

PERHAPS THE WORLD'S GREATEST CHERRYPICKER

Eric Li Cheung of New York City is a truly amazing young man. Only 16 years old as this is written, Eric has already established himself as one of the most gifted and perceptive numismatists to appear on the scene in many years. He also has a legitimate claim to the title of "World's Greatest Cherrypicker"; he has purchased numerous coins at well below their true market value by correctly concluding that they were scarce—or even rare—varieties. Four years ago, at the tender age of 12, Eric prepared an essay embodying some of his keen insights on how to go about cherrypicking coins successfully.

How I Profit from Cherrypicking

BY ERIC LI CHEUNG

Attribution of die varieties is not just for fun. There are people who are willing to pay more than type coin values to purchase these coins. Not everyone has the time to research die varieties, though. In fact, not everyone knows what a die variety is. However, persons who specialize in die varieties and search for them are willing to spend more than type coin money in order to obtain particularly scarce varieties. If you discover a coin with a scarce and desirable die variety, you can often make money.

The rarity of a die variety can essentially be based on the life of the die that struck it. Coins struck on dies that broke more easily are scarcer than those coins struck from sturdy dies. Coins struck on dies that lasted are more common. Rarity of die varieties is usually based on the late Dr. William Sheldon's rarity scale, as follows.

R-1: Common (over 1,000 available)
R-2: Fairly common (501–1,000 available)
R-3: Scarce (201–500 available)
R-4: Very scarce (81–200 available)
R-5: Rare (31–80 available)

CHOICE AND RARE 1806 QUARTER

Lot No. 314
(Enlarged)

314 **1806** Browning 10. **Choice Brilliant Uncirculated. High R-6.** Rich, blue-gray in color with rosy highlights in the centers. Both sides are semi-prooflike. Struck from State III of the dies, as described by Breen in his update of Browning. An important rare variety of the date, made more desirable by being **one of the finest known.** *(SEE COLOR PLATE)*

Ex George F. Scanlon Collection (Stack's, October 24, 1973, lot 947); earlier, ex Charles Jay Collection (Stack's, October 27, 1967, lot 141).

This Quarter was attributed by twelve year old Young Numismatist Eric Li Cheung during his week-long practicum at Stack's in January of this year (his attribution was confirmed, of course). Quarter collectors will recognize Eric as the author of an attribution guide for Bust Quarters that has been well received by the fraternity. Stack's has been happy to provide resources and facilities to enable ANA recognized YN's like Eric to work with important coins they might otherwise not be able to study. We found Eric to be a remarkable young man whose numismatic talents will one day be recognized nationally.

Figure 12-7. Stack's Coin Company of New York City graciously hosted a week-long visit for Eric Li Cheung. Eric attributed this lot under the wise supervision of Stack catalogers. *Photo courtesy Stack's. (Copyright 1996 by Stack's. All rights reserved.)*

R-6: Very rare (13–30 available)
R-7: Extremely rare (4–12 available)
R-8: Unique or nearly so (1–3 available)

Die varieties are referred to by variety numbers. References have been written for the attribution of Colonial and early U.S. coinage. Die varieties for half cents, large cents, half dimes, dimes, quarters, half dollars, and dollars are most commonly and currently referred to by Cohen, Sheldon, Valentine, Davis, Browning, Overton, and Bolender numbers, respectively. These numismatists cataloged these die varieties by sequentially numbering them. In addition to that, they assigned a rarity rating to the varieties described (Figure 12-7).

Coins which some dealers have in their junk boxes can be valuable treasures. At a local show, I found a 1796 Draped Bust large cent. It was graded About Good. I bought it for $3. It turned out to be a Sheldon-99, which the late Dr. William Sheldon listed in his book as a Rarity-7 (today it's about R-6). A number of dealers, independent of one another, each offered me $175 for it. I also found two 1818 Browning-10 quarters, graded Good, which I bought for $25 each. These coins are listed as R-6. Dealers offered me $80 apiece for those coins.

I've only described a tiny sampling of my cherrypicking finds. Many people are unaware of die varieties. As a result, you can often purchase a low-grade coin that is very rare and sell it for a huge profit.

I have an equation for finding the value of a coin with a die variety:

DATE/MINT MARK + CONDITION + COLLECTORS' DEMAND (FOR THE COIN BOTH AS A REGULAR DATE AND VARIETY) + RARITY OF THE VARIETY = VALUE

The demand for the date is just the popularity of the date and type combination, disregarding the variety. The demand for the variety is essentially the same thing, except it takes into account the popularity of the particular variety or error. For example, overdates, overstrikes, missing parts, die breaks, and die cracks increase the demand.

There is no established value for rare die varieties, but your use of my formula should give you an idea of how much your varieties are worth.

CHAPTER 13

"INSIDER TRADING" OF RARE COINS

Honest, if you buy this coin I promise I'll bid that coin to three times the level that it's listed on the sheet for now. It's the only one known. I can bid it up to any level you want. What level would you like me to bid it up to?

—Well-known market-maker with a coin
listed in a certified coin population
report as the only one graded for that grade.

During my years as a coin trader, I've witnessed many examples of insider trading and observed very closely the way that information is disseminated—its ethical use, unethical use, and uneven distribution in this field.

RARE-COIN INSIDER TRADING

Just what *is* rare-coin insider trading? Outsiders perceive it as the manipulation of the coin market for material gain by people who take advantage of their knowledge of inside information, knowledge not available to the general coin-buying public. In point of fact, however, "insider trading" is a nebulous term not only in the coin market, but also in the securities industry. There is no universally accepted or court-sanctioned definition for Wall Street insider trading, so no one should expect a specific definition for rare coin insider trading either.

A number of prominent coin dealers capitalize on their knowledge of insider information to make advantageous deals. In fact, this goes on so routinely that even Ivan Boesky would be impressed. The methods of market manipulation in this field are almost endless. Yet up to now, few investors have tapped the profit potential inherent in this freewheeling situation.

People in this field don't have government agencies monitoring their day-to-day activities. For this reason, and because the coin industry is relatively small in size, savvy investors can put themselves in the same advantageous position—the same insider position—as major dealers.

For example, an investor can purchase a coin that he or she knows is the only one of its kind to which a certain grade has been assigned by a given grading service, and then make arrangements to have a dealer bid up the value of that coin.

An investor can get friendly with a dealer and learn from that contact, on a confidential basis, that five rare coins of a certain type and date were submitted by the dealer for grading and will be coming onto the market soon.

INSIDER INFORMATION AND RARE COINS

Insider information is used routinely, of course, in many different aspects of daily life. And it's used in ways that are legal and ways that are not.

Suppose your local congresswoman knows that certain property will soon be the site of a major development, and suppose she tips off her cousin, who then makes an investment in the area. That's leakage of insider information.

Suppose the chairman of the Federal Reserve Board is drafting a statement on interest rates that's likely to have a dramatic effect on the securities industry. Any number of his colleagues or associates might conceivably be aware of what he's preparing to say, and this insider information might enable them to make—or advise their friends to make—some highly lucrative deals.

Although this kind of insider information permeates the coin field, I don't believe it to be a major problem. There are mechanisms in place that will limit to a great degree, or even prevent, insider trades. And as I have noted, this industry is relatively small; insider information doesn't remain secret very long.

With that said, I must point out that there *are* certain types of insider information that have put some people at a tremendous advantage in the coin field and have left others at a great disadvantage.

Selling Off Right Before a Massive Downturn

We saw a good example of this phenomenon in July 1988, when coin dealers at the annual convention of the American Numismatic Association were stunned by the announcement that coins supposedly certified by the Professional Coin Grading Service had turned up in counterfeit plastic slabs. Apparently some dealers learned of the situation before the announcement was made—and based on this information, gained through insider contacts, they immediately sold many of their PCGS-graded coins. Some of the coins they sold were in counterfeit slabs and, like virtually all the coins of this type, these were overgraded and therefore overpriced. But even the coins in genuine slabs were worth substantially less following the announcement, because the scandal shook market confidence (at least for a short time) in PCGS coins as a whole. This was a clear instance where knowledge of insider information helped certain dealers significantly.

Price Manipulation

Another common use of insider information in the coin market is price manipulation. Often this involves coins with very low populations, coins that have been graded in very small quantities in a given grade by a particular grading service.

From the insider's standpoint, the ideal population is *one*. The chances for price manipulation are maximized when a dealer owns the only coin of a certain kind to which a given grade has been assigned. This information can be obtained by studying the population reports issued by the major grading services. So long as the dealer is certain that no other coins of that type and that grade are available, he or she can bid up the price of that coin on the teletype system. (If another example happened to exist, the dealer would be obliged to purchase it at his or her bid price if the coin's owner belonged to the same trading network and chose to accept the bid.)

Suppose this coin is listed initially at $2,500 in the *Certified Coin Dealer Newsletter* (or *Bluesheet*), the standard weekly price guide for coins that have been independently certified. And suppose the dealer offers progressively higher bids, upping the ante to $5,000, to $6,000, and finally to $7,000. After $7,000 has been offered for several weeks, the publishers of the *Bluesheet* may raise the coin's listed price from $2,500 to $7,000. At that point the dealer will sell it to someone who is unaware of what has been going on, perhaps to another dealer unschooled in the ways of such games or perhaps to an unsuspecting collector or investor. The dealer may even offer a "discount": With the *Bluesheet* price at $7,000, maybe the coin will be offered for "just" $6,000. And then, when the dealer stops bidding $7,000 for the coin and has sold it for $6,000, its price will go back down to where it was before and where it belongs: $2,500.

The Inner Circle

Collectors and investors can avoid this type of manipulation by doing business with dealers who are not only honorable, but also members of the coin market's inner circle—that is, dealers who know the ins and outs of population reports and will not themselves fall victim to this kind of scam.

Keep in mind that dealers themselves can be victimized if they don't stay fully informed on all the factors involved in determining the value of a coin. If they don't pay close attention to population reports, they too can be deceived by price lists where the value reflects manipulation rather than real demand. They may think they're getting a bargain when someone comes up to their table at a show and offers them such a coin at a price well below the *Bluesheet* level. And they'll pass this "bargain" on to a customer, not because they too are trying to take advantage of someone, but because they themselves aren't very knowledgeable.

In many cases it is wise to do business only with someone who is an authorized dealer of NGC or PCGS or both. On request, both organizations will provide a current list of their authorized dealers.

Collectors, investors, and dealers, too, should watch closely for signs of volatility in any specific area of the market. This is especially true of areas where few coins have been certified and where, for that reason, one dealer can control a complete population. Great volatility in any particular area doesn't mean that coins are being traded rapidly; it may mean that a dealer has manipulated that portion of the marketplace—manipulated it upward and then sold the specific coin or coins, causing bid levels to drop precipitously.

PCGS has the following anti-self-interest policy posted in its grading room.

Graders!!!
PCGS Anti-Self-Interest Policy

PCGS graders *cannot* do any of the following:

1. Grade their own coins.
2. Grade coins they submit for clients or other dealers.
3. Grade coins they have a financial interest in (split-profit deals, etc.).
4. Verify any of the above coins.
5. Participate in *any* discussion whatsoever—inside or outside of the grading room—either before, during, or after the coins are in the grading process.

Fiduciary Responsibility

PCGS graders *cannot* use any information obtained inside the grading room before the information is available in the general marketplace. More specifically graders cannot do any of the following:

1. Buy coins from a dealer based on information obtained in the grading room. If a grader finds out who a coin or group of coins belongs to while the coins are in the grading process, that grader cannot contact the submitting dealer for the purpose of purchasing the coins (or obtaining first shot, etc.) until *10 days after* the dealer has received his coins back from PCGS.
2. Sell or buy coins and/or coin positions based on information obtained in the grading room.

Any grader who has one substantiated violation of item No. 1 or who shows a consistent pattern of violating item No. 2 will be immediately terminated.

THE BAD OLD DAYS

In the early 1980s we witnessed market practices that were far less ethical than those we have today. Dealers at that time often drove up bid levels in *The Coin Dealer Newsletter* (or *Greysheet*), the standard weekly price guide for all U.S. coins. They did this on a constant basis. And they didn't have to concern themselves with rules and regulations requiring them to buy such coins if those coins were offered.

Circa-1980 dealers could take a coin listed for $400 in *The Coin Dealer Newsletter,* bid $600, $700, $1,000—and keep bidding higher and higher amounts on the teletype system. In those days they had no real obligation to purchase any coins that people sent; coins were not certified then, and we didn't have a sight-unseen system. The dealers would simply send the coins back, saying they didn't meet their high grading standards.

Dealer promotions and price manipulation played a big part

in the marketplace confusion over grading standards. In driving up prices, dealers were looking to make bigger profits on coins they already had; they had no interest in buying such coins from anyone else. Thus, as people sent them coins, these dealers just shipped them right back. A number of people would then submit coins of the next higher grade, since the artificially inflated price levels were high enough to justify selling even these at the quoted bids. Again the dealers would send the coins back. In some cases dealers were offering to buy coins graded MS-65 at a certain price, and people were sending them coins graded as high as MS-67; even then the coins were returned.

Today's Improved Market

Although manipulation does occur today, it's much more difficult to drive up price-guide levels—especially those of certified coins, since dealers must be willing to buy any coins that are offered. This discourages the unscrupulous from trying to manipulate prices of the more common certified coins, where hundreds or even thousands of examples may exist.

As growing numbers of coins are certified, population reports will list far fewer one-of-a-kind coins. Already the number is dwindling, even among supergrade coins bearing the very high MS and proof numbers that grading services assign quite sparingly. In most cases enough coins are available to protect against price manipulation. Today supergrade commemorative coins appear to offer the best opportunities for manipulators—and the greatest risk for potential victims—because these coins exist in very limited numbers in certified grades of MS-66 and above.

Clearly the coin market doesn't have a perfect trading system. But in a world where no system is completely perfect, today's system is certainly far better than yesterday's.

PROMOTIONS OF COINS IN NEWSLETTERS

Newsletters serve as yet another way to promote coins and influence their prices. Some mass-market coin dealers publish their own newsletters and use them on a regular basis to promote the coins they have for sale.

Often it's possible to anticipate such promotions—even without being a true market insider—simply by analyzing which coins these dealers have promoted in the past.

When dealers send newsletters to thousands upon thousands of collectors and investors, obviously they can't use them to promote coins of which just three examples, or even 300, are known. They have to select coins that exist in more promotable numbers. Among the series that combine sufficient numbers with broad-based popularity are Morgan silver dollars, Saint-Gaudens double eagles, and commemoratives.

Dealers stage promotions for these and other popular coins on a regular, systematic basis. They may promote Saint-Gaudens double eagles one month, Morgan dollars the next month, and commemoratives the month after that. If you haven't seen the Morgan dollar promoted in one of these newsletters in a while, you can be quite certain that its turn will be coming very soon. And that might be a good time to buy Morgan dollars—before the promotion hits, with all its attendant hype, and prices go up in response.

I recommend that you get on the mailing lists of all the large dealerships that publish and distribute such newsletters. Often they're quite informative and even entertaining, and they can help guide you in charting the direction of the market.

INSIDER ECONOMICS

Paul Taglione, a former principal of the now defunct New England Rare Coin Galleries, has written a number of valuable books and articles analyzing the coin market's inner workings. Taglione and his company became targets of a Federal Trade Commission lawsuit charging them with unfair or deceptive acts or practices in or affecting commerce. Despite this, and to some extent *because* of this, his insights on the market are fascinating and illuminating.

The following is an excerpt from Taglione's book, *An Investment Philosophy for the Prudent Consumer* (Numismatic Research and Service Corporation, Boston, 1986).

Across the expanse of market actors currently active in the Numismatic Markets, technical numismatic knowledge and comprehension of the economics of the various Numismatic Markets is, in my view, extremely variable in depth and quality. An amazing number of market actors do not possess adequate technical knowledge of areas in which they trade. Incredibly enough, very few market actors seriously study the economics of the Numismatic Markets in which they participate. Any private numismatic investor can obtain an edge in a specialized area and, I am perfectly convinced, any private investor can obtain a general edge in even wider areas of the Numismatic Markets. **The "investment edge," as I see it, involves a wide-ranging knowledge of the economics of the area in which one wishes to invest.** A first step in obtaining this knowledge is researching and examining the supply side of an area. How many examples of this coin exist? How many come to market? Is the supply of this particular coin or class of coins inelastic to increased demand? The next step is obtaining a knowledge of the size, intensity, and quality of demand. This step *must* begin at the level of the individual buyer. What sort of market actor demands and desires this coin? Does the acquisition of this coin *satisfy* a preference or does it *stimulate* a preference to acquire more coins? In my opinion, the quality of demand is much more important than its size or intensity. The size or intensity of demand can be the result of dictated preference and if quality of demand is taken to include endurance and continuity (which I take it to include), then it becomes obvious that demand which derives from dictated preference is markedly lacking in these qualities. Another step in obtaining the investment edge is investigating the parameters of price at which buyers can and do acquire material. Obviously the demand for a common coin is much more sensitive to price than is the demand for a rare coin. An investor must exercise a great deal more caution in acquiring a common coin in terms of price than is required for obtaining a rarity whose market appearance in and of itself generates a value for the acquisition opportunity. Perhaps the best investment edge of all is the recognition that the edge is complicated and varies from area to area and from time to time. Part of this recognition is an awareness that choosing the elusive and storied "right dealer" might not be an edge at all; it might be a disadvantage!

How to Minimize Acquisition Costs

When the market is at or near the low, as reflected in the *Certified Coin Dealer Newsletter* or the regular *Coin Dealer Newsletter,* often you can buy coins at a discount—that is, at a price below what the newsletters indicate. That's when you're in your ideal acquisition phase.

In many cases dealers may be willing to tell you how much they paid for a particular coin (and again I urge you to buy only certified coins). If so, you may be able to negotiate an advantageous price.

It's risky to buy uncertified coins at auction. You may find yourself buying into a trap. You may be buying a coin that was graded only Proof-63 or Proof-62 by a certification service, but then was broken out of its plastic holder and put into the auction as Proof-65.

Time after time after time, I serve as a consultant to institutions and individuals who have coins that were "no-graded" by NGC or PCGS, coins with defects so serious that they couldn't be certified and encapsulated. Yet many leading auction houses (the finest in the nation, in some instances) are willing to take these coins and put them in their sales and give them glowing descriptions.

How to Sell High

The way to sell coins high is to take certified coins, crack them out of their holders, and consign them to a dealer for sale at auction. Chances are, the dealer will take attractive color photographs of those coins, give them a nice display in a glossy, impressive catalog—and indicate they're in a higher grade.

Normally, you shouldn't sell coins at auction during times of climatic extremes—in other words, in the summer or in the winter. Of course, there are exceptions. If the market is heating up, for example, it might be a good idea to sell in the summertime.

In most cases it's not a good idea to sell in the wintertime, even if the auction is taking place at a coin show in an area where it's warm and the show is a popular one. Traditionally, such auctions haven't produced the absolute highest prices for consignors.

Auction-House Grading

Not all auction catalogs overstate the grades of their coins. Sometimes, in fact, the opposite is true—and in such cases shrewd bidders may be able to pick up real bargains.

Suppose a consignor goes to an auction house and says, "You people are the most competent coin graders in the world; grade these coins the way you want to." The auction house, not wanting to be accused of overgrading and wanting to make its realized prices more impressive, may assign conservative grades to the coins. This has been known to happen in an estate sale. Lawyers representing the estate will consign the coins to an auction house, and you'll find MS-65s being graded in the catalog as MS-63s.

Often, however, the scenario is diametrically different. Someone will go to an auction house with a package of coins and say, "Listen, I know NGC would grade these coins MS-63; but unless you call them MS-64 or 65, I'm not going to consign these coins to you." Even a so-called reputable auction house is likely to take those coins and abide by the wishes of the consignor.

There's nothing unethical about what these auction firms are doing. They don't necessarily grade according to the standards set forth by NGC or PCGS. Some auction firms have their own grading standards; therefore they can take a certified coin—a coin that's been graded conservatively by an independent grading service as MS-64 or 63, and for which you've paid a 64 or 63 price—and legitimately grade it MS-65 after cracking it out of its holder.

Maximizing Grades

I was fascinated by a very interesting deal with an auction house. There were coins that NGC had graded About Uncirculated-58, but when they were taken out of their holders they were cataloged as MS-62s and realized handsome prices of thousands of dollars apiece. As an MS-62, one of these coins sold for $5,400 plus a 10 percent buyer's fee. When it was in its slab as an AU-58, dealers did not want to buy it. One dealer refused even to make an offer on this coin; he said he wasn't interested.

In another case, an institution took dozens of MS-63 gold coins that were no-question 63s to an auction house that cataloged many of them as 65s. The coins did not bring big prices, though.

Another coin group involved PCGS MS-64 Premium Quality Morgan dollars. A very large grouping of these coins was presented to an auction firm that was willing to crack them out of their holders, grade a number of them as high as MS-66, and include color photographs in its catalog. With very few exceptions, the remainder of the coins were cataloged MS-65. An auction firm that maximizes grades is still not an assurance of high prices realized.

Coins Grading MS-63 to MS-67

The grading band between MS-63 and MS-67 is one of greatest concern to consumers. We're likely to see a trend toward fuller description within that one small area than in all the rest of the spectrum. Grades 1 through 62 are almost a non-issue compared with that part of the spectrum between 63 and 67.

A high-quality 65—one that almost grades 66—is clearly worth more than a minimum 65 price. In all cases investors should stick with Premium Quality coins, but try not to pay any premium.

INNER-CIRCLE DEALERS

Finding bargains in certified coins involves a great deal of judgment, and I don't like making generalizations in this area. You really need to consult your coin advisor and find someone you can trust implicitly. Many coin dealers are reputable, but not all are knowledgeable enough to help you in this area of the market. When it comes to these particular types of coins, you really need a dealer who's a member of the inner circle.

You can find inner-circle dealers by checking ads in coin publications and noting which ones are affiliated with both the Professional Coin Grading Service and the Numismatic Guaranty Corporation. Determine who these authorized dealers are; there are listings. Both organizations scrutinize their dealers for financial integrity and trustworthiness. In fact, dealers who are members of NGC are pledged to arbitrate any dispute regarding NGC-related coins through that service; so if you deal with an NGC-authorized dealer who's listed in the ads, you can be certain the dealer has been prescreened closely and will arbitrate any dispute.

COST AVERAGING

Cost averaging is a technique familiar to people in financial fields. Essentially, it's a way of cushioning a loss when one investment goes down in value by purchasing a second example of the same item at the lower price.

Suppose you buy a coin for $10,000 and it plunges in value to $1,000. To cost average, you buy another coin just like it—a coin of the same denomination, date, and grade—for $1,000. What you are doing, effectively, is splitting the difference. Now you can take the attitude that you really paid $5,500 apiece for the two coins: the sum of their prices ($11,000) divided by two. It's unlikely that the market value of either coin will rebound all the way to $10,000, but chances are good that after dropping in price so sharply, the coins will regain at least part of the lost ground. They may rise to $5,000 or even $7,000 apiece. And at that point you'll break even or come out slightly ahead.

Cost averaging is a psychologically soothing way to rationalize the fact that you overpaid for a coin or bought it at the top of the cycle.

LATE-DATE HYPE

Beware of late-date coins in plastic slabs. Although the rare coin market has benefitted greatly from the certification of coins by independent grading services, certification has led to unfortunate abuses in this one area.

The problems involve late-date coins in exceptional condition—coins such as proof or Mint State Jefferson nickels, Roosevelt dimes, and Kennedy half dollars. Even in the highest grades these coins are extremely common, but certain unscrupulous dealers have found a way to market them at greatly inflated prices as if they were much rarer and more valuable. They submit the coins to one of the grading services, get them certified and slabbed at a very high grade such as Proof-68 or MS-67, and then sell them for far more than they're really worth—sometimes two or three hundred times as much.

HOW TO SELL SLABBED COINS PROFITABLY

When liquidating certified coins, you must decide whether they are high-end, low-end, or mid-range coins of the designated grade. After this is established, the investor should adhere to the following rules of thumb:

- Coins that are premium-quality or high-end and nearly qualify for the next higher grade should be broken out of their certified slabs and sold at public auction at a negotiated higher grade. Sometimes an auction company will guarantee a minimum price. Some auction firms may even agree to reimburse the consignor for the value of the coin at its sight-unseen grade if it should bring a lower price after being broken out of its holder and sold at auction.
- Coins that are low-end—just-made-it coins that might be given a lower grade if they were cracked out of their holders—should be sold on a sight-unseen basis.
- Coins that are in between—neither high-end nor low-end but simply decent, accurately graded coins—can be sold on a sight-seen basis to other dealers at a reasonable negotiated price. These coins can also be sold at public auction in their slabs.
- When selling certified coins that are just-made-it coins, or even reasonably decent coins for the grade but not premium quality, be absolutely certain to deal only with an autho-

rized dealer of the grading service in whose capsules these coins are slabbed. I can document many cases in which individuals have gone to unauthorized dealers with certified coins encapsulated by grading services; resenting the independent services with which they have no working relationship, these dealers have said, "This coin is worthless; I'll give you $50 for it," when the sight-unseen price on the coin was as much as $3,000. Dealing with *reputable* dealers isn't enough; you must deal with dealers who have been screened by the grading services.

HOW TO NEGOTIATE AUCTION CONTRACTS

If the time comes to negotiate an auction contract and you find yourself with coins of substantial value to consign, you may want to seek legal counsel about a Uniform Commercial Code filing statement, according to Leonard H. Hecht, a lawyer in New York. This can be quite important, and I suggest you consult your attorney for further details.

When you negotiate with an auction house, you also may want a cash advance. All these points are negotiable, depending on how much your coins are worth.

Many coin auction firms use a 10-10 commission structure—that is, they charge the consignor 10 percent of the prices realized for his or her coins and receive a like commission from each of the buyers.

If your holdings are sizable (and most auction firms won't accept a consignment worth less than a couple of thousand dollars), you should negotiate for a lower rate. Auction houses often reduce the seller's fee to 7 percent, 5 percent, or even less. In some cases they have been known to waive a seller's fee altogether in order to get a consignment. And if they want a consignment badly enough, some auction firms will even provide a rebate to the seller, giving him or her a share of the buyer's fees.

Because there's so much room for auction firms to maneuver on their fees, heirs to estates should be especially vigilant and cautious. Suppose you've inherited a coin collection worth four or five million dollars, and you've hired a so-called independent consultant to help you decide how and where to sell it. Quite conceivably, one auction firm may have contacted your consultant with a tempting offer: "Convince your client to auction that collection through us, and in exchange we're prepared to pay you a percentage of the prices realized." Not being a coin collector yourself, you may have limited knowledge of what's involved and may decide to use that particular auction firm based on the counsel of someone who, behind the scenes, has a vested interest in the outcome of this transaction.

AN ANALYSIS OF PRICES REALIZED

Given the same coins, all the topnotch auction firms get about the same price levels from their buyers. Usually the big difference is just how big a chunk of the proceeds you, the consignor, will receive and how much the firm will keep for itself. From your standpoint, how much you get—not what the coins sell for—is the real bottom line.

Let's say one firm wants to charge you a 20 percent fee and won't give you any money in advance. Meanwhile, a competing firm is willing to guarantee you $800,000 on your $1 million collection, willing to give you a check for it up front without interest, and even willing to waive the seller's fee; in fact, this firm is willing to pay *you* a percentage or two of the buyer's fee. It seems pretty obvious which is the better deal from your standpoint. You certainly shouldn't listen to any hype you hear from the firm that wants to charge you 20 percent.

What counts is the financial deal, not how big a name the auction company has. It comes down to a matter of numbers, so pick the best ones. In some cases you can even negotiate for minimums—the minimum prices realized for certain coins. This is especially true in smaller auction sales.

The Three Keys to Value

Three basic factors determine the value of a coin.

- First and foremost is the level of preservation—how many nicks or scratches or flaws a coin has.
- Second is the collector base—how many collectors are interested in a particular coin series. A certain Lincoln cent may

have a mintage of 500,000, and that's a lot of coins. But if there are a million collectors of Lincoln cents, then 500,000 becomes a relatively low number.

- Third is the number of coins extant or available. If only 50 examples of a given coin are available, but only 40 people want one, the value of the coin isn't going to be very high.

It's the interrelationship of these three factors that determines how much a coin is worth. Ideally, you want a high-grade, low-mintage coin with a broad collector base. Although mintage figures can guide you, they can be misleading because in many cases significant numbers of coins have been melted or otherwise lost since their manufacture.

HOW TO GET OUT AT THE TOP

Getting out at the top requires a degree of good luck. However, you can do a great deal to improve your luck if you keep a close eye on the market and develop good instinct.

The signs to watch for here are the opposite of those that enable you to buy at the bottom.

- When you see coins going up in price dramatically and hear people talking about these increases, that's when you should sell.
- If you hear that a limited partnership is buying $50 million worth of coins, that's a good time to sell.
- If you hear there's a limited partnership that now has $80 million and is almost in its acquisition phase and coins are a great investment, but you look and don't see any other limited partnerships behind it, think about this: When these people go to sell all these coins, who's going to buy them? That could be the top; that's the time to sell.

But don't be guided strictly by marketplace signs. From a personal standpoint, the best time to sell is if you've made a profit, or if you want to cut your losses and get into something else. If you buy something for $1,000 and it increases to $10,000, that's fine. What's wrong with taking a small profit? It doesn't hurt.

The coin may go up another 10 or 15 percent—but so what? You've sold and you've made a profit, and that's what's important. If you can sell and make a profit, that's the top for you.

THE ABSOLUTE TOP

Don't ever think you can sell at the absolute top, because you can't. The finest experts in this industry can't do it: but there are the people who think they can manipulate the marketplace, control the price guides, bid coins up to whatever levels they want, and then sell them off to unsuspecting customers. In many cases their best-laid plans backfire, and they fail to get out at the top. Sometimes they end up selling off hundreds of thousands—even millions—of dollars' worth of coins at the bottom of the cycle because they're in a cash-flow crunch.

You can't predict with any certainty what is going to happen in the coin field, even in the very near future.

CHAPTER 14

COINS AND THE INFORMATION SUPERHIGHWAY

The Computer Revolution has permeated—and permutated—virtually every area of society, and the rare-coin market is no exception. In just the last few years, really since this book's first edition was published in 1996, computers have moved from being merely an option to becoming almost a necessity for people who buy and sell coins on a regular basis. For all but beginners and dabblers, access to the Internet is practically as important today as access to price guides and reference books. A computer has become almost as vital a tool as a magnifying glass or a high-intensity lamp for viewing coins. And knowing how to travel the Information Superhighway is as crucial to success as knowing how to navigate the aisles on a major coin show's bourse floor.

Even die-hard traditionalists who resisted the revolution during its early stages have resigned themselves to the changes' inevitability. In 1996, I reported in this book how the leadership of the American Numismatic Association had rebuffed my attempts to expand the use of computers—and specifically e-mail—in carrying out its regular correspondence. "I may be a

Figure 14-1. Computerization at NGC. *Photo courtesy Numismatic Guaranty Corporation of America, Inc.*

dinosaur," one of those leaders admitted in casting a vote against the suggested conversion, but he nonetheless voted no, saying he wasn't convinced that computer communication was really as cost-effective as advocates claimed. Since then, the ANA has seen the light and embraced the new technology, maneuvering around the remaining pockets of resistance.

Viewed on the road map of history as a whole, the few years since 1996 are just inches on a journey of thousands of miles. Yet during that brief time, computer technology has insinuated itself into virtually every aspect of the rare-coin marketplace, leaving the dwindling "dinosaurs"–those who resist and rebuff it–to watch the passing parade in disbelief and bewilderment as they fade faster and faster toward extinction. Coin dealers now use computers to manage their inventories . . . monitor coin and bullion prices virtually minute by minute . . . keep in touch with developments in the market, the hobby, and the wider world as well . . . and contact colleagues and customers quickly, inexpensively, and efficiently. Dealers who conduct auction sales of coins, or purchase coins at other dealers' auctions, are shifting significant portions of their business to the Internet. Even the United States Mint is using an Internet Web site now to sell its proof and mint sets and other premium products to collectors; in fact, it is encouraging on-line purchases, as opposed to mail and telephone orders, by offering price breaks to people who buy its products via computer. It isn't far-fetched to project that within just a few *more* years, on-line sales may account for the lion's share of transactions in the coin market, or at least in certain segments of that market.

Meanwhile, collectors are using the Internet, too, in ever greater numbers and with ever greater proficiency, navigating skillfully among the numerous Web sites, chat rooms, and on-line bulletin boards that furnish information, offer coins for sale, and bring together people of similar interests. To a great extent, these on-line destinations have taken over roles that coin clubs used to play; indeed, new *on-line* clubs have sprung up in recent years. And while traditional coin clubs are suffering in some cases as a result, there is ample evidence that the new technology—aided by such bonanzas as the 50-state Washington quarters—is bringing many newcomers into the hobby.

Coins and Computers

Forward-looking dealers began using computers in the mid-1980s to buy and sell coins on a sight-unseen basis through computerized trading networks. Later in the decade, major grading services undertook experiments involving the use of computers to help grade coins and the largest grading service, PCGS, even unveiled a prototype called The Expert—a computer which was programmed to grade Morgan dollars. Unfortunately, both of these promising ventures failed to achieve their potential because the coin market entered a lengthy slump as the Eighties ended, causing entrepreneurs to trim their sails. But today, many millions of people are utilizing computers in even more personal and fundamental ways, and the new technology's role is constantly expanding as a wondrous new millennium starts to unfold.

The Computer Revolution has now reached into the homes of Americans virtually everywhere—including enormous numbers of current and potential coin hobbyists. Anyone who owns a computer and a modem can gain quick access to sprawling on-line services, where like-minded people await to chat and share information. Accessing one of these services typically requires only a local phone call; an answering modem connects you with users all around the nation—and even all over the world. Once on-line, you can tap into seemingly endless stores of information compiled for the membership of the service. Or, if you prefer, you can correspond with others by sending and receiving electronic messages.

THE INTERNET

Most people have heard of the Internet, but many have no idea what it is. Briefly, it is a loosely connected universe of computer networks and bulletin boards that enables computer users to gain information on an almost endless range of human knowledge. As this is written, it embraces many thousands of

Figure 14-2. *On-line coin merchants are changing the landscape, both at conventions and in the marketplace.*

separate "newsgroups," or series of public messages and responses dealing with related topics. Perhaps the most popular segment of the Internet is the World Wide Web, where computer users can find in-depth information on subjects of special interest to them—including coins.

The Internet was developed as a means for the U.S. military establishment to communicate quickly and efficiently with scientific researchers doing government work at colleges and universities. It has long since outgrown that narrow role, however. Today, tens of millions of people actively surf the Internet on a regular basis in the United States and Canada. Numerous service providers are available. For a flat monthly fee—typically about $20—they will furnish software and access to the Internet through a modem with a local telephone number. On-line services also offer Internet connections, as well as other services such as e-mail capability and access to a wide array of chat rooms. These have become a great deal more affordable since this book's first edition was released. At that time, for example, America Online was charging a fee of $2.95 per hour for connection to its network, and many AOL customers routinely ran up bills of hundreds of dollars a month. Since then, AOL has established a flat monthly fee that provides unlimited access for $21.95 and access for shorter periods for even less. Similar flat-fee access also is available through other on-line services. By making Internet access more affordable, these new fee arrangements have helped stimulate even greater travel on the burgeoning Information Superhighway.

COIN COLLECTING ON-LINE

As the benefits of computer technology grew increasingly apparent throughout the 1990s, more and more coin dealers, hobby organizations—and even individual collectors—began making use of the Internet to publicize their activities. Despite the reservations of some elected officials, the American Numismatic Association was among the first to take significant steps in this direction. The ANA first went on-line in June 1993, staking out positions on the CompuServe and Prodigy on-line services. The following year, it established a presence on the

Internet as well, greatly expanding its exposure to prospective new members. These efforts were initiated by Robert J. Leuver, the ANA's executive director from 1987 through 1997, who was a vocal advocate of using computer technology to get out the word about the hobby in general and the ANA in particular. Today, the ANA provides many services to its members and the public at large at its Internet site on the World Wide Web: http://www.money.org

As the 1990s wore on, we saw a proliferation of coin-related "billboards" on the Internet. I set up a Web site, for instance, for my own company, Scott Travers Rare Coin Galleries Inc. of New York City. I use this to provide helpful information about the coin marketplace, including detailed excerpts from books that I have written about rare coins. To visit the Scott Travers Rare Coin Consumer Protection Home Page, head for http://www. inch.com/~travers/travers3.htm

IMPORTANT NUMISMISMATIC WEB SITES
Auctions
    eBay
    www.ebay.com
    Teletrade
    www.teletrade.com

Grading Services
    ANACS
    www.anacs.com
    Independent Coin Grading Company
    www.icgcoin.com
    Numismatic Guaranty Corporation of America, Inc.
    www.ngccoin.com
    Professional Coin Grading Service
    www.pcgs.com

Information Resources
    Abacoin Article Archive
    www.abacoin.com/resources/articles/index.asp

Certified Coin Exchange
www.atchou.com/cce.html
Coin Club Locator
www.coinclubs.com
Coin Universe Library
collectors.com/articles/index.html?universeid=81
Coin Zone Article Archive
coinzone.com/CoinResources/articleindex.asp
Scott Travers Rare Coin Consumer Protection Homepage
www.inch.com/~travers/travers3.htm
U.S. Coin On-line Encyclopedia
www.coinfacts.com
U.S. National Numismatic Collection/Smithsonian Institution
americanhistory.si.edu/csr/cadnnc.htm
Worldwide Coin Show Directory
coinshows.com

Organizations

American Israel Numismatic Association
www.amerisrael.com
American Numismatic Association
www.money.org
American Numismatic Society
www.amnumsoc.org
British Art Media Society
www.bams.org.uk
Canadian Numismatic Association
www.nunetcan.net/cna.htm
Canadian Numismatic Research Society
www.nunetcan.net/cnrs.htm
Classical and Medieval Numismatic Society
www.nunetcan.net/cmns.htm
CoinMasters On-line Coin Club
www.coinmasters.org/mainpage.html
Combined Organizations of Numismatic Error Collectors of America
hermes.csd.net/~coneca

Early America Coppers
eacs.org
Gold Institute
www.goldinstitute.com
International Bank Note Society
www.public.coe.edu/~sfeller/IBNSJ
John Reich Collectors Society
www.logan.com/jrcs
Numismatic Bibliomania Society
www.coinbooks.org
Numismatic Literary Guild
www.numismaticliteraryguild.org
Professional Numismatists Guild
www.pngdealers.com
Royal Numismatic Society
www.rns.dircon.co.uk/index
Society for U.S. Commemorative Coins
www.money.org/sum-carmody.html
Society of U.S. Pattern Collectors
www.uspatterns.com
Token & Medal Society
www.angelfire.com/id/TAMS/index.html

Periodicals
Canadian Coins News
www.vaxxine.com/trajan/coin.html
The Celator
www.celator.com
The Coin Dealer Newsletter
www.greysheet.com
COINage magazine
www.coinagemag.com
Coins magazine
www.krause.com/coins/cm
Coin World
www.coinworld.com
Numismatic News
www.krause.com/coins/nn

World Coin News
www.krause.com/coins/wc

Book Merchants
Bowers & Merena Galleries, Inc.
www.bowersandmerena.com
Brooklyn Gallery Coins & Stamps
www.brooklyngallery.com
Charles Davis Numismatic Literature
www.abebooks.com/home/numismat
George Frederick Kolbe Fine Numismatic Books
www.numislit.com
Krause Publications
www.krausebooks.com
The Money Tree
www.moneytreecoin.com
Numismatic & Philatelic Books of Santa Fe
www.santafebooks.qpg.com
Scott Travers Information Services
www.pocketchangelottery.com
Stanton Printing & Publishing
www.jtstanton.com

Federal Reserve Banks
Atlanta
www.frbatlanta.org/
Chicago
www.frbchi.org/
Minneapolis
http://woodrow.mpls.frb.fed.us/
New York
www.ny.frb.org/
Philadelphia
www.libertynet.org/~fedresrv/fedpage.html
St. Louis
www.stls.frb.org/

U.S. Department of the Treasury/Mint/B.E.P.
www.bep.treas.gov/

www.treas.gov/mint/
www.usmint.gov/

E-mail Addresses for Editors of Publications
Beth Deisher
Editor, *Coin World*
bdeisher@coinworld.com
Barbara Gregory
Editor, *The Numismatist*
anaedi@money.org
David C. Harper
Editor, *Numismatic News*
harperd@krause.com
Ed Reiter
Senior Editor, *COINage* magazine
EdEditor@aol.com
Marcy Gibbel
Managing Editor, *COINage* magazine
CoinMag2@aol.com
Robert R. VanRyzin
Editor, *Coins* magazine
vanryzinr@krause.com

BUYING COINS ON THE INTERNET

There has been exponential growth in the amount of business conducted by buyers and sellers on the Internet. When this book first appeared in 1996, most people were wary of carrying out transactions via computer. Even many progressive individuals who had their own computers and used them to obtain information and communicate with others were hesitant to take the additional leap of faith involved in making purchases on-line. Their caution was prudent, for at that point the security surrounding transmittal of credit-card information and other personal data was far from perfect. Today, that protection is considerably more reliable, and buyers who exercise normal caution should find their on-line shopping as safe as more traditional approaches—and probably a lot more convenient.

This is not to say that purchasing merchandise on the Internet is risk-free. Although the mechanisms surrounding such transactions may provide adequate safeguards against interception by wrongdoers, there's a very real danger of being ripped off by unscrupulous *sellers,* and that danger clearly exists in transactions involving rare coins.

On-Line Auctions

Internet auctions have become an important method of selling rare coins. Traditional auction firms have recognized the potential of the burgeoning new technology and established a growing presence on-line. In general, their Internet sales are legitimate and ethical, and offer opportunities for buyers to obtain desirable coins more quickly and easily than through the normal methods of the past. High-quality digital images and detailed descriptions often accompany listings for these coins, giving prospective purchasers instant access to a kind of on-line "catalog" without the time and expense of obtaining a printed version from the auction firm.

Unfortunately, the same advantages that make Internet auctions attractive to legitimate businesses and their clients have also caught the attention of less reputable companies and individuals. They, too, conduct Internet sales, but without the safeguards and ethical considerations buyers are used to getting—and still receive on-line—from more established firms with names and reputations to uphold. Rip-off artists are encouraged and emboldened by the relative lack of restraint and regulation in this still untamed frontier, where swaggering sellers are free to come and go like shady traveling salesmen hawking shoddy wares to unwitting victims.

Government agencies are striving to bring order to the chaos that confronts them on the Internet. To date, however, their efforts have achieved only limited success. Like marshals policing the wide open spaces in the Wild, Wild West, they find themselves trying to track down Computer Age villains in a landscape that is vast and largely lawless. To make matters worse, some of the sophisticated Internet companies that facilitate on-line sales have chosen to remain above the fray, not only refusing to be "deputized" as crime fighters but actually seeming to coddle and protect the guys in black hats.

On-Line Auction Abuses

Wherever technology leads, fast-buck artists are sure to follow. With the coming of computerized coin auctions, we have seen a proliferation of abuses carefully tailored to capitalize on the weaknesses of the system. Those weaknesses stem in no small measure from the fact that many on-line auction companies, including the industry's far-reaching volume leader, eBay, take a laissez-faire approach to the business being transacted, ostensibly at least, under their aegis. These companies contend that they are merely go-betweens, providing the venue where on-line auctions occur but playing no role in the actual sales—and assuming no responsibility for anything untoward that may occur.

Any number of abuses can and do occur. For starters, unethical sellers frequently select inferior material to offer in on-line sales, treating these impersonal, long-distance auctions as dumping grounds for the dregs in their store stock or the merchandise they sell at coin-show bourses. This way, they don't have to face their prospective victims up close and personally. Then they assign high reserves to these coins—that is to say, prices below which the coins will not be sold. In doing so, they place themselves in a no-lose situation: If some unlucky bidder is ignorant and/or foolish enough to offer the high amount (or pay even more), they've made a healthy profit on a less-than-healthy coin. If the excessive reserve isn't met, they just hold on to the coin and keep inserting it into future sales until it inevitably sells.

Knowledgeable buyers possess the ability to grade coins with reasonable accuracy. Lacking this, or as a second layer of protection, they rely on the judgments of major third-party certification services. But these are not the buyers targeted by disreputable on-line auctioneers. Rather, they are aiming at novice collectors or people who don't collect coins at all but might be enticed to do so by glitzy presentations and the false sense of security imparted by the fact that a sale is taking place under the umbrella of eBay or some similar well-known on-line firm. To give themselves wiggle room to avoid potential charges of price gouging, the dealers almost always limit their on-line offerings to "raw" or uncertified coins—coins that have not been examined, graded, and encapsulated in hard plastic holders by one of the major services. This gives them leeway to assign whatever grade suits their purposes, and deprives their customers of a valuable safeguard.

Tips for On-Line Bidding

Before clicking a mouse to transmit even the smallest bid for an on-line auction lot, you should review and adopt the following recommendations.

Check out the dealer and make sure he or she is legitimate and reputable. There's a good chance you will encounter dealers you've never done business with, or perhaps never even heard of, when you take part in an on-line auction. That in itself isn't necessarily cause for concern or suspicion; this is a new field, and it has attracted not only new buyers but also new sellers. It *is* cause, however, for caution. You need to do some detective work—the same kind you would do if you were planning to buy a new car or hire someone for home improvement work. Check to see whether the dealer is a member of the Professional Numismatists Guild (PNG), an industry organization that polices its members' ethics and offers arbitration to settle disputes. Browse through on-line message boards used by coin collectors and check to see whether the dealer has been the subject of any complaints from customers. Go one step further and post a message yourself seeking information about the dealer. After all this, if nothing negative surfaces, proceed—but very slowly and carefully at first, until you're fully satisfied with the dealer's business practices and the quality and value of the coins.

Never buy uncertified coins on-line. Unless you are an experienced collector with the knowledge and ability to grade coins accurately yourself, you probably should buy only certified coins in *any* situations involving significant cost. But this caveat is true in *all* transactions that take place in on-line auctions. Not surprisingly, you will find few if any certified coins in Internet auctions conducted by dealers with questionable ethics. That's because reliable price guides are readily available with current market values, or value ranges, for coins that have been certified by the major grading services. Unethical dealers prefer to assign the grades and prices themselves, rather than have them determined by independent experts. And you can be certain they never, ever err on the low side.

Learn all you can about market values, even when buying certified coins. By purchasing certified coins, you assure yourself that the *grade* of a given coin is accurate, or at least very close to the mark. But that alone is not enough; you also must determine the *value* of the coin in that particular grade. This can be done quite easily by checking a current issue of *The Certified Coin Dealer Newsletter* (familiarly known as the *Bluesheet*), a weekly price guide reporting market values for coins that have been certified by one of the major services. Even then, you should adjust your bidding downward when vying for certified coins in on-line auctions. That's because they're likely to be low-end coins—coins that barely qualified for the grade that was assigned to them. This is the last place you would ever find *high-end* or premium-quality coins, so this is the last place you should ever overbid.

It's easy to understand why on-line coin auctions are so popular. They offer instant access to a wide array of material—and instant gratification when you're declared to be the winning bidder. This is one case, however, where winning isn't everything; in fact, it may be the worst possible outcome for the "lucky" winners. The *real* winners may be the bidders who dodged a financial bullet by finishing out of the running—and the so-called "successful" bidders may end up holding not only the coins they bought but also the proverbial bag. To avoid this trap, arm yourself beforehand with all the knowledge possible about both the dealer and the coins and then bid conservatively—or, if you have the least bit of doubt, don't bid at all.

Figure 14-3. *eBay's vice president, Andrew Coleman (left), in conversation with Heritage Capital Corporation's cochairman of the board, James L. Halperin. eBay and Heritage are at technology's cutting edge in numismatic transactions conducted over the Internet.*

The eBay™* Phenomenon

I've alluded several times to the hands-off attitude major online auctioneers take toward the abuses that occur on Internet sites that bear their names. Of these auction firms, eBay is the largest—and while abuses in eBay auctions may or may not be worse than those in other Internet auctions, it's clear that dubious practices do occur there, and their numbers are magnified by the sheer size and scope of the company's spawn. It's also apparent that eBay has not responded aggressively to numerous complaints by buyers who believe they were victimized in these sales. On the contrary, eBay officials have sought consistently to disassociate their company from both the abuses and the abusers, and disavowed responsibility for both. They liken eBay's role to that of a hotel that rents an auction room to the actual sellers, and thus bears no legal responsibility for the sale itself, but only for the condition of the premises. But this is not the

---

*EBAY is a trademark of eBay Inc.

impression many—probably most—on-line bidders have when they participate in these sales. They assume understandably that eBay screens sellers before permitting them to use its auction "premises." And, more important, they assume that eBay will investigate apparent abuses and take action against abusers when complaints are substantiated. The reality is decidedly very different.

One of the attractions of buying coins on eBay is the simplicity of the bidding process. To start this process, a prospective buyer first goes to *www.ebay.com* and registers as an eBay member. There is no charge. This enables him or her to browse through a base list for something of interest, or to look for a specific coin by using eBay's search engine. Next, the potential bidder scrolls down to the bottom of the page, enters the amount of the bid and clicks the review button. At this point, he or she reviews the bid, enters a user ID and password, clicks the "place bid" button—and with that, the bidding is complete.

Simple enough, right? Yes, but behind this uncomplicated facade lurks a plethora of potholes, pitfalls, and perils. And though eBay has no problem lending its name and prestige to the entry process, even signing up potential bidders as members of eBay, not as clients of the dealers leasing its site, it's nowhere to be found when those members try to extricate themselves and leave with their pockets unpicked. In short, the front door has "eBay" emblazoned upon it in large, bold letters, but the exit is unmarked and the message that's implied is "Just go away and leave us alone."

Because of my reputation as a consumer advocate, hundreds of people have written to me with grievances about their experiences in eBay coin auctions. Many complain about overgrading and other misrepresentation. Some say the coins they got were scratched, discolored, or otherwise defective. I've even had complaints from buyers who got *nothing:* Disreputable dealers simply took their money, ran, and never looked back. Disturbingly, these grievances have had a common thread: Time and again, the victims have sought eBay's help and gotten very little, if any, satisfaction or assistance.

eBay's Self-Serving Position

On the one hand, eBay boasts proudly of its status as "the world's on-line marketplace," conveying the image of great size and, by implication, great strength. On the other hand, it refuses to flex its considerable muscle when it learns of apparent wrongdoing in its vast domain. Instead, it shrinks almost reflexively into a legal shell, repeating its mantra that it is not responsible—and cannot be *held* responsible—for the actions of the people who use its on-line marketplace. It bills itself as the "modern incarnation of the traditional newspaper classified advertisement, automated and accelerated for the twenty-first century." But reputable newspapers screen their classified advertisers, and cooperate fully with victims and law-enforcement agencies when readers who purchase merchandise through those ads are defrauded. Complaints by consumers and reports in major newspapers state repeatedly that eBay, on the contrary, is evasive and elusive when confronted with evidence of questionable activity, including outright fraud. In addition, critics say, it is slow to take action against offenders—even when the evidence against them is overwhelming—and it frequently metes out minimal punishment, or even none at all.

Authorities who prosecute fraud cases involving eBay auctions report that they do so *in spite of* eBay obstructionism. In July 1999, for example, a Southern California man pleaded guilty to mail fraud in connection with a number of eBay auctions. He admitted posting consumer electronics items for sale on eBay, collecting about $37,000 from bidders, then failing to deliver any merchandise. "eBay was not immediately available to comment," a Reuters dispatch reported. "However, a source close to the investigation said the company was 'not terribly cooperative' in the case." As of June 2000, at least 10 people had been prosecuted since 1998 for engaging in auction fraud on eBay, according to the Federal Trade Commission.

There has been considerable publicity regarding purported fraud in eBay auctions involving sports memorabilia. In July 2000, the *National Law Journal* reported that a California lawyer, James Krause of San Diego, was seeking class-action certification for a suit charging eBay with negligence in connection with the sale of unauthenticated—often fake—sports memorabilia. Krause, too, was stonewalled by eBay officials, but he took strong exception to the company's position. "If you look at what a live auctioneer does and compare it to what eBay does, they're exactly the same," he said. "The interchanges between eBay's buyers and sellers are exactly like the interactions between auctioneers and the audience, with the same give and take."

One place where eBay finds it difficult to ignore the allegations of fraud is in its filings with the Securities and Exchange Commission, where it is obligated to provide full disclosure on any activity with potential implications for the value of its stock. In its filing with the SEC on March 31, 2000, the company had this to say:

> We believe that government regulators have received a substantial number of consumer complaints about us which, while small as a percentage of our total transactions, are large in aggregate numbers. As a result, we have from time to time been contacted by various federal, state, and local regulatory agencies and been told that they have questions with respect to the adequacy of the steps we take to protect our users from fraud.

In that same filing, eBay claimed that it cooperated with law enforcement agencies in combating fraudulent activities, but said it didn't expect improvement in these activities any time soon. "We are likely to receive additional inquiries from regulatory agencies in the future, which may lead to action against us," the company told the SEC. "We have responded to all inquiries from regulatory agencies by describing our current and planned antifraud efforts. If one or more of these agencies is not satisfied with our response to current or future inquiries, the resultant investigations and potential fines or other penalties could harm our business."

An Exchange of Correspondence with eBay

In preparing the second edition of *How to Make Money in Coins Right Now,* I gave eBay an opportunity to answer objections from critics and present its side of the story. The responses I received were curt, evasive, and even hostile. Far from discrediting the critics, these wary, legalistic responses served to validate their complaints.

In a letter dated May 4, 2000, to Robert Chesnut, eBay's associate general counsel, I posed a series of ten questions relating to the company's positions, policies, and activities. The questions were as follows:

1. What responsibility does an electronic auctioneer have?
2. Does eBay take the position that eBay has to register its auctions in the states and cities in which it does business?
3. If eBay takes the position that it doesn't, do you believe that eBay is required to register in California under California Business & Professional Code Sec. 5700 or in Virginia under Va. Code 54-824.1 et seq.?
4. Do you believe that eBay is regulated by the California Auctioneer Commission?
5. Are eBay dealers licensed auctioneers?
6. Do you think that eBay is facilitating sales that are not consistent with the respective laws of the states?
7. Does eBay feel it has traditional liability in cases of misdescription or misrepresentation?
8. What liability does eBay think it has in the case of counterfeit coin sales?
9. What liability does eBay have when a sold item turns out to have been stolen several owners ago?
10. Does eBay comply with New York City Department of Consumer Affairs regulations relating to auction bids and reserves?

The response I received came not from lawyer Robert Chesnut but from a public relations man—Kevin Pursglove, eBay's senior director of communications. And he made it clear that no answers would be forthcoming for my questions.

"While Rob [Chesnut] and several other members of our legal team do occasional media interviews about specific eBay trust and safety programs, it has been our practice to decline interview requests about broader legal theories and positions," Pursglove said. "We have refused these requests due to obvious attorney-client privilege issues that could be raised by such interviews. We appreciate your interest in eBay and hope you can understand why eBay, like so many companies, respectfully declines requests for legal counsel to publicly discuss such legal theories. We wish you well with your current book."

Seizing on the suggestion that eBay lawyers might be willing to answer questions about "specific" issues, as opposed to broader legal matters, I then distilled a single specific question:

> My firm, Scott Travers Rare Coin Galleries, Inc., a New York corporation, never sold coins over eBay, but might do so soon. My firm does business from New York, NY. Do I or a representative of my firm need to have an auctioneer's license with the New York City Department of Consumer Affairs in order to sell coins over eBay?

Pursglove's reply was succinct: "With regard to your question, as with any other business venture you may consider you should consult with a New York attorney to ensure that your actions comply with the law."

To this, I replied: "I gather from your response that you believe my actions would be those of an auctioneer rather than a consignor since only an auctioneer and not a consignor must 'comply with the law.' Unless I hear from you to the contrary, I will so presume and inform my readers accordingly."

This seemed to rile Pursglove. "You may not make such a presumption," he fired back. "The reference to 'the law' below means generically all laws. eBay does not give legal advice to individual users on their particular business situations."

"Thank you for your clarification," I quickly wrote back. "I now assume from the information you have provided that persons should not consign to eBay unless and until they have consulted a lawyer. If I don't hear from you to the contrary, I will assume that this is what you mean and inform my readers of your advice."

By this time, Pursglove seemed to be growing weary from all the evasive action he was taking. This was his final response:

> Your last assumption is also incorrect. We regret that we were unable to accommodate your request for an interview on eBay legal issues. We understand and respect your deadline and desire to obtain accurate information, but we are simply not able to assist you further. We are concerned that your unconfirmed assumptions about eBay's position on these issues could lead to inaccuracies. To avoid any possible misunderstandings, please assume nothing about our position, and do not communicate any official or unofficial eBay advice or position to your readers.
>
> We will not comment further on your questions or assumptions. You may not, however, assume from our silence that we agree or disagree with your positions—only that we have no additional comment. Have a nice day!

A Legal Opinion

Armen R. Vartian is a Manhattan Beach, California, attorney who serves as legal counsel to the Professional Numismatists Guild. He prepared a column that addresses Internet coin transactions for submission to *Coin World,* the hobby's newspaper of record. Here is what Vartian wrote in Spring 2000, slightly abridged from his original submission:

> Collectibles transactions on the Internet have increased at a tremendous rate. Most major coin dealers have the bulk of their retail offerings available on-line, and the traditional numismatic auction houses are encouraging Internet bidding at their sales. Huge amounts of business are done on smaller sites, by e-mail, and in nonnumismatic auction venues. eBay, not a numismatic specialist by any means, is now one of the largest sellers of rare coins in the country (I just visited its site, and there were over 75,000 coin and currency items being auctioned).

Is this a good thing for collectors? The Internet should not be seen as a revolution for collectors, but rather as an easier way for them to do business with reputable people with whom they are already familiar.

Just as with mail order, in Internet transactions there is always the risk that retail buyers will send money to someone who does not then deliver the items purchased. However, the Internet allows such fraud in ways that weren't economic, or even possible, in the context of mail order. Buyers' relatively easy use of credit card numbers in Internet transactions gives fraudulent sellers better access to those numbers than ever before. It also enables dishonest sellers to cheat buyers out of $50 here, $100 there, amounts which aren't enough to keep the mail order crook in business, but which serve the new on-line thieves just fine given the relatively low costs of operating in the Internet. Such amounts are difficult or impractical to recover through the courts or through government agencies, most of which are far more interested in major scams focused in one area than in small crimes committed on a large scale nationwide. Even identifying the criminals can be difficult on the Internet because of the generally casual attitude toward identification.

Another risk which has been magnified by the Internet is the risk of buying overgraded or misdescribed merchandise. Looking at some nonnumismatic sites such as eBay, I am amazed at the volume of uncertified coins, modern and bullion coins, and private commemorative coins which are up for auction. For the most part, these are items which traditional numismatic auction houses would advise consignors to wholesale, because the profit to be made doesn't justify the costs (i.e. commissions) of selling at auction. If the sellers of these items are making much money, they must be selling at considerably above the coins' market value, which doesn't sound like a good deal for the buyers. In addition, with no central numismatic authority reviewing lot descriptions, nothing stops a crafty seller to misdescribe what he or she is selling. Yes, the buyer must beware, but the Internet brings such sellers to unwary buyers a lot more easily than was possible before.

What about the "feedback" systems and "safe harbor" protections on sites such as eBay? I'm not convinced that these address the fundamental problems satisfactorily. Recently, a class action lawsuit, *Gentry et al. v. eBay, Inc.,* was filed against eBay in San Diego Superior Court by a group of collectors who purchased fake autographed sports items on eBay. The plaintiffs allege that eBay's "safety" programs contributed to enormous damage to autographed sports memorabilia consumers because eBay allowed feedback from anyone, regardless of whether or not the person had ever conducted a successful transaction with the person whom he or she was rating. The plaintiffs allege that the dealers who sold them fake merchandise all had eBay "stars" and "power seller" ratings, with "Most, if not all, of these Positive Feedback ratings . . . self-generated or provided by other coconspiring dealers." The lawsuit also alleges that eBay received "an alarming number of consumer complaints" about the defendants, and "a number of warnings from government agencies that a substantial amount of forged sports memorabilia was being auctioned on eBay." Despite these complaints and warnings, the plaintiffs allege, eBay did nothing, allowing the practices to continue "for the sole purpose of reaping millions of dollars in profits for itself."

As for the "safe harbor" concept, it looks a lot better on paper than in practice. Traditional numismatic auction houses guarantee delivery, and back those guarantees with their own money. The nonnumismatic Internet venues, if they have any safe harbor at all, buy insurance policies. Claims are subject to deductibles, as well as to the length of time it takes the insurer to pay up, and other restrictions on coverage. It can take months to recover on a safe harbor claim, and chat rooms are full of complaints from disgruntled buyers who say that they filed claims and never received anything. I'm not aware of any formal statements by eBay responding to any of these allegations; in my personal opinion, eBay tends to be reticent about making such statements. But the picture seems plausible and, if true, isn't a pretty one.

Of course, unlawful or unethical behavior is not a risk if a buyer does business with a reputable coin seller through its Internet site. But the long-standing numismatic dealers and auction houses were easy to contact even before the Internet, and it is dubious whether the marginal benefits of doing business with these dealers over the Internet justify exposing buyers to the explosion of other, not-so-reputable sellers out there.

THE MAIN POINTS OF THIS CHAPTER

If you have made the decision to purchase coins on-line, remember these three important points which have been elaborated on earlier in this chapter.

- Check out the dealer and make sure he or she is legitimate and reputable.
- Never buy uncertified coins on-line.
- Learn all you can about market values, even when buying certified coins.

HOW TO SUBMIT COINS TO GRADING SERVICES

There are many ways to crack a coin out of the holder of a grading service. Here are a few:

- An NGC holder comes apart after a good hit by a flat hammer on each edge. After a twist or two, the holder should come apart.
- PCGS holders can be opened by using sheet metal nippers (a plier-type tool with the cutting edge perpendicular to the handle). Just cut the holder on the edge across from the coin and the holder breaks in two. The insert ring with the coin will then slide out.
- For removing coins from any type of slab, some people use a bandsaw. With this method, the coin is left sandwiched in the holder so that it doesn't have to be handled. Practitioners of this method make a few straight cuts well away from the coin. This leaves small squares of plastic on each side of the coin which lift off. "By using the bandsaw," writes an advocate of this method, "I don't have to worry about striking the slab with a hammer or jamming something between the front and back."

You do *not* have to crack a coin out of its holder to have it upgraded. Here is some advice from Anthony Swiatek:

To Cross or Not to Cross
BY ANTHONY SWIATEK

The coin(s) in question can be submitted (for a fee) via your dealer to NGC or PCGS using their Certified Pregrade or Crossover service. At NGC, the other service's slab is evaluated. Should NGC agree with the listed grade, the holder will be "green-dotted" with a self-sticking removable coding label, indicating crossover acceptance. If NGC does not concur, a "red-dot" coding label is applied. The dealer can indicate on the submission invoice whether to be called if "green-dotting" occurs for crossover into the NGC holder and how quickly he or she needs the coin(s) returned. If no instructions are given, the coin(s) is returned in its original holder.

At PCGS, if a coin crosses via its Crossover service, it is automatically placed into a PCGS holder, unless instructed otherwise, and returned to the submitter. If it doesn't cross, the coin is returned as received. The coin(s) is never downgraded, as long as you do not crack it out of the holder and send it in "raw."

Assume that you believe the certified coin held in your hand is undergraded. The grading label indicates the coin is MS-64, but you believe it to be an MS-65. This coin can be sent in by your dealer (for a fee) to NGC for its Designation Review or to PCGS for its Regrading service. Should either service agree that your coin should be rated higher, the coin will be sealed in a new holder, along with its accompanying grading insert label attesting to the new grade. If the service does not agree with your grading mastership, the coin will be returned as submitted.

PCGS

PCGS accepts submissions through authorized dealers and directly from PCGS collectors club members.

PCGS Fee Schedule

Service	Fee	Turn-Around Guarantee	Phone Grades
Economy*	$15	no	yes
15 Days*	$30	no	yes
5 Days*	$50	no	yes
2 Days*	$100	yes	yes
6 Hours* (coin show only)	$100	no	no
Bullion Gold Ex.	$20	yes, 10 days	yes
World*	$25	yes, 30 days	no
Crossover	available for all service levels	depends on service level	yes
Guarantee†	$25	no	yes
Reholder	$5	no	n/a
Mech. Error	$0	no	n/a

*Regrade Service is available.

†Fee is refundable in certain cases.

PCGS authorized dealers agree to the following regarding impaired or altered coins:

(a) Dealer acknowledges that PCGS will not grade coins which, in the judgment of PCGS, bear evidence of harsh cleaning, artificial toning, damaged surfaces, altered surfaces or PVC damage, or other similar impairments or evidence of coin "doctoring," as described below. Dealer agrees that it will not knowingly submit any coins for grading which have been altered in any way, and acknowledges that the determination as to whether a coin should be graded shall be made by PCGS in accordance with its standards. However, because the determination by PCGS to reject such impaired coins will require a review by PCGS's grading experts, Dealer will be required to remit, as set forth herein, the standard grading fee for any such coins that are submitted to PCGS.

(b) Dealer shall not, directly or indirectly, "doctor" coins. Coin "doctoring" involves the alteration of the appearance of a coin to attempt to increase its value, and may involve, among other things, adding substances to coins (such as, among other things, putty, wax, facial oils, petroleum jelly, or varnish); treating coins with chemicals (such as, among other things, potash, sulfur, cyanide, iodine, or bleach); heat-treating coins to alter appearance; rematting ("skinning") proof gold; "tapping" and "spooning" (i.e., physically moving surface metal to hide marks); filing rim nicks; or repairing coins (retooling metal). Dealer and PCGS agree that PCGS would suffer irreparable damages if Dealer were to engage directly or indirectly in coin "doctoring" and that PCGS shall be entitled to preliminary and final injunctive relief for any breach of Dealer's obligation not to "doctor" coins.

NUMISMATIC GUARANTY CORPORATION OF AMERICA

NGC accepts submissions through its authorized dealers/members and from members of Certified Collectors Society and ANA members.

NGC Fee Schedule

Service	Fee	Turn-Around	Description
Walk Through	$125	Same-day Service	*For those times **when you want to move your inventory fast!*** Your coins are graded and returned within hours.
Dispatch	$85	24 Hours	*A great service for a great price* with a great turn-around time. We receive your coins in the morning; out they go the next day.
Express	$50	5 Working Days	*Within a week,* your coins are back. You can submit coins valued up to $10,000.
Early Bird	$28	12 Working Days	*Choose this economical service* for your coins valued up to $5,000. A convenient service with very few restrictions.
Goldrush	$20	5 Working Days	For $5 Liberty, $10 Liberty, $10 Indian, $20 Liberty, and $20 St.

Service	Fee	Turn-Around	Description
			Gaudens all dates, valued up to $1,000. World coins valued up to $500 are also acceptable, all common dates. 5-coin minimum.
Economy	$15	21 Working Days	*Now you can afford* to have your lower-valued coins graded. Accepting non-gold U.S. and World coins valued at $300 or less. 5-coin minimum.
Prescreen	50-coin minimum for coins valued over $300, $5 per coin; 100-coin minimum for coins valued under $300, $1 per coin	10 Working Days	*Let us do the work!* We'll pregrade your raw coins for you by selecting those pieces which meet your predetermined minimum grade. The coins which make the minimum grade will then be written up for you and submitted under the tier of your choice. We ask only that you send your raw coins in groups of 50 or more and that they all be of the same type.

INDEPENDENT COIN GRADING COMPANY

ICG accepts submissions from its authorized dealer network, as well as from the public.

ICG Fee Schedule

Tier	Turnaround Time	Grading Fee	Requirements
1-Day	1 day	$100	All US coins.
5-Day	5 business days	$50	All US coins valued at $10,000 or less.
15-Day	15 business days	$30	All US coins valued at $5,000 or less.
5-Day US Gold Special	5 business days (5 coin min.)	$20	$20 Saints and Liberties, $10 Indians, Liberties and $5 Liberties, valued at $1,000 or less (any date as long as value is under $1000).
Economy*	21 business days (5 coin min.)	$15	All Non-Gold US coins valued at $300 or less.
Regrade	Same as selected tier	Tier price	Any ICG coin may be submitted for regrade.

Tier	Turnaround Time	Grading Fee	Requirements
Crossover	Same as selected tier	Tier price	Any coin already encapsulated by another grading service. If ICG grades the coin the same or higher, the coin will be encapsulated in an ICG holder.
Pre-Screens Variety*	Call or write for prices. 5 additional days to selected tier (no economy submissions).	Selected tier plus $5.	All US coins. ICG will examine for ICG recognized varieties.
ICG Guaranteed Quality Controlled		$24	Any ICG coin that in your opinion ICG has overgraded. Grading fee and postage are refunded if ICG lowers the grade of your coin. Please refer to the ICG Guarantee for more information about additional compensation.
Reholder	3 business days	Free	For chipped or cracked ICG holders.

* Estimated turnaround time

ANACS

ANACS accepts submissions from the public.

ANACS Current Service and Price List
(DOES NOT INCLUDE SPECIAL PROMOTIONS)

- **REGULAR-SPEED SERVICE**
  - 1–9 coins $12 per coin
  - 10+ coins $10 per coin

- **5-DAY EXPRESS SERVICE**
  - 1–4 coins $21 per coin
  - 5+ coins $15 per coin

- **2-DAY EXPRESS SERVICE**
  - $39 per coin

- **1-DAY EXPRESS SERVICE**
  - $59 per coin

- **6-HOUR WALK-THROUGH SERVICE**
  - $99 per coin

- **FAX SERVICE**—$5 per order

- **ATTRIBUTION RESEARCH SERVICE**
  An additional $5 per coin

- **PRESCREEN SERVICE**
  Coins in other grading services holders.

- **RE-EXAM SERVICE**
  Coins in ANACS holders. Fees for re-exam and
  prescreen are the same as listed above.

- **ANACS REHOLDER SERVICE**
  Regular speed, $5 per coin.

- **TELETRADE SERVICE**—5 coin minimum
  Regular Service—$8 per coin
  5–Day Express—$14 per coin

- **PVC RE-EXAM**—$5 per coin

A quantity discount is available on submissions of 100 or more coins for all services except
Teletrade.

RARE COINS AS SECURITIES

BY DAVID L. GANZ*

Are rare coins securities, or are they just coins? There's no easy or specific answer to that question because the courts of the nation are split on the issue—and there is no ready resolution in sight.

The short answer to the question is that a coin is always a coin, but sometimes coins can be sold in such a way as to make them into a security. When they reach that status, coins become subject to a host of government regulations, and a prospective liability to purchasers.

Rare coins are not generally thought of as being a security. Stocks and bonds are the most traditional types of wholly regulated investment vehicles. By contrast, the purchase and sale of rare coins is almost entirely unregulated.

Coins generally lack the attributes traditionally associated with a security: fungibility (the ability to exchange one for an-

---

*David L. Ganz is a New York City lawyer who is a past president of the American Numismatic Association.

other without noticeable difference); homogeneity (substantially identical pricing for identically described individual components); divisibility; and representation of a defined value of an otherwise regulated entity.

However, there are some coins that meet this definition—typically a generic, slabbed (or encapsulated) coin. What is always at issue is the manner in which the coins are sold to the ultimate purchaser that can transform them from a mere coin into a security.

The Securities and Exchange Commission has been curiously silent on whether or not coins are securities, except for the Brigadoon Scotch case, which determined that investment contracts for rare coins were indeed a security.

Based on the sales presentation by the seller (but not the supplier), the sale of rare coins can constitute an investment contract or a security under the laws of several states.

As with every investment vehicle that is not a stock or bond, the analysis of whether or not coins sales are a security begins with the test set forth in the seminal case of "SEC v W.J. Howey & Co.," where the U.S. Supreme Court set out a three-pronged test for determining whether a transaction involves an investment contract. In Howey, the Supreme Court defined an investment contract as (1) an investment (2) in a common venture premised on the reasonable expectation of profits (3) to be derived from the entrepreneurial or managerial efforts of others.

Just as Howey was the seminal case that demonstrated that a security went beyond stocks and bonds, the principal authority that establishes that the sale of rare coins can constitute a security is "SEC v Brigadoon Scotch Dist. Co. (Federal Coin Reserve)."

The Brigadoon Scotch case involved an entity known as the Federal Coin Reserve, which marketed rare coins as an investment vehicle. The Brigadoon Scotch Court noted at the time, Federal Coin Reserve "stimulates sales by advertising in such media as airline magazines, journals used in the medical profession and other similar outlets. It does not advertise in publications specifically addressed to amateur or professional coin collectors."

The description of what Federal Coin Reserve offered its customers is set forth in the brochure explicitly. Federal Coin Reserve promised professional selection and supervision; reinvestment of capital gains; accounting services; diversification; daily bidding; insurance; tax advice and consultation; depository vaults; and a claim that "The Federal Coin Reserve looks forward to a minimum appreciation of 100% every five (5) years. . . . " (Brochure, p. 17).

The defendants in Brigadoon Scotch (Federal Coin Reserve) denied that they were selling securities and instead asked the Court to take at face value their claims that the items offered for sale (rare coins) are just that—a mere commodity—and that there was no investment contract, which would be required as a finding under federal law.

The Brigadoon Scotch Court said, "regardless of the nature of the ultimate sales here, FCR's analysis is not in keeping with the law because an investment contract is determinable not only by the nature of what the sellers actually sell but equally by what character the investment is given . . . by the terms of offer, the plan of distribution, and the economic inducements held out to the prospect. In the enforcement of an act such as this it is not inappropriate that promoters' offerings be judged as being what they were represented to be." (citation omitted)

In Brigadoon Scotch, as indeed with almost every other investment-type case involving rare coins, "FCR customers purchase their coins as an investment for the purpose of making a profit," rather than for the purpose of collecting coins as an amateur numismatist.

The Brigadoon Scotch court put the issue succinctly: The crucial inquiry is "Whether the efforts by those other than the investor are the undeniably significant ones, those essential managerial efforts which affect the failure or success of the enterprise."

The determining factors in those schemes was that "what was being sold was an investment entrusting the promoters with both the work and the expertise to make the tangible investment pay off." Glen-Arden Commodities, Inc. v. Costantino.

If a seller promises to (or does) manage the investment or uses his/her expertise to help or hinder the valuation changes in rare coins purchased, the coin sale could be a security.

CONTACT THE AUTHOR

The author welcomes your comments and reports on how well you did following the suggestions given in this book. Although there is no guarantee of an answer, every inquiry will be carefully studied.

Scott A. Travers

Scott Travers Rare Coin Galleries, Inc.
P.O. Box 1711, F.D.R. Station
New York, NY 10150-1711

Telephone: 212/535-9135
Facsimile: 212/535-9138
E-mail: travers@pocketchangelottery.com
Internet: http://www.inch.com/~travers/travers3.htm
http://www.pocketchangelottery.com

INDEX

Scott Travers ranks as one of the most influential coin dealers in the world. His name is familiar to readers everywhere as the author of five best-selling books on coins: *One-Minute Coin Expert, The Coin Collector's Survival Manual, Travers' Rare Coin Investment Strategy, The Investor's Guide to Coin Trading,* and *Scott Travers' Top 88 Coins Over $100.* All five have won awards from the prestigious Numismatic Literary Guild. He served from 1997–1999 as vice president of the American Numismatic Association, a congressionally chartered, nonprofit organization. He is contributing editor to *COINage* and a regular contributor to other numismatic periodicals, and he has served as a coin valuation consultant to the Federal Trade Commission. His knowledge of coin values is used to update his annual price guide, *The Insider's Guide to U.S. Coin Values.* His opinions as an expert are often sought by publications such as *Barron's, BusinessWeek,* and *The Wall Street Journal.* A frequent guest on radio and television programs, Scott Travers has won awards and gained an impressive reputation not only as a coin expert, but also as a forceful consumer advocate for the coin-buying public. He has coordinated the liquidation of numerous important coin collections, and he is president of Scott Travers Rare Coin Galleries, Inc., in New York City.